RAISING BOYS WHO DO BETTER

For our big-hearted boys and
the men we hope they will become.

'It is easier to build strong children than to repair broken men'
Frederick Douglas

'I have a son, who is my heart. A wonderful young man,
daring and loving and strong and kind'
Maya Angelou

'I'm a man. Not yet, not today, maybe tomorrow'
Ezra, age 2

UJU ASIKA

RAISING BOYS WHO DO BETTER

A HOPEFUL GUIDE FOR A NEW GENERATION

CONTENTS

INTRODUCTION

We need to have a conversation about boys. This invitation is for parents of boys, as well as anyone who cares about the young males in their lives and the men they will become. That includes parents of daughters, aunties, uncles, godfathers, grandmothers, teachers, community leaders. That smiling neighbour chucking my kids' footballs back over the fence for the umpteenth time. We all need to be a part of this conversation.

Our society is in flux, and so much of what's changing is how we think about manhood and what we are willing to accept from the dominant male culture. As a womanist (an intersectional term for Black feminists, as coined by *Alice Walker*), I am trying to raise my sons with strong, womanist values. There is so much to unpack, including lessons from my own upbringing.

On 12 March 2021, the day that Sarah Everard's murder was confirmed, I put up a post on Instagram. It was an image I had seen of graffiti on a wall with the words 'PROTECT YOUR DAUGHTER' crossed out and replaced with a bold new call to action: 'EDUCATE YOUR SON'.

The post attracted hundreds of likes and reached close to 25,000 accounts. It captured something many of us were feeling, especially women who were fed up with the same old narratives around female safety and self-respect. *What was she wearing? Did she cry for help? Was she intoxicated? How late did she stay out? Was she – whisper it – asking for it?*

Social media was aflame with the anger of those of us who have spent too many nights, evenings and early mornings glancing over our shoulders. Keys between our knuckles, emergency contacts on speed dial. We were tired of womanhood being put on trial while men watched from the sidelines, as if they weren't part of the problem. As if they weren't the problem itself.

Sarah was walking home, and she did everything 'correctly', and still she was attacked by a man who swore to protect his fellow citizens. It was time to turn the spotlight on men and what they could be doing better. Stop warning women how not to get assaulted and teach men not to assault in the first place. *Educate your son*. It was time to read the writing on the wall.

That week, I had been invited to speak about race, gender and intersectionality on two panels for International Women's Day. It was the cruellest irony to hear of Sarah's fate as, worldwide, we were being urged to #ChooseToChallenge sexism and the status quo. But the bone-tiredness and broken-heartedness I felt wasn't just about Sarah Everard.

My sense of mourning was compounded by a feeling of erasure. Watching the outpouring around Sarah's loss, my heart rose and sank. What about Blessing Olusegun, Bibaa Henry and Nicole Smallman, and all the other women of colour who had been murdered or disappeared? Didn't their lives matter too?

Every parent feels a tightening in their chest at the news of another child who never made it home. As a mother of Black boys, this feels both urgent and deeply personal. I am parenting at the intersection of race and gender. Barely a teenager and a tween, my sons are already seen as potential threats in some circles, but their Black skin also makes them walking targets.

How can we do better for our male children? How can we raise our sons to be kind, conscious, empathetic, and accountable?

I'm hardly the only person fretting about this. In recent months, almost every major newspaper has published think pieces on what some call the 'boy crisis'. I've sat with fellow mums and dads, swapping stories and concerns. We're worrying if we've said enough, done enough, what more we should be doing.

In August 2021, the *Observer New Review* published a cover story titled 'How To Raise A Boy'.[1] Writer Tom Lamont interviewed me, alongside several authors including Bobbi Wegner (*Raising Feminist Boys*) and Sonora Jha (*How to Raise a Feminist Son*). During our conversation, I asked Tom about his own experiences. He told me his challenge was figuring out how to parent a 'very boyish boy' when he wasn't especially laddish himself. He felt somewhat out of his depth.

Many parents are grappling with the question of how to bring up decent kids in a culture riddled with hypermasculinity. Bobbi Wegner made a point about avoiding the phrase 'toxic masculinity', as she doesn't find it helpful. Yet it's arguable that masculinity at its most extreme and unchecked is like a toxin. It's the poison gas that has fuelled everything from global wars and nuclear bombs to colonialism, capitalism and the climate emergency.

As the *pandemic* swept the world in 2020, it became obvious that the countries faring worse were those run by hypermasculine caricatures: men who boasted about shaking hands despite all the warnings. Men who thought they could shrug off the virus with a pithy slogan. Men who mocked people wearing masks as 'feeble'.

Brazil´s death toll was skyrocketing when former President Jair Bolsonaro told his nation: 'All of us are going to die one day. There is no point in escaping from that, in escaping from reality. We have to cease being a country of sissies.'[2]

The actual word he used was *maricas*, which is slang for 'small girls', and also a homosexual slur.

Sonora Jha has spoken about the macho resistance to wearing face masks and how this idea of masculinity was literally killing people. Even men who weren't against face coverings in theory were less likely to wear them correctly. I used to spot so many of them around town, masks dangling under their chins like 'Hey, I'm cool with masks, but also, I'm a man. Covid can't catch me.'

My husband wore a mask on public transport, but as a cyclist, he wouldn't be caught dead in a helmet. Recently, he got himself a snazzy new electric bike. He waxes lyrical about whizzing around the city, down steep hills and giddy inclines, tearing through Hampstead Heath after dark. One evening, he was zooming along at top speed when his rucksack flipped off the handles and onto the road ahead. It took every muscle in his body to brake hard enough to stop himself from crashing. Abiye was a whirr of adrenaline when he got home and shared what happened. The boys were gawping. I pictured my husband lying on the road, his head cracked open.

'It's a good lesson, anyway,' he said. 'I probably should take more care.'

I asked if he might consider wearing a helmet.

'Nah, babe, but don't worry. I'm unbreakable.'

He thumped his chest.

Of course, there are plenty of women around town without masks or helmets. But let's face it, none will be thought of as less womanly because she's chosen to protect her life or the lives of those around her. We don't have to prove our femininity by pretending we're superhuman.

Like many kids their age, my boys have grown up on superhero myths. This never used to bother me. I'm a comic book fan myself, and I love a good origin story. I thought it was cute when my then three-year-old insisted I address him only as 'Batboy' for the foreseeable future, or when his younger brother would fall asleep in his Spiderman suit. The *Black Panther* movie was a game changer and T'Challa will always be my king. Wakanda Forever.

Yet more and more these days, I question these stories we tell our boys about what it means to be real men. Powerful. Unbreakable. More than human. Even when it's just a comic, the message bleeds through like ink.

Watching my sons fill out and grow into themselves is one of the joys of motherhood. It's a bittersweet feeling and a scary one too, because they are entering a zone where I know they have to leave me behind, a path they must walk alone.

Before you know it, the boy in the superhero costume is an adult with an invisible 'S' carved on his chest. How can we encourage them not to carry the universe on their shoulders? How can we ensure they understand there's more to success than earning billions and launching a penis-shaped rocket into the stratosphere?

RAISING BOYS WHO DO BETTER

When the patron saint of toxic masculinity, Piers Morgan, tweeted off another vile comment targeting Black women, I mentioned it to the boys. My youngest said: 'Who is Piers Morgan?' Indeed. Sadly, we can't shield them from the Morgans of our age for ever — but we can teach them better ways.

I know I've raised good boys. They are kind, funny and smart. Every time I feel like humanity is hurtling off a precipice, I look at my children and I'm filled with hope. Then I turn around and they're on the floor, punching each other. I remember how much work lies ahead. As we say in Nigeria, our road is far.

So, I'm talking to parents and teachers, community leaders and psychologists, grandparents, siblings and neighbours. I'm listening to boys and their mates. I'm speaking to my brother, cousins, uncles and nephews. I'm opening up conversations with my husband and sons. I'm reflecting on the way I grew up and how I've mothered my boys so far. I want to examine what worked, what still needs work and whether certain things can be fixed – or is it already too late?

My first book, *Bringing Up Race*, focused on storytelling over strategies. *Raising Boys Who Do Better* is about stories too, primarily. It's about rewriting the narrative on boyhood while holding myself and others to account. Hopefully, you will find some answers too or at least feel reassured that you are asking the right questions.

The challenge of raising boys in the twenty-first century is immense, but it's also exciting. We're living through a time when more of us are ready to have hard conversations, share intimate and vulnerable experiences, and parent with courage and self-awareness. Everything it means to be a man today is up for debate. At times, this can feel like a crisis. Or maybe it's a renaissance.

---

* Please note that I've used terms like boy, male and masculinity inclusively to refer to people who identify or experience life as male.

PART 1
LIFE

WITH
BOYS

HOUSE
OF BOYS

You could say I was ambivalent about boys before I became a mother. My earliest attachment to a male was to my father and I loved him dearly. I also had a brother and, frankly, I could take him or leave him. Don't get me wrong, I love my brother too, but as a little sister our relationship was a pendulum swinging between adulation and aggravation. At primary school, he was in the top year when I was at the bottom and we might as well have been in separate universes. I'll never forget how excited I was to sit next to him for dinner one time when he was school prefect. For the entire meal, he didn't so much as glance in my direction and we ate in silence. He doesn't remember it, but I was crushed.

From my starting point of ambivalence, I now find myself the mother to two sons and a stepson. When you are the only female in a house of boys, people often wonder how you cope. Where do you position yourself between the farts and manspreading? I shrug and roll my eyes, but for the most part, it's a blast. A whirl of energy, physicality, banter and the best hugs ever. I'll admit there are times when I feel like an oppressed minority in my own home, especially when it comes to the state of the toilets. However, I wouldn't swap these guys for anything.

So here I am, writing a whole book on the topic, though please don't think of me as some kind of boy-whisperer. Like many parents, I only claimed expertise before I actually had kids of my own, though I well remember those carefree days when I gleaned everything I knew by watching films like *Parenthood*, tutting through episodes of *Supernanny*, or flicking curiously through my sister's copy of *What to Expect When You're Expecting*.

I imagined myself as a calm, controlled mum whose kids wouldn't throw tantrums in public, like the ones I'd seen banging their heads against supermarket trolleys. Certainly my child wouldn't dare to raise their voice at me, let alone swear like the tween boy I once overheard telling his mum to 'go fuck herself' on the train. I mean, I'm Nigerian. My child wouldn't even know how to shape their mouth to begin.

I also decided that, if I had boys, I wouldn't give them toy guns. Why encourage such violence in kids? Nor would I limit them to the bricks, balls and automobiles that seemed to sum up the masculine imagination.

I would foster any interest in dolls or play kitchens and promote toys that crossed gender boundaries.

I could never have foreseen my sons' instant attachment to things that go zoom and stuff that goes boom, and I wasn't prepared for my firstborn, Ezra, turning me into a trainspotter. At school, we used to laugh at the 'anoraks', those nerdy, obsessive types who (for reasons still unknown) spent their spare hours hanging around stations and gathering obscure data, but I'm not sure I actually knew any trainspotters in real life. Until I met my first son. Nothing thrilled Ezra more than a trip to our local station to watch the trains come in.

'Choo choo!' he'd scream, waving frantically at the odd passenger grinning and waving back. One of our regular outings was to St Pancras Station to watch the trains or the Eurostar arriving and departing, followed by hot chocolate and cake at the station cafe. Riding to Greenwich and back at the front of the driverless Docklands Light Railway trains would send him loopy with delight. The most exciting times were if a train driver on his break would allow Ezra to climb into the front carriage of an actual train, sit in the driver's seat, and steer us on an imaginary voyage.

Aside from an enjoyable afternoon spent riding vintage steam and diesel trains along the Epping–Ongar railway, I can't say I was as enamoured as my son. I had little interest in trains beyond romanticizing about one day travelling on the Orient Express. Reading *Thomas the Tank Engine* on repeat made me want to stab my eyes out.

But it wasn't just trainspotting that got my boy worked up. Ezra loved anything that moved. The bin men were his heroes, with their big vans and shiny jackets. His jaws would slacken in awe at the sight of a fire engine or ambulance. He'd spend happy hours lining up all his Hot Wheels and toy trucks or driving a plastic vehicle along every surface of our home. Ezra's very first word was 'car'.

Of course, he had other playthings too. As his primary sidekick for years, I liked to think I was helping to round out his interests. He read eagerly, identifying words off the page from an early age. We'd host teddy-bear tea parties and soft-toy discos, although these often devolved into furry boxing matches. There were mornings at playgroup when Ezra would tussle with other boy toddlers over the dolls, although this had more to do with who got to wield the dolly pushchair than who got to play dress-up or feeding.

Quite simply, watching my son at play challenged my feminist notions about how boys and girls weren't so different. Something primal was clearly at work here. Or was it? I decided to speak to Abi Wright, the co-founder of *Festival of the Girl*, an organization dedicated to championing young girls and promoting gender equity. Her insights revealed that, far from being something innate, most of these behaviours can be attributed to our environment:

> **I really want more people to understand what gender stereotyping is and that we all do it, even if we're trying not to, because we've all been brought up on that for hundreds of years. And why that has such an impact on both boys and girls, but particularly on boys. They say [gender stereotypes are] set in kids by age four, but it's definitely before then. The minute you find out what the sex is, the world will come crashing down on that child.[1]**

A world of gender-reveal parties with pink or blue balloons. Nursery walls decorated with trucks or unicorns. Shopping aisles with products segregated by pastels or camouflage. Babygros that state: 'Here Comes Trouble' or 'Pretty Little Princess'. These messages are like a stealthy surround-sound playing out in our subconscious, no matter how much we think we're immune to them.

A BBC documentary series titled *No More Boys and Girls: Can Kids Go Gender Free?* explored whether the reason we haven't achieved gender equality is tied to how differently we treat boys and girls. One episode showed adults offering stereotypically gendered toys to babies depending on whether the baby was dressed as a girl or a boy. When they were made aware of it, the adults were shocked to realize what they were doing.

Abi notes that what many of us may perceive as being 'boy traits' or 'girl traits' are really down to individuality rather than gender.

We're all just different people, and we like different things. My two would fit perfectly into gender stereotypes if my second had been a boy. She loved cars, trains and climbing up on things. My eldest is more stereotypically 'girly', but they're just two different people. I didn't own a dress. I do understand that we are creatures that need to label things for our own understanding. That's why schools have such an impact on our kids; they're trying to find their tribe. In a way, the 'girl' and 'boy' label is the easiest label to use, but I don't think people understand how incredibly detrimental it can be.

You might wonder what's so harmful and yet gender stereotyping can limit a child's potential and their self-perception. For those who don't conform to traditional gender roles or identities, it can lead to discrimination and mental-health challenges. But what if you're parenting a boy who seems to be bursting at the seams with pure boyishness?

Journalist Tom Lamont has written in the *Observer* about how he felt stumped as a 'beta' dad raising a visibly 'alpha' male. He told me that his older daughter was more easy-mannered, and that he'd expected his son to be similar in temperament, or at least to take after him. Boy, was he wrong.

Parenting them has been like two completely different jobs, like a career change almost. When they were a tiny bit younger, I'd make little videos filming what one was doing. There would be my son hurtling around on the trampoline or toying with explosions and death and my daughter would be hunched over a sewing machine.[5]

I'm amused by these images and wonder what Tom and his wife make of their children slotting so neatly into their gender roles.

'My wife and I certainly didn't proactively encourage this, but also I don't subscribe to the theory that there are these innate boy v. girl characteristics,' he says. So how does he explain his son's behaviour and temperament? Like many experts, Tom acknowledges that identity is a rich and complicated field that's part nature, part nurture and a whole lot of culture. After all, our babies are learning from us constantly.

'I've always been interested in the little sub-verbal clues we give each other. I think that happens with kids quite a bit; for so long you're communicating with them in non-verbal ways. You don't think you model gender stereotypes and a lot of us parents are scratching our heads about this, but who knows what kind of unconscious encouragement nudges I'm giving my son to act out?'

This was interesting to me, that as someone who didn't fit the traditional boy mould growing up, Tom might be tacitly giving licence to his son to take on that mantle.

'Maybe a part of me likes what I see in him,' he muses.

I wonder how much of our children's identities — their behaviour and desires — are driven by other people's expectations and that basic human need to fit in?

Shortly before Ezra turned three, I enrolled him at nursery. I was getting ready to have another baby and looked forward to a couple of child-free hours. He was a little shy to settle in at first, but on the third morning when I picked him up, Ezra was buzzing. He told me he'd had the best day ever.

'We did so much peeling, Mummy, and I peeled all the boys. It was so fun!'

'That's great, sweetheart,' I replied, with a bemused smile.

What was he peeling exactly? Were they doing some kind of craft activity involving oranges? Pleased to see my boy so excited, I didn't give it a second thought.

The next day, I took him to our local stay-and-play centre. Ezra made his way to a box of stickle bricks in the corner. I watched as he carefully pushed two long, rectangular bricks together into the rough shape of what I quickly discovered was supposed to be some kind of gun. I only deduced this because he was pointing it straight at me.

'*PEEL, PEEL, PEEL!*' he shouted, clicking his fingers as each imaginary bullet came flying at my chest.

Oh. So that's what he had loved doing so much.

You can listen to psychologists and fellow parents and your own liberal feminist instincts debating the pros and cons of giving kids toy guns. You can avoid buying toy guns as a matter of conscience. Then you watch helplessly as your toddler points a brick, or a twig, or his bare fingers at you, and shoots.

My sister Nkiru once remarked on how her daughter used to come into her bedroom, sit at her dressing table, and smear her creams, lipsticks and powders all over her face. Then her son would come in and turn those potions and lotions on her dresser into an elaborate game of Risk; a rudimentary battlefield where perfumes were deadly sprays and the smudge of lipstick on tissue was a bloody flag, waving surrender. And surrender she did. 'I never planned to buy him toy guns at first, but he made his own anyway. So, in the end I gave in.'

I gave in too. I didn't encourage war games, nor would I ever buy my child a toy that looked like a semi-automatic weapon. However, I'd let them have water pistols and glow-in-the-dark light sabres and bubble swords to smash around. When their birthday gifts revealed Nerf rifles, it no longer fazed me, apart from those tiny orange foam bullets sending me into a decluttering frenzy. Even after they had outgrown most of their toy box, the laser-tag pistols they got one Christmas could still keep Ezra and Jed cheerfully sniping each other for hours.

When Ezra was invited to his first laser-tag party at age ten, he came back singing his own praises.

'I'm so good at shooting, you have no idea.'

My friend Jo, whose son was the birthday boy, confirmed it. Ezra was top of the score sheet. I was impressed and ever so slightly alarmed.

When does nurture give up and instinct take over? Are we too quick to surrender to what we believe are masculine urges to shoot and conquer and compete? Should I have told my preschooler that 'peeling people' was too rough, and spent more time guiding him towards calmer, quieter fun instead?

According to the experts, there's no harm in gun play for kids – so long as they're playing safely and consensually – and it goes without saying that no child should have access to actual weapons. However, imaginary weapons are preferable to lifelike guns.

In her article 'Bang bang! You're dead', parenting coach Pennie Brownlee surmises that when kids are allowed to construct their own weapons, as opposed to being handed realistic AK-47s, for instance, it actually stimulates 'hundreds of thousands of connections in the child's brain' that allow them to process overwhelming emotions. Citing research by Swedish paediatricians and the American National Institute of Play Science, she points out that such richly imaginative play can be beneficial and actually work as an antidote to violence later in life.[6]

Children often use made-up weapons and other aggressive play to make them feel more powerful at a time when they have little power in reality. Games like these can even help a child work through difficult feelings and worries about the violence they see in society. Also, as my three-year-old discovered, going on a pretend 'peeling' spree with your mates can be so much fun.

It takes me back to school holidays in Nigeria, when my siblings and cousins and I would play cowboys. We'd watch Clint Eastwood movies and run outdoors to reenact *The Good, the Bad and the Ugly*. The girls thought we were as tough and badass as the boys. However, for the most part, we weren't as fixated on gunning each other down or beating each other up. We'd be indoors singing Diana Ross songs into the mirror while the boys made nunchucks out of cut tree branches, broken bed springs, nails and bicycle chains.

When we were little, a nursery rhyme told us that boys were made of frogs and snails and puppy-dog tails. Ask me now, as a mother, and I can tell you about LEGO and race cars; boys bouncing off tables or trees, spinning off scooters. Balls, boards, climbing frames. Toddlers with cuts on their cheeks and their mothers' hearts on their sleeves. I can also point you to boys in tutus and tights or stripy leggings. Fairy wings, face sparkle or rainbow nail polish. Boys who wear heels and dresses or grow their hair to bum-length. Geeky boys obsessed with coding, model trains, kitchen science or an alphabet of dinosaurs. Boys who prefer glitter or slime or colouring or poetry. Musical boys strumming or rapping in their bedrooms.

Boys are all the above and so much more. Today, a boy can be anything he wants to be. And yet, too many of our boys still feel trapped by ancient ideas of what a boy is supposed to be.

What comes to mind when you think of the word 'boy'? I interviewed a range of voices on this question, and I also asked my sons to poll their friends, who were aged between twelve and sixteen. Here are some of their responses:

SPORTS AND EDUCATION

'I think of blue because of the view that boys are supposed to wear blue and not pink, which I disagree with. When I think of a boy, I also think of sports because boys usually do more sports compared to girls.'

'When I think of the word "boy", I think of the colour blue and a male child. Just from personal experience, I think boys are more active and playful than girls tend to be.'

'Things that come to my mind are sport and activity but also a sense of power and control over what you want.'

'I see a boy as someone with less authority than a man.'

I was struck by how limiting some of their responses sounded. Several of those surveyed by my sons are boys I know personally, some I've known since they were little. These are boys who I would describe as creative and caring, funny and sweet. They are foodies, gamers, skateboarders, artists and geeks. Yet what instantly sprung to mind for them were thoughts of sport and action, power and control, and of course the colour blue.

From parents of boys, it was fascinating to hear more variation, although similar themes did crop up, such as noise, chaos, sports, sweat and mess. What came across strongly was the depth of pure love and affection parents feel for their sons; something not often expressed in stereotypical portraits of boyhood.

I spoke with comedian, actor and author Rob Delaney, the father of four boys, who told me that when he thinks of the word 'boy': 'I think of the joy I get from smelling their sweaty head after they've been playing outdoors. My oldest is eleven, so none of them stink yet.'[7]

Rob might enjoy discovering that even when they start to stink, you crave that closeness with your boys. The scent of a newborn baby's head has been proven to be as intoxicating as a drug. But you can get just as high from sniffing a boy you've loved and raised to the age of chin hair and Lynx. I still inhale the smell of my teenagers' locks, although I do it surreptitiously!

Broadcaster and writer Chine McDonald said that the word 'boy' conjured up: 'Big hearts, tireless energy and an insatiable appetite for adventure.'[8]

Eve Rodsky, writer and domestic-equity campaigner, boiled it down to four words: 'Courage. Resilience. Care. Love.'[9]

In a conversation with sisters Jen Audrie and Lisa Lynn, authors and hosts of the podcast, *Dear Patriarchy*, Jen was surprised to find herself tearing up when I asked what 'boy' meant to her. Her answer made me well up too.

I don't know why that made me so emotional. Boys are so special, and raising them is so loaded. Because they're

RAISING BOYS WHO DO BETTER

sweet and kind and loving but at the same time, from a very young age, they're put on a pedestal and kind of treated like little gods. But then so much is expected of them. They're told you can do whatever you want, have whatever you want. Then there are all the rules like 'don't cry, be tough'. There's a lot. Boy is a lot.[10]

I feel this deeply as a mother of sons. Is it possible to raise a boy who can feel truly free if he is weighed down by all these assumptions and biases and expectations, before he's figured out who he is and what he wants from life? It truly is a lot for a child to cope with and a lot for a parent to untangle too.

For Tom Lamont, the word 'boy' made him think of: 'a mess around their mouth or face, energy, chaos, making triple the amount of noise in any playground or park. My son comes to mind, I guess, my own youth comes to mind.'

However, on reflection, the plural 'boys' evoked something much less benign.

''Boy', singular, I think of with fondness but 'boys' in the plural has a different connotation to me; it seems there's more tension behind that word, more confused feelings. Maybe that's always the difference between the individual and the collective. When you think about individuals, you think of people close to you. Forty-year-old men might potentially refer to each other as boys. It could also be the summons to a stag weekend, and not all of those things have great connotations.'

I completely get what Tom is saying. For me, the thought of 'boys' as a collective can bring up that age-old ambivalence. As for 'men', that's even more complex.

On 15 March 2019, in Christchurch, New Zealand, a twenty-eight-year-old Australian man walked into two mosques with a Mossberg 930 semi-automatic shotgun and an AR-15-style rifle and opened fire. He was arrested on his way to a third mosque, and later pleaded guilty to fifty-one murders, forty attempted murders and engaging in a terrorist act. It was the deadliest mass shooting in New Zealand's history and resulted in the country's first sentence of life without the possibility of parole.

The gunman livestreamed fourteen minutes of his attack on Facebook. He also emailed out a seventy-page manifesto titled 'The Great Replacement', an allusion to a White supremacist conspiracy known as 'Great Replacement Theory' that suggests White people are being overtaken by non-Whites across Western societies. 'The Great Replacement' hit headlines again in 2022 after a mass shooting by another alt-right supremacist at an African American church in Buffalo, New York that claimed ten Black lives. These killings represent White male fragility at its most deadly, but they're only one part of the puzzle.

Whenever I hear about a mass shooting, I wonder about the shooters' parents. What kind of relationships did they have before their sons started to withdraw and turn to thoughts of destruction? Was their parenting part of the problem, or was there something inborn, a kink in the system, a twist in the genetic line? Do they have sweet memories of their tiny ones saying things as innocent, or troublingly prescient, as 'Peel, peel, peel'?

What makes a killer? There might never be a simple answer, but there is one troubling certainty: the majority of mass shooters are men.

'Men commit the overwhelming majority of mass shootings for basically the same reasons they commit most violent crimes.' This is a statement to CNN from 2018 by Dewey G. Cornell, a licensed forensic clinical psychologist and director of the Virginia Youth Violence Project at the University of Virginia. He added: 'Men tend to be more violent than women because of a complex interaction of evolutionary and psycho-social factors. Men tend to be more aggressive and less inhibited by empathy, and men in distress seem to be less willing to turn to others for help.'

Less than two weeks after the Buffalo shooting, an eighteen-year-old man fatally shot nineteen children and two teachers at Robb Elementary School in Uvalde, Texas. I will never forget the photos of the children, who were aged between seven and ten, shared in news reports. Their sweet little faces pictured in happy, carefree times. Some of the children had received special awards earlier that day for their schoolwork. The gunman was barely an adult himself. He had bought two assault rifles just after he turned eighteen. Right before the school shooting, he shot his sixty-six-year-old grandmother in the head.

By the following month, US newspapers had published more than 20,000 articles about both the Buffalo and Uvalde shootings. However, just thirty-seven of those articles pointed to toxic masculinity as an underlying factor, despite statistics that reveal that men are 98 per cent more likely than women to commit mass shootings. Of every mass shooting in North America since 1982, only three of the shooters has been a woman.

In 2019, the American Psychological Association released its first statement on traditional masculinity, describing how it harms boys, men and society at large. The report attracted a backlash from right-wing pundits and commentators, who worried that it was painting all men in a negative light. Yet, politics aside, we need to address the cold hard facts.

The APA report describes how men are three times more likely to die by suicide than women. Men live shorter lives than women, often because they take more risks and seek help less often. Men commit 90 per cent of homicides in the United States and they are also 70 per cent of homicide victims. Whether we call it traditional or toxic, fragile or rigid, the hardline culture of masculinity can have deadly consequences. It is a killer hiding in plain sight.

In the documentary film *The Mask You Live In* directed by Jennifer Siebel Newsom for The Representation Project, it's heartbreaking to hear the boys featured, ranging from school kids to young adults, talk about trying to take up a man-shaped space in a man's world. They describe the pressures of growing up to fit the 'man box', a rigid set of codes around what it means to be considered a 'real' man. 'The Man Box' is a concept popularized by A Call to Men founder Tony Porter, whose TED talk on the topic has been viewed more than three million times. Porter based it on the work of Paul Kivel, an educator, writer and activist originally from San Francisco, California.

Kivel is one of the co-founders of the Oakland Men's Project in San Francisco, California. For more than forty-five years, he's been leading workshops and training for schoolkids and adults on social justice, violence prevention and raising boys to manhood. One of his most influential concepts is the 'Act Like a Man Box', this idea of performative and restrictive masculinity and how it harms everyone. Paul and his team developed a curriculum based on conversations, role play, prompts and exercises to explore male socialization.

He says: 'We were really looking at the expectations of what it meant when boys are told to be a man, man up, act like a man. Boys immediately, wherever we went, could identify those ideas they'd been taught, such as be aggressive, don't make mistakes, be strong, get loads of girls.'[18]

For the exercise, Paul would draw a box around these codes or rules and label it. Then he'd open up a conversation about the names that boys get called when they dare to step outside the box.

'The boys very quickly threw out a litany of words like wussy, pussy, wimp, punk, fag. Then we have a conversation around what those are words for and what it feels like [to be called them]. How it links to sexism and homophobia.'

Paul would then lead boys through an exercise to examine what it costs boys and men to be in that box.

'Things like not showing affection, getting into fights, being fearful of appearing to be queer. Boys have already paid that cost. They know they don't fit in that box and that somebody is going to find out that they're not tough enough.'

Kivel is one of many experts who are using the Man Box methodology to get men and boys to open up.

'It's very powerful when boys hear other boys talking about not fitting into that box, because when you're out in the playground, you feel like you're not meeting the standard and there's something wrong with you.'

An Australian study of 1,000 men aged eighteen to thirty revealed that those who are more rigid in their masculine ideals, who force themselves more tightly into this Man Box, are also more prone to violence towards themselves and others. What's devastating to me is that inside every Man Box I can imagine a little boy, simultaneously hiding himself and desperate to be seen.

In a report by Promundo and Unilever titled 'The Man Box: A Study on Being a Young Man in the US, UK, and Mexico: Key Findings', the authors state:

> **Young men in the Man Box, it seems, experience some reward for meeting these societal expectations. They are doing what their parents, partners, friends, and media sources are telling them to do, and they can therefore feel a certain confidence and comfort in who they are. However, the Man Box also exacts a high cost in terms of mental health. It tells men they should always be tough no matter the circumstances, which no one can do. It tells them to act strong even when they feel uncertain. In other words, it tells them to be someone other than who they are.**

When I think of the word 'boy', I think of my sons in their sweetness and wildness and humour and rough edges and soft spots. I think of the life that I want for them and for all our children. A life of joy and ease, where everyone can breathe. When I think of 'boys', I envision the world as a house of boys pretending to be men. A giant Man Box, if you will. Many feel lost inside it, yet more are taught to sacrifice themselves to keep it standing. Yet a house is just a construct and a construct is just another word for a story. We need to tell ourselves and our children better, more expansive stories about boyhood and masculinity. It's time to deconstruct and build something new.

In the wake of the mass shootings in Christchurch, a group of schoolchildren came together to perform a haka as a way of honouring the victims. If you've seen the All Blacks rugby team performing a haka, you might recognize it as a Maori battle cry; a show of manly strength. Feet stamping, eyes rolling, tongues hanging and puffed-out chests. It looks like masculinity at its most amped up.

However, the haka can be performed by people of all ages and genders. The New Zealand women's team, the Black Ferns, have their own version of the dance. When the air shimmers on a hot summer day, Maori legend says it's Tane-rore, the son of sun god Tama-nui-te-ra and his wife Hine-Raumati, who embodies summer, dancing for his mother. This light, quick motion is the foundation for all haka.[21]

The children doing the haka for the schoolfriends who died were a mix of boys and girls, White and Indigenous, moving in sync. It's an incredibly beautiful and emotional performance. The first haka they sang, 'Tika Tonu', featured advice to a young man from his father.[22] These lyrics are especially poignant:

Tika tonu atu ki a koe, e tama

Hiki nei koe aku whakaaro, pakia!

He hiki aha to hiki?

He hiki roa to hiki?

I a ha ha!

E tama, te uaua ana

E tama, te maro

Roa ina hoki ra

Te tohe o te uaua na

E tau nei

Be true to yourself, my son!

My concerns have been raised about you, so pay attention!

What is this problem you are carrying?

How long have you been carrying it for?

Have you got that? Right, let's go on.

So, son, although it may be difficult for you,

and son, although it seems to be unyielding,

no matter how long you reflect on it

the answer to the problem

is here inside you[23]

A simple message worth repeating: Be true to yourself. The answer is inside you.

Conversation and Reflection Prompts

What comes to mind when you think of the word 'boy'?

What stories did you inherit around boyhood or gender when you were growing up?

Did you have set expectations about boys before you became a parent or caregiver?

How does your boy match or defy stereotypes?

How has becoming a parent reinforced or changed your view on boys?

Do you let your boy play with toy guns?

Do you agree that the world is a house of boys?

What do the lyrics of the 'Tika Tonu' haka mean to you as a parent?

ACT LIKE A MAN BOX

Try this exercise with your son or with a group of boys (girls can play too). Discuss what it takes to free yourself and live outside the box, not just as boys but as individuals. How can you make this a regular practice?

MOTHERS AND SONS

I f you want to piss off Kirstie Beaven, editor of *Sonshine* magazine, you only have to say two words to her. It's a phrase that makes the hairs on the back of her neck stand in protest. You might have used this phrase yourself, or seen it on T-shirts or bumper stickers or splashed across social media.

'There's a hashtag called #BoyMom which boils my blood,' she says, half-laughing, half-growling. 'It's all the stereotypes, i.e. your house is full of dirt, and football boots are everywhere, towels on the floor, hashtag boy mom. I feel like that's what springs to mind when I think of the word "boy", except the boys I know aren't so one-dimensional.'

Surely, though, as the mother of a son as well as a daughter, Kirstie can relate on some level?

No, it just does not speak to me at all. I'm parenting two different personalities and I don't think their gender is anywhere near as important as whether they're introverts or extroverts, or how resilient they are, how much sensory input they need, what activities bring them joy. I've taken my daughter to play football and stood on the cold, rainy, muddy field watching her play football, which is the typical #BoyMom

Kirstie observes that when you have one of each, it's harder to stomach those stereotypes. 'There are plenty of days when my daughter is the one charging round the house and yelling at the top of her voice,' she notes. 'Also, I learned in lockdown that one of my kids can't have a good day unless they've been outside and run around, and for me, that happens to be my daughter. She's like a puppy.'

I get where Kirstie is coming from and I sympathize, but I have to confess: I do identify as a #BoyMom. I've probably used that or a similar hashtag over a dozen times when sharing anecdotes about my kids on social media (not necessarily about football or muddy boots, despite nodding my head fiercely at that description).

Out of all the women I interviewed, none really saw themselves as a traditional 'boy mum'. However, I can confirm that most of the boy mamas I know feel we belong to a special club. There's no secret handshake. All we need is a look. A silent understanding that passes between us. For we have been to the other side. Our eyes have seen things we can never unsee. And we wouldn't have it any other way.

From playgroups to nursery, primary and secondary, sports teams and after-school clubs, the closest friends I've made since having kids have been fellow mothers of boys. We gravitate to each other as our kids tumble into each other's orbits. This might not be your experience; in fact, I'd encourage you to do things differently. Boys who grow up with close female relationships are more likely to see and treat girls and women as whole individuals. If you can, try to introduce more female friends into your little boy's life and maintain cross-gender friendships as he grows.

When Ezra was a baby, he had a girl pal called Esra. Jed was besties with Eve, whose brother Jake was in Ezra's year. They were so cute together and we couldn't stop ourselves from planning their future weddings and imagining how beautiful their kids would be. However, over time and distance, these friendships faded, and the boys became much more about their male crews.

I know at least one boy in the mix who had maintained a close friendship with a girl since we all hung out together at Stay and Play. By their tween years, however, she had a huge crush on him, and he was either blissfully unaware or playing it off, according to his mother. It felt like boy-and-girl friendships were either doomed to cooling off or turning into a 'will they/won't they' Cameron Crowe romcom. In actuality, while boys and girls often split down gender lines as they enter pre-school, mixed-gender friendships become more common as they approach adulthood. Of course, sex can get in the way. A 2015 study by a Norwegian University suggested that males and females often misread each other's signals: she interprets his attraction as friendliness, while he interprets her friendly behaviour as sexual interest. However, millennials are more likely to see friendships between males and females as normal. According to a 2020 YouGov survey, eight in ten (84 per cent) Britons believe men and women can be friends, compared to 6 per cent who don't.

Whatever one believes, according to everything from classic literature to greeting cards to that vintage sailor's tattoo, there's nobody who owns a boy's heart like his beloved mama.

The mother–son relationship is the stuff of Freudian legend, fodder for Hitchcock movies and mother-in-law jokes. The archetypal mother-and-son spectrum veers from the Madonna and Child to Agrippina and Emperor Nero. An iconic, virginal beacon of pure love, or an obsessive, manipulative woman who would watch the empire burn if her son could sit on its ashes (legend has it that Nero ordered his mum's death when she got a bit too *motherish*).

Needless to say, neither of these extremes speaks to me. Yet I have felt the tug myself, something I can't explain: a love for my boys beyond reason.

When I asked author Eve Rodsky what surprised her most about mothering boys, she said: 'How close I am to them. How much we share together. Our deep connections in a heart-centred way.'

Perhaps it's got nothing to do with mothering boys and everything to do with being a parent. I asked educator Zahara Chowdhury the same question and she said: 'What surprises me is just the overwhelming amount of love and care. I'm so in love with him and my daughter. It's really difficult, almost impossible, to imagine my life without them. It scares me.'[4]

Jen Audrie of the *Dear Patriarchy* podcast told me that having a boy created a big shift in her feelings around men in general.

> **When I left my last job, it was because of sexual harassment, which I'd faced throughout my career. I did kind of have a hardened heart towards men, and unfortunately boys as well, although at no point did I transfer that to my unborn child. I think that, since having my boys, it really helped me not just understand on a**

cerebral level, but also in my heart, that the patriarchy is not men, it's the systems. I think learning that changed me, also seeing my sons and falling in love with them in a very different way that's sometimes hard to understand. There's such a deep tie, I think, between mothers and sons. But it also helped me fall in love with my husband more because I could see that little boy in him.

In a Netmums poll of 2,500 parents, more than half of mothers said they had a stronger connection with their boys. Ninety per cent admitted treating their sons more favourably than their daughters. I'm fascinated by this. Experts surmise that it's because women are more self-critical and more likely to see themselves in their female children. They've experienced their own mothers' disapproval and they continue that cycle with their daughters. In the Netmums poll, mothers tended to judge their daughters more harshly, while describing their sons as 'funny, cheeky, playful and loving'. My niece Mayowa accuses her mother Nkiru of playing favourites with her brother Seyi all the time. I had to laugh when Nkiru told me how she usually responds: 'He's not my favourite. He's just my son.'

#BoyMom

Before I announced the sex of my first child, strangers predicted it for me. I was living in Lagos at the time, and despite being in a happy relationship I had no immediate plans of having babies. One afternoon in June, a bout of suspected food poisoning sounded alarm bells. I bought a pregnancy kit from a roadside kiosk, paying 500 naira (about 80p) for the news that would change my life for ever. A visit to the doctor revealed I was already two months gone.

Despite taking so long to realize I was pregnant, I had a strong sense that it was a boy. As the weeks passed, people on the street would meet my growing belly with knowing smiles.

'Ah, Mama Bomboy. Well done.'

'Well done' is a common greeting in Nigeria, but it was also advance praise for my achievement. In West African pidgin, 'bomboy' refers to a plump and healthy baby boy. Calling me 'Mama Bomboy' was both guesswork and invocation. May I be blessed with a male heir. For a daughter might earn her bride price one day, but, even in 2005, a son was the ultimate prize. One reason why is that Nigeria is a patriarchal society where a male child is more likely to carry on the family lineage and to support his parents financially in their old age.

I can't say how I knew I was having a boy, but I felt his presence strongly. Maybe it was the shape of my bump (a myth) or the heightened sex drive (pure facts). When the ultrasound scan affirmed it, I was giddy with expectation.

I wore my bump and the conferred titles with pride. Mama Boy. Mama Bomboy. I wept at the baby shower when my cousin's wife gifted me a hooded towel embroidered with 'Baby Cole' (my married name) in light blue thread. I played Lauryn Hill's ode to her son, 'Zion', on repeat, screeching along to the part where she sings 'my joy' over and over until her voice cracks. But it wasn't until Ezra was in my arms, squinting up at me, that my heart cracked wide open.

Hello, baby boy. My joy, my joy, my joy.

When I learned I was expecting baby number two, I pictured a boy. A teeny replica of Ezra who could wear his hand-me-downs. But I also dreamed about having a girl. I'm not into fairies and florals but I did fantasize about shopping in the pretty section. Boys' clothing seemed to be dominated by checked shirts, dungarees and T-shirts covered in trucks. My husband used to joke that he didn't have girl sperm in him. On some days, though, he wondered about life with a 'mini Uju'. I wondered too.

However, I had lost a baby at twelve weeks, before finding out that I was pregnant again a month later. At six weeks, I was rushed back to hospital, bleeding. The baby was intact, the doctors assured me. But at each visit, I would hold my breath as the probe rolled over my tummy, praying silently: please, let there be a heartbeat. Please.

For the eighteen-week appointment, we weren't fussed about finding out the sex. All we wanted was a baby who was healthy and, most importantly, alive. When the scan technician pointed at the screen and asked if we could 'guess' what we were having, my husband and I burst out laughing. There it was, unmistakably. Another boy. A brother for Ezra and a hat trick for Abiye, whose first son Isaac would turn thirteen after the new kid arrived. We couldn't contain our delight.

One of the blessings of having another son is that you have a fairly good idea of what's coming. I was no longer worried about some of the tough first calls I'd had to make with Ezra like leaving my baby to cry himself to sleep (nope) or whether to vaccinate my infant (trust the science). To circumcise or not? It wasn't even a question. Also, I adored being a boy mum. I was a sucker for his cheeky energy. The way he'd pull me into his arms and profess his feelings for me.

'I love you, Mummy. You're my nice girl. You're beautiful.'

Mama Bomboy. As an African, you're welcome to pop out as many sons as your womb can handle. But in the West, it's a different story. When you announce you're having another boy, it's not always met with unbridled enthusiasm. The general sense is that one boy is fun, two boys are a handful, three or more boys are a disaster waiting to happen.

I remember standing at a bus stop with Ezra when I was heavily pregnant with Jed. A woman beside me asked if I knew what I was having.

'Another boy,' I replied, smiling.

'Oh,' she said. 'Shame.'

I'd barely had a chance to register what she'd said before she put her hand over her mouth.

'I'm so sorry, I don't know why I said that.' She was flushing. 'I've got two boys myself. I guess it's just that people always expect you to want one of each.'

There are few things heavier than the weight of other people's expectations. Ivanka Poku, a mother of gorgeous twin boys, found herself becoming increasingly enraged by the response to her third pregnancy.

'If one more person says "Oh no" after I tell them I am expecting a third boy, I'm going to punch them in the face.'

Like me, she was carrying a 'rainbow baby'; a pregnancy after a miscarriage. She was delighted that her boy was healthy and felt that her family would be complete. Yet comment after comment insinuated that she'd be missing out on a baby girl and that she was only adding more trouble and chaos to her life.

On an episode of the popular *On Boys* podcast, a trio of mothers shared some of the most offensive comments they'd had while out with their male offspring: 'You remind me of a little Russian lady trying to count up all her monkeys in a cartoon.' Or this one, delivered within earshot of the other children: 'What's wrong with your husband's sperm?'

If you are a mother of boys, everybody has an opinion. Boys are loud, aggressive, hectic, destructive, sporty, messy, rambunctious, smelly, rough. Boys will wear you out. Boys will leave you high and dry when they grow up and start families of their own. I'll admit there's a sprinkling of truth to some of these stereotypes. However, there are infinite layers to the male human and what he can be and do.

My friend Vicki tells me she feels mildly offended when, since the birth of her daughter, people say stuff like: 'You must be so happy now that you've got your girl.'

'It's such an insult to my boys,' she says, 'and of course, I love my little girl and my eldest, but it's my middle son who's most like me. Also, all these stereotypes that boys will leave you . . . I'm Greek. They never leave! Greek men stay with their mamas for life.'

When I mentioned I was writing about boys, my friend Mercy clapped her hands.

'Boys never stop breastfeeding! Make sure you put that in your book. I have two in secondary and my eldest is twenty-four, but it's as if they're still permanently attached.'

Back in the day, older relatives would tease my boys for clinging to me. They'd warn me that I was spoiling them or that the little one would find it hard to go to school when the time came. Some raised their eyebrows because I breastfed each of them until they were eighteen months old. Obviously they'd never come across those extended breastfeeding lactivists who nurse their children practically until they leave for uni.

At a London salon one time, I was breastfeeding a then thirteen-month-old Jed. He was finally drifting off to sleep when my stylist, a fellow African, walked over. She stopped in her tracks.

'What is he doing?' she practically yelled at us. 'Oh my God, I can't believe it.'

She tapped my baby's head.

'Stop that now!'

Jed pulled off and blinked at her.

'Grandpa, you're still sucking?'

She told me that her son, now almost one, had nursed until nine months and she thought he'd never quit the habit.

'Boys love the breast too much.'

They may have given up the boob long ago, but I'm still super-close with my boys. It's hard to know where to draw the line sometimes, though. Most days, I'm reasonable about them growing up and moving on at some point. Then there are moments when I think their future partners will have to hack them free from my cold dead fingers. Will I ever be ready for my son to put his arms around another woman and call her his nice girl?

They say it's harder for mothers than fathers to cut the cord, and it's hardest of all for mothers of sons.

Maybe it's primal; an instinct in us to protect the weaker sex. Because, as it turns out, male superiority is something of a myth. Human females are more resilient, outlasting males from cradle to the grave. Premature baby boys have a 50 per cent greater mortality rate than girls. Even full-term boys don't fare as well. Around the world, more boys are born each year, but they are less likely to survive.

In a CNN interview, professor Ray Catalano (school of public health, University of California, Berkeley) described the male infant as "a relatively frail organism".

He said: 'For every society, for every year, the human being most likely to die [prematurely] is male infants. And that's true for every society that we have data for.'

A boy finds it harder to adjust outside his mother's womb. Baby boys cry more than girls and generally need more comforting. In pregnancy, a female foetus can manage with the placenta alone, while a male foetus grows more slowly and consumes more of his mother's calories. Essentially, if you are expecting a boy, you give up more of your life force. That's one theory why mothers who only have sons are statistically more likely to die after age forty-five. Read that again and weep. Stats like these really piss me off when I'm trailing after the boys, picking up their socks.

'Look at this mess. You people will not kill me before my time. Do you realize mums of boys are more likely to die early?'

Jed doesn't look up from his screen.

'Did you even hear me?'

He lifts his headphones. 'Sorry, Mum. I hope you don't die young.'

He grins and returns to his phone.

As I stomp through the living room, collecting debris, part of me is amused, part of me is boiling. Another part of me acknowledges that I'm digging that early grave with my own shovel. So why don't I just put the shovel down?

Gonca Senocak, a mother of a teen boy and a tween girl, blames it on boys being more needy.

'When I compare my kids, Adasu has always been so independent. Mehmet is older but he would let me do everything for him if I let him.'

Am I biologically wired to sacrifice myself for my male offspring, despite my feminist beliefs? Are mothers to blame for raising men who prowl the earth like it owes them something?

All that being said, we can't be at fault for everything, surely? Society is quick to point the finger at us. It's worse for working-class Black mothers, commonly accused of everything from breaking up the family unit to draining the social welfare system and letting Black boys run amok.

The flipside of this is when mothers come down extra hard on their sons, and mothers of colour can be the harshest. We know that our boys need skin as thick as armour, and we are the ones who have to build it up. You can see this 'tough love' in African, Asian and Latino culture, but overall, it doesn't seem to breed tough boys. It breeds men who are entitled and fragile, or resentful and insecure.

Vanessa Walters, author of *The Niger Wife*, has experienced this from both Jamaican and Nigerian culture. She asserts that mothers need to be a soft place for their boys. 'The mother–son relationship is probably the most important, even if not necessarily the closest. Men don't get a lot of empathy from the world, so they really need their mother for a source of unconditional love.'[9]

We have a huge responsibility as mothers holding up half of the world, but we can't bear the weight alone. Especially when, thanks to the patriarchy, our bodies are never fully our own.

What is an earthquake? Is it what happens when our female ancestors turn over in their graves? Or when the earth finally opens her mouth to tell her story? On the day that Roe vs Wade was overturned, many women felt the tremor. The ground rocked, my insides screamed with rage. I spoke about it with Ezra and Jed, and they were surprised, but their response was a vague echo of their father's – that is, that the US Supreme Court can suck it. It was really no skin off their noses. These seismic shocks are never as great for men.

Educate Your Son. The message is loud and clear, but how can we do this effectively when so much is theoretical for them?

After a biology class at school that describes the menstrual cycle, Jed tells me he's glad he's not a woman. That doesn't stop him from showing me a meme comparing labour pains to getting kicked in the nuts.

'Ultimately, neither a man nor a woman can ever really know which is worse,' he says, knowledgeably.

Amused, I dig up a video in which men are strapped to devices that mimic period cramps. The men are writhing in agony.

'And those are monthly cramps,' I inform him. 'And labour pains are about a thousand times worse than cramps.'

Clearly, I've won this argument, although apparently only in my head. My boys still aren't convinced there's anything quite like taking a hit to the family jewels. *It's OK*, I sniff, *this isn't a contest*. It's about basic human care. You don't have to suffer the same to have empathy for the people in your community.

Unfortunately, empathy isn't what's being fed to boys from Man Box culture, and you won't always find it in your male partner if he's been raised under the same systems.

Lisa Lynn of the *Dear Patriarchy* podcast tells me she's most frustrated when she clashes with her partner over the way she's trying to bring their son up against a tide of macho programming.

> **My partner has three children from a previous relationship. One of them is a girl and while it grinds my gears a little bit that he needs to have had a girl to understand some of these patriarchal concepts, she has been an excellent way for me to illustrate to him the damage of patriarchal conditioning and toxic masculinity. But it does sometimes feel like when you're on empty anyway, when you have to educate the person you're living with in order to see your humanity – because that's very much how it feels sometimes – and to protect the developing sense of humanity that your son is getting, that's when I'm most close to getting really frustrated.**

Author Chine McDonald admitted she's sometimes wracked with worry about bringing up her two boys.

'I recently read Laura Bates's *Men Who Hate Women*, and I feel the weight of responsibility of parenting boys that don't grow up to be "incels" who hate women. I feel the weight of responsibility of raising boys that will smash the patriarchy, not prop it up.'

If the thought of having to teach your son about smashing the patriarchy, Roe vs Wade, period pains, feminism, gender diversity, racial justice, capitalist structures and myriad other things stresses you out, take a breath. You don't have to serve it all up at once and they don't have to drink it all in one gulp. The best education is your mother–son relationship. How you engage, how you nurture, how you create a secure attachment, how you help them regulate their emotions, how you facilitate conversations, how you inspire curiosity and critical thinking. Most of us never learned conscious parenting from our own caregivers. We are figuring it out and so we need to have patience and make space for mistakes. Parenting is one long stumble towards love and acceptance.

Dr Cara Natterson, author, paediatrician and host of *Puberty Podcast*, gave me some excellent advice in this regard. She said the main thing we can all practise as parents and caretakers, everyone who touches the lives of kids, is permission to take a do-over.

> **If you as a parent say to a five- or ten- or fifteen-year-old, "I got that wrong," you're modelling that it's OK to fail, but also to take the do-over and try it a different way. There's so much power to this kind of modelling and, to me, that's how we raise up kids regardless of their gender. That's how we empower them to be good humans.[10]**

The main thing I've learned is that there's real joy in being a boy mum, so long as you don't let the hashtags lock either of you in. There should be no gatekeeping of affection either. Too often, boys get shamed for their attachment, and that can be the first shove down the one-way chute to hypermasculinity hell.

Even in 2023, one of the quickest ways to emasculate a man is to call him a 'mama's boy'. And yet, the number-one predictor of success for a boy is his relationship with his mother. Studies show that a healthy mother–son bond improves their behaviour, boosts academic performance, helps boys resist peer pressure, decreases risky behaviour, helps keep them off the streets. Boys with close attachments to their mums are less likely to have underage sex, get hooked on drugs or alcohol, join gangs, experience depression or anxiety, act out aggressions or wind up in prison. They are more tuned in to their emotions and less caught up in performing masculinity. Overall, true mama's boys make for better life partners and happier, more resilient human beings.

On 13 October 2021, comedian Joanna Neary shared an anecdote on Twitter that went viral: 'Yesterday, a male teacher openly mocked my son for turning back at the school gate to wave goodbye to me. Today, my son said he wants to stop waving from now on. This is how it starts.'

Thousands of people responded, most decrying the teacher's toxic masculinity and the cage that society puts boys in from birth. Others spoke about the power of teachers to shape or wreck lives, and how children of all genders are often taught to quash their feelings in order to fit in. A few commenters pointed out that the teacher was probably raised under a set of 'real men' rules; that he was a victim too.

My favourite response came from author Simon Young: 'This is really sad to hear. Tell your son I'm forty-five and still practically dislocate my shoulder waving to my mam when I leave her house.'

Tell your sons that real men wave at their mothers. Real men have feelings and aren't afraid to let the whole world know. Tell your sons that it's OK to express who they are at any given stage.

It's OK to wave at your boys too, kiss them, smell their heads. Because they are growing, and you never know when it's the last time you get to feel their fuzz-free cheek against yours or a hand that still fits inside your palm. I look at how much my sons have changed since the pandemic, and my heart sighs.

Sooner than you imagine, the baby they placed in your arms wrapped like a Jedi will be a teenager trying to rest his bristly chin on your head (or maybe your shoulder, if you're taller than me). It is astonishing to see the child you once carried in your arms become someone you look up to.

At bedtime, mostly we fist bump, but every now and then, my seventeen-year-old pulls me in for a hug and pats my back; a strange role reversal that's comical and rather sweet.

The walls above our door frames are smudged with finger marks, evidence of Ezra and Jed stretching to test their wingspans.

Every door in our home records a memory of a boy who crawled, toddled and walked through it many years ago.

'Remember when I couldn't reach the doorknob?'

'It took me so long to be able to unhook that latch!'

'Isn't it funny that just last year I couldn't see through this peephole?'

We are the doorways our children pass through, slamming in their wake. Our bodies bear the smudges of their fingerprints. The notches that show how quickly they've grown. Too quickly.

Sooner than we know, our boys will square their shoulders and stride into manhood. They might never look back. But if they do, I'll be right here, waving. Or throwing up my gang sign, #BoyMom.

Conversation and Reflection Prompts

Are you a typical boy mum?

In what ways do you (and your boy) defy stereotypes?

What do you think distinguishes the mother–son relationship?

If you have a child of another gender, do you or they feel you play favourites with your son?

What is your favourite thing about mothering a boy?

And the most challenging or surprising?

How do you feel about raising a mama's boy? Has your opinion shifted from reading this chapter?

CHALLENGE

Go on a mother–son date (you don't have to call it a date!). Think of some things you can do together that might challenge the boy-mom or mama's-boy stereotypes. You pick one suggestion. Let him pick another one. Make this a family tradition.

HOW NOT TO RAISE A CHAUVINIST

read a good piece of advice somewhere that when your child says 'Look at me' what they're really saying is 'Witness me'. Pay attention. Show me that I matter. So, I do my best to give my sons my fullest attention whenever they say, 'Mum, look', which has happened approximately 13.7 billion times during my relatively brief career as a mother. 'Mummy, look!' One kid goes flying and tumbling over the sofa in a stunt that could break every bone if it goes wrong. 'Mummy, watch me!' Another kid on a scooter doing turns and spins on the pavement edge as cars hurtle past. 'Mum, check this out!' The latest expletive-filled music video. As a writer-in-residence (aka work-from-home parent), the timing doesn't always suit. But whenever I can, I put down whatever I'm doing and try to lean in. Of course, sometimes this attentiveness comes back to bite me in the other cheek. Like when my sixteen-year-old looks up from his phone, amused.

'Hey, Mum, pree this.'

Witness me.

I stroll over and he shows me a clip of a women's NBA player missing a basket in spectacular fashion. The ball lurches into the air and soars blissfully past the hoop as if it's on a journey to live a better life, somewhere at another stadium. The clip is cut to reaction shots of famous NBA players holding their heads, falling to the ground stupefied, or laughing hysterically. Ezra's chuckling as he replays it.

'That is a serious *L*. Some of these air balls are crazy.'

It's funny, I'll admit. However, my inner activist is bristling. I'm quick to point out there are countless male ballers who miss shots regularly. Why do they keep turning women into memes? WNBA players deserve more respect.

'Yeah, but let's face it, nobody wants to watch women play basketball. I mean, they can't even dunk.'

Ezra's grinning wickedly now, primed for my comeback.

'You know, all you're doing is giving me more material for my book. I'm going to quote you throughout.'

He shrugs. 'All publicity is good publicity.'

When you live with teenagers, or teen boys in my experience, you learn to take banter like one of the lads. Most of the time, I dust my shoulders off and keep rolling. After all, I know where they really stand and getting into a 'he said, she resisted' scenario can be like digging myself into a one-woman hole. However, sometimes, there's an underlying edge. Because the balance of power outside our home means that, no matter which way I turn, I will hit a wall marked 'Patriarchy'. When Ezra or Jed or their dad slides a blatantly sexist joke into conversation to wind me up, it grates because we all know that this is how so many people actually think. So while I'm biting my tongue at Ezra's WNBA comment, I'm making a mental note to Google: 'Can women dunk?'

Apparently, I'm not the first person to consider this question. Google searches that come up include: 'Can women dunk?', 'Has a girl ever dunked a basketball?' and my favourite: 'Is it illegal for women to dunk in the WNBA?'

According to one stat, as of 2020 there had been twenty-seven total dunks by women in the entire history of professional US basketball leagues. An article in *Slate* discusses why there are so few dunks in the women's game, putting it down to a huge gap in 'leaping ability' between men and women. Once a cisgender male hits puberty, typically he can jump higher than 95 percent of females, regardless of whether he's shooting for a basketball rim or leaping over a pole vault.

I skim over a report about Oklahoma State basketball player Toni Young, whose coach banned her from dunking after she did one in practice and broke her arm in three places. Instead, I'm eager to tell my boys what I've learned: that girls can dunk, as a matter of fact. Although I already know how they'd respond:

'Twenty-seven total dunks? Are you serious right now, Mum?'

Effectively, I would only be proving their point. Of course, this isn't really about dunking. It's about slamming on the idea that women are lesser beings because we can't reach the rim so easily. It's about taking a sledgehammer to that patriarchy wall and smashing a hole right through it. Except that we shouldn't reach for a sledgehammer. As Audre Lorde said, the master's tools will never dismantle the master's house. We need to get creative if we want to take this shit apart.

A male chauvinist's sense of fragile self-worth partly hinges on the knowledge that when it comes down to it, they can overpower most females by sheer size and strength. From another angle, this is partly why very few women can ever feel 100 per cent safe from the threat of male violence. Some men love to bring up competitive sports as a sign of male dominance. In fact, a 2019 YouGov poll showed that an astonishing one in eight males believed they could win a point against Serena Williams in a tennis match. Male chauvinists will gloat that Serena might be 'the GOAT', but she'd never beat Nadal or Federer. That's why the Men's Final is the grand finale at Wimbledon. It's also why the whole world stops for the hundred metres men's race. We admire female sprinters, but none can match Usain Bolt.

I don't want my sons thinking women's sports aren't as relevant as the men's games. Yet as I write this, my own double standard is giving me a side-eye. When England won the Women's Euros, it felt like a landmark moment. I relished seeing the Lionesses dancing on a table at a press conference, to the inevitable outrage of some commentators. However, before the tournament, I have to admit that I could barely name any players on the England women's team.

On the popular podcast *The Guilty Feminist*, host Deborah Frances-White and her guests always begin with the phrase: 'I'm a feminist, but . . . ' and then reveal some of their not-so-feminist confessions. It's a funny and relatable take on how women can betray our better instincts. We can't bang on about feminism without acknowledging the ways in which we fall short, for we are all works in progress and unpacking our own chauvinism is an essential part of this work.

My name is Uju and I'm a feminist but . . . I'm helpless with DIY. I have never mowed a lawn. I'm the first to comment on a newsreader's hair and clothing (to be fair, I do this with any gender). Typically, my heart melts when my husband cries in movies, but occasionally, I cringe. My alter ego is a cross between Ruby from *Black-ish* and Jack Bauer from *24*. Sometimes I buy pink products just so no one else in my house uses them. I'd rather watch Arsenal men's football than women's.

What about you? What are your 'feminist but' confessions? Don't skip past this if you're a man; as Chimamanda Ngozi Adichie said, we should all be feminists. The fact is that male chauvinism undeniably has its grip on all of us, some tighter than others. One school of thought dates the concept of the patriarchy back to around 12,000 years ago, when agricultural life began. Humans settled in groups and started owning resources that needed defending by the strongest males present. Nowadays, in pretty much every patriarchal society – that is, most modern societies – the vision of the ideal man is almost identical: physically superior, commanding, decisive, emotionally in control, ready to take on anything. These are qualities that might look good on the battlefield but, in everyday life, this archetype can be extremely limiting for boys and men.

The original definition of 'chauvinism', which defined it as 'a belief in your country's superiority' has evolved to become interchangeable with 'sexism', and for good reason. It's the same aggressive, colonizing mentality that seeks to dominate the planet that also wants to hold women down. Long before intersectionality became a theory, sexism, racism and capitalism worked as an unholy trinity.

The word chauvinism comes from Nicolas Chauvin, who was supposedly a die-hard devotee of Napoleon. It's questionable whether Chauvin actually existed, but his name has been etched in history. The term 'male chauvinist pig' sprung up around the Civil Rights era, and was used to describe extreme nationalism, aggressive masculinity and the oppressive State. It also harks back to the 'pig laws' of the post-slavery American South, when a Black person could face prison for stealing a three-dollar pig. Today, 'pig' is a term that's become inseparable from the long and corrupt arm of the law.

Hollywood actor Steve McQueen, once described as 'paranoid, aggressive and macho', stated: 'They call me a chauvinist pig. I am and I don't give a damn.' Unfortunately, some men claim it as a badge of honour. Yet no matter how porcine his demeanour, calling someone like the infamous 'pussy-grabber' Donald Trump a 'pig' is an insult to the friendly creatures. After all, pigs are highly intelligent, social and playful animals with excellent spatial-mapping skills.

Perhaps we could speak of 'male chauvinist trees', although it doesn't quite have the same ring to it. Actually, it's not trees that are the problem, but 'male' trees planted by botanical chauvinists. Ask Tom Ogren, a horticulturist who's spent years warning about botanical sexism and its environmental effects. If you've noticed yourself sneezing, wheezing and rubbing your eyes more frequently lately, blame the proliferation of male trees in urban parks and gardens.

Male trees are evolutionarily designed to spread their pollen far and wide (sound familiar?) to help fertilize females' seeds. But since urban foresters have been over-planting male trees, pollination is out of control. Ogren (whose wife suffers from allergies and asthma) began investigating why all the trees in his neighbourhood were male. He came across advice in the 1949 USDA *Yearbook of Agriculture*: 'When used for street plantings, only male trees should be selected, to avoid the nuisance from the cottony seed.'

Apparently, the fear was that female trees would drop their seed pods and fruit all over the place, making a big mess for us to clean up, whereas male pollen would simply wash or blow away. However, Ogren says female trees don't actually produce seeds or fruits without any males present. In fact, female trees trap and remove large amounts of pollen from the air and turn it into seed. So, his solution to creating an allergen-free environment is to plant more female trees.

In a truly millennial moment, Ogren's rather obscure theory was picked up by an influencer, Ellie Botoman, whose post went viral on TikTok, garnering around 2.9 million views according to *BuzzFeed*. It sparked debates around botanical sexism, capitalism and the patriarchy.

But here's the rub: my husband and our youngest son are both plagued by allergies and start coughing, sneezing and chugging antihistamines each April. However, if I mentioned male trees and botanical sexism, they would laugh me out of the room. I don't blame them either. It sounds like feminism gone barking mad (pun intended).

My real question here is this: how do we get men and boys to care as much when the status quo is so comfortable for them? Or, even if it makes them uncomfortable, how do we get them to engage when there are centuries of programming to unravel? Sometimes I listen to my sons in a family debate, and their inclination to lead with maleness rather than insight, and I wonder: is it too late for them already?

Where to begin? One way is to focus on engaging boys in thought-provoking conversations around male identity and the wider culture. It's also helpful to start tuning in to more conversations yourself.

I was listening to author Michael Ian Black on a podcast talking about a fake Spanish-language game show on *Saturday Night Live*. *'Quien Es Mas Macho?'* has comedian Bill Murray asking contestants which of two celebrities is more macho. Black said any one of us can play this game with practically anything. Try it now and I'll bet we have the same answers. What's more macho, coffee or tea? A German Shepherd or a poodle? Butter or margarine?

It's essentially a game about masculinity and social coding. Black explained that butter is more masculine because margarine was created for healthier eating and showing that you care about your health has been socialized as a feminine thing to do. He said: 'Anybody will be fluent in this language by the time they're around age five, and if you choose to deviate from this as a boy, you risk being mocked, made fun of, teased.'

I played this game with my then thirteen-year-old. First, I explained the *'Quien Es Mas Macho?'* rules. Then I started with a question about a TV show we'd watched, *How I Met Your Mother*.

'Who is more macho, Barney or Ted?'

Jed responded, 'I think I have to say Barney.'

'I would say Barney as well, but interesting that you hesitated. Barney isn't obvious even though he's a more obviously macho guy. At the core he's very sensitive. Who is more macho, Hulk or Spiderman?'

'Hulk.'

I compared two men who had played for the Arsenal men's team.

'Kolasinac or Nketiah?'

'Kolasinac.'

'Now we're going to play it with completely random things. What's more macho, a mug or a teacup?'

'A mug.'

'What is more macho, a pillow or a cushion?'

'A cushion.'

'A piece of paper or a notebook?'

'A piece of paper.'

'Ketchup or mayonnaise?'

'Ketchup.'

'A bar of soap or hand sanitizer?'

'Hmm . . . Hand sanitizer.'

'That's a tricky one for me as well. Spaghetti or noodles?'

'Spaghetti.'

'It's interesting that you instantly have an idea of what is more macho? Why do you think that is?'

'I actually have no idea. Maybe it's what I like more or something.'

'So, are you identifying with the macho or with the other thing?'

'The macho.'

'And what makes you feel like you need to identify with the macho?'

'I'm male.'

'Do you understand what macho means?'

'Not a hundred per cent.'

'What's your sort of best guess at what it means?'

'Maybe like a stereotypically strong person who does a lot of things to seem, like, cool and strong.'

Jed had no idea why, but these ancient codes are passed on and written into us by the time we start school. After researching my first book, *Bringing Up Race*, and discovering how racial identity is constructed, I was fascinated by the similarities with gender constructs.

Just as with race, by the time they are three months old, babies can distinguish between people of different genders. Around the same age that young children are forming set ideas around racial differences, a two- or three-year-old is also establishing a sense of themselves and others according to the gender label. By age five, owing to the conscious and unconscious messages they receive from society, kids have quite strong ideas about boys, girls, how they look, who does what and who matters more.

A *Daily Mail* article charmingly titled 'Five-Year-Old Children are Inherently Sexist' describes a study of hostile and benevolent sexist attitudes held by children of that age group. Unlike hostile sexism (the more obvious type), benevolent sexism involves attitudes such as, 'women need doors held open for them,' or 'women are better homemakers'. Benevolent sexism sounds benign, but it's a breeding ground for the microaggressions that chip away at female progress.

As kids grow older and develop a less reductive understanding of gender roles, their hostile sexism tends to reduce. However, while girls tend to shrug off sexist attitudes, benevolent sexism lingers for boys at age eleven, most likely because the patriarchy is everywhere and boys have more to uphold. For while young girls are encouraged to see themselves without limits, young boys are socialized to prop up the Man Box and its limiting belief system.

Gender bias affects kids globally, as outlined by a Save the Children survey of around 1,900 fourth graders – nine- and ten-year-olds – in West Africa (nearly 1,400 in Sierra Leone and another 400 or so in Côte d'Ivoire) and around 500 kids of the same age in America. In response to sexist statements like 'boys are smarter than girls' and a 'wife should obey her husband', up to 70 per cent of boys in the West African countries and a quarter of girls agreed, as did 40 percent of US boys, versus 5 percent of girls. In the US, close to 70 per cent of boys and girls agreed that housework is a mother's job.

According to the World Economic Forum, only fifteen countries will close their gender gap within the next half-century. It will take 208 years to reach gender equity in the US at the current pace of change. In the UK, the expectancy is seventy-eight years. In other words, it's unlikely to be within our lifetimes. However, there's some hope for our children and we can make a difference while we're still here too. Parents and caregivers can help kids challenge sexist, misogynistic, chauvinistic attitudes from an early age through a combination of thoughtful conversations, critical questions, storytelling, role play and role modelling.

When talking to children about race, I've encouraged parents to speak openly, factually and positively about how we are different and also how we are the same; to foster critical thinking by asking open-ended questions, and to raise curious kids who ask big and small questions too. To read and watch alongside their kids and discuss what comes up. To model the behaviours they'd like to see in their children, and to affirm hope and resistance through inspirational stories and figures from history and the present day. All these techniques can be applied to raising gender-equal children too.

If you'd like to role-play some situations, here are some simple scripts I've shared on challenging racist comments that also work for shutting down sexist ideas. You can try these with your kids or use them with your peers.

Respond to questions and statements that seem imbued with sexism with the following:

Why would you say that? Have you thought about it this way?

What do you mean by that? Here's what I've learned.

Is this what you actually planned to say? This is how it came across.

Do you realize what you said is harmful/sexist/illegal? Hear me out and I'll explain.

Or try direct statements:

That's not funny. That's not kind. That's not cool. That's not clever. That's not OK. That's not fair. That's not true. That's sexist.

Affirmations are essential too, by teaching children of all genders to be inclusive and teaching kids to claim themselves. For instance: *Girls can play football. Boys can play with dolls. Anyone can carry pink/blue/ rainbow bags. You don't have to be a boy or a girl to wear this outfit. I am who I say I am, and I hope you feel free to be yourself too.*

Of course, children learn most from watching the adults around them, so it's important to examine your personal biases and behaviours and to start discussions with your household about the changes you'd like to see.

For author Eve Rodsky, it all begins at home. 'The last frontier of equity is in our homes. We need to reimagine home.'

Through her book *Fair Play* and its follow-up documentary, Eve works tirelessly to show how society benefits when men and women are equal partners at home. Women feel less stretched, more supported, and men also gain hugely from being more actively involved. Eve's husband Seth is one of the voices in her documentary and she describes his journey as 'beautiful'. Being aligned with her other half is one reason her sons feel free to challenge the status quo.

'Zach and Ben are athletic and present as sporty, and yet they watch their sister, help her wipe her tush, they are in care roles early.'

Eve's quick tip on reshaping masculinity for the modern age? 'Start by learning to wipe your little sister's vagina from front to back when she is a baby.'

'Act Like a Man Box' pioneer Paul Kivel became a stay-at-home dad in the 1970s, when it was far less common.

My partner was a science professor struggling against the male dominance of her profession and against the idea that if she wanted tenure, she couldn't have kids. Also, because we both grew up with traditional families and male/female relationships modelled, we had to be very intentional about shifting those roles. We actually wrote a contract laying out our hopes and expectations, and checking in every couple of years to see how we were doing.

After a couple of years, they discovered they had simply reversed roles. 'And that's not what we wanted; we wanted more equality and more balance. It takes a lot of intentionality and commitment and openness to re-evaluate how it's going and to get through the really deep socialization that's constantly reinforced outside the home.'

When bringing up two boys and one child who identifies as non-binary, Paul and his partner gave them chores to teach essential life skills and to help see themselves as contributing to the family, regardless of gender. 'They were all learning to cook dinner one night a week. They were all balancing the check book and writing checks for the monthly bills.'

Kivel told me the rewards of being a stay-at-home dad were life changing. 'For me, it was personally transformative to be there every day, interacting with, caring for and learning from our kids. It changed my relationship not just with my kids, but to myself, to my body and my feelings. My thinking about the world.'

The average twenty-first century man is doing a ton more housework and childcare than his forefathers. However, studies show that across Western democracies, the percentage of 'daddy care' peaked around the turn of the millennium. Twenty years later, progress has stalled.

In recent times, there's been much discussion about the 'mental load' that women carry on top of housework and childcare. The invisible and thankless task of keeping up with appointments, playdates, birthdays, homework, holiday bookings, family errands, outings, after-school runs, making sure the toilet roll doesn't run out. Et flipping cetera. Discussions are happening, but for most women the load still feels heavy.

I enjoyed an *On Boys* podcast episode where a guest talks about how she's raising her kids to share the mental load by asking questions, so they learn to notice what needs to be done around the house. I love this idea, especially in today's world, where attention is currency. If you can get your kids to drop their phones to notice their surroundings, you're on the right path. In fact, raising children to be *acomedido* (attentive and helpful) is common practice in Mexican and Indigenous cultures.

No matter your child's age, you can encourage them to notice what matters, whether it's about housekeeping or change-making. Ask questions like *What have you noticed? Does this seem right to you? Is it fair?* Start young and most kids will be willing participants because children are innately tuned in to what's fair and what's not fair.

There's an Italian social experiment captured on film where this plays out rather sweetly. Following a UN report on the average woman getting paid 35 per cent less than a man, the filmmakers asked boy and girl duos to decorate a Christmas tree in exchange for a reward. Once the baubles are hanging, each boy receives a jar full of sweeties and each girl receives a jar that's half empty. It's funny and telling to see the kids' reactions.

'But I did the same job. I even helped him,' one girl points out.

The film wraps with the kids redistributing their goodies more fairly, although one girl does have to prise the jar from her teammate's arms. If only it were so easy in the real world.

In our household, I can't claim we're modelling true equity. For a Nigerian man, I'd describe my husband as a feminist. He cooks dinner most Sundays, he does laundry, he was very involved in baby care (although my boobs did the midnight milk round). Yet like many modern couples, we've hit stumbling blocks over stuff like who keeps the home running and who's at the pub. Despite some of our quirkier characteristics, it's been a fairly traditional modelling of 'him outdoors, her in the kitchen' since our youngest was in nappies.

So, how do I cope? By making peace with the fact that I'd rather do an extra set of dishes than hammer in a nail, carry bedframes or meddle with wires behind the TV. We don't split down the line, but he takes care of plenty when he's home. For couples and families who need more help in sharing the load, Eve Rodsky created the Fair Play Card Deck, a fun game that allows you to talk about and to divvy up household tasks and responsibilities.[17] (See Resources and Recommendations, page 253.)

Where I know I can do better is in teaching my boys to do more. Our sons have done basic household chores since they were little, but I'll admit there's stuff they get away with because they're boys. I'm a feminist but . . . my seventeen-year-old can't boil a pot of rice. If my son was a daughter, she'd be cooking jollof by now. OK, since I've confessed this in writing, you have to hold me accountable. By the time this book comes out, my sons will be cooking rice. In the mighty name of jollof, amen.

When I interviewed Jed about what boys could do within the home for more equality, he answered: 'Help more with cooking, cleaning, doing stuff all around the house. Don't just sit with your leg up on the sofa.'

We both laughed, because his standard pose is spread out on the sofa, leg up on the arm, in a manner we've come to know as 'Jed just Jedding'. The irony is not lost on either of us.

Eve wrote the book on domestic equity, but it's not a done deal for her either. She says, 'I see my sons, who every day are in an internal battle between how we're trying to raise them at home and what's outside our doors. For example, my son Ben's in fifth grade, very popular and confident and a gender ambassador in many ways. He brought his lunchbox to school, and he said all of his friends were dogging him all day because he was using a purple lunchbox. He didn't want to bring it to school after that. This is from a kid who's super-confident.'

She observes that while her sons are aware of the Man Box, they can't escape it entirely. However, she's proud of how they question gender norms. She recalls a trip to her alma mater, the University of Michigan, with her son Zach.

We started to play a game of pool while watching a Michigan women's volleyball game. Two men came into the bar and started demanding a remote to watch NFL Sunday football, saying who in their right mind put this on women's volleyball. My son was shocked and said to me afterwards, "I did. I wanted to watch women's volleyball".'

Being a boy is complicated, Eve acknowledges, especially in the age of TikTok misogynists.

'My sons introduced me to Andrew Tate; they said I would "hate him".'

Personally, I hadn't even heard of Andrew Tate until an article I read in August 2022 brought him to my attention. Educators and activists had been voicing their concerns over Tate's domination of TikTok's algorithms that was helping him spread misogynistic attitudes particularly to teen boys. His infamy seemed to peak at the end of 2022 after a very public Twitter showdown with climate-change activist Greta Thunberg, shortly after which Tate was arrested on separate charges of human trafficking.

Eve says it's important to have conversations about figures like Tate that aren't about shaming, but on trying to understand what attracts boys in the first place.

'We unpacked his stereotypes one by one. "Women are weaker than men" – what does he mean by that? Physically? What about emotionally? What does weak mean? Men like Andrew Tate require unpacking, then dismissing.'

After I read that article, I decided to unpack Andrew Tate with my teenage son.

'Have you heard of Andrew Tate?'

He smiles.

'Yeah, he's funny. Why?'

'I've just read an article about him that troubled me.'

'He says a lot of things but you can tell he doesn't mean most of what he says. It's just jokes.'

'Like what?'

'I mean, he does say stuff about women. You know, like how women should stay in the house. It's a bit over the top, but it's tongue-in-cheek. He's just a very traditional guy. He doesn't actually say anything that's directly hateful.'

So many red flags go up in my mind, I'm surprised they don't burst through my skull. I try to maintain a calm expression.

'This article says otherwise.'

Eye roll. 'Have you watched any of his videos? He doesn't just go on about women either, he talks about other stuff.'

'I'm interested in why he's so popular. At the time of this article, he's got one of the biggest accounts on TikTok and Instagram.'

'Yeah, and he doesn't even post his videos there. It's other people posting it.'

'OK,' I say, aiming for a measured tone. 'The thing about someone like him is that you have to be careful, because even if he's not saying anything directly hateful, that type of messaging can be insidious, especially if it's wrapped up in humour. Is he a comedian?'

'No, he's an ex-MMA fighter.'

And a multi-billionaire, according to Tate. More conservative sources estimate his actual fortune around £30 million. Tate has claimed to be a trillionaire. An image of Tate dressed as Dr Evil in *Austin Powers* pops into my mind. There are no trillionaires recorded on any Rich List.

I can see my boy's shoulders starting to hunch, his chest folding in slightly; he's reaching for his phone. I talk a little faster.

'So, what he says about women doesn't sound traditional, it sounds pretty backwards. And while you might see it as a joke, there are a lot of impressionable kids and young men who take it seriously. It's worrying how he's being pushed to the top of your feed. Remember how I've always asked you to question stuff and to look for the story behind the story. What's Andrew Tate's story? Why is he saying all this about women and who is he trying to reach? Why is he the number-one guy on TikTok?'

The teen is focused on his phone now, chin defiant. He doesn't understand why he's getting a lecture. After all, he's not some kind of Tate groupie. Not like the guys I find on a Twitter thread later who all call Tate their 'Top G'.

'I'm not lecturing, I'm just trying to understand.'

Damn it, I sound like a lecturer. I'm often encouraging parents to 'try not to lecture'. Ask questions. Challenge ideas with grace. Most importantly, listen. Your goal is to have a conversation with your child, not talk at them. Yet here I am failing my own advice, again. Sometimes it matters too much, and my emotions take over.

Stepping off my podium, I try again. I explain that I realize he's not a Tate minion, but this is bigger than Tate. It's about recognizing how social media plays with our minds, why controversy gets the biggest platform, how easy it is for toxic ideas to seep into the mainstream, slick as butter on hot toast. It's about staying aware (I'd say 'woke' if it didn't make me sound like a dick) and knowing when to switch off.

The next day, my kids tell me they've found the female equivalent to Andrew Tate. Her name is Drew Afualo and she's got even more followers on Instagram. I should hear what she's saying because it's really horrible to guys. She disses men all the time, she body-shames them, it's outright misandry. Have I heard of the term? It's hatred against men.

'Yes, I know about misandry.'

They look up one of her videos on TikTok. It's titled 'Terrible Men' and cut with screenshots of men trying to slide into her DMs. Many of the comments are from men calling her out on her sexist double standards.

'Well, that's no good either,' I agree. 'I'm curious, is she talking about terrible men she's dealt with specifically, or about men in general?'

'It doesn't matter, because the stuff she says hurts all men. Especially when she's saying rude things about the way a guy looks. It's collateral damage.'

I nod.

'Fair point, and this works both ways. One comment from an influencer with a huge platform can have a massive ripple effect. That's why we have to be careful about what we consume and also what we share. You never know how it will affect people day-to-day.'

Actually, I do know a little about the impact of videos by the likes of Tate. Overnight, I had read more about this shiny, yappy persona. His content has been linked to a rise in toxic masculinity on social media, as well as outright sexism in schools. His prime audience appear to be teenage boys who are drawn to the tough-guy exterior and lap up his views on everything from why women are innately weaker to how to win at life, Tate-style. His narrative plays into the hands of those who feel like women and minorities are becoming too powerful, that males (and White men in particular) are an endangered species.

On Instagram, author Scott Stuart (@ScottCreates) reshares a clip from an influencer showing how quickly you can be funnelled from an Andrew Tate video into an alt-right stream. He starts by opening TikTok and clicking 'like' on Tate's clip at the top of his feed. Soon, his feed is dictated by similar clips, and, in less than an hour, he's being shown a video by alt-lite pundit Ben Shapiro. I send this clip to the boys on WhatsApp. Jed responds with a 'horrified' emoji, his brother doesn't bother opening it. He wants me to stop talking about Tate; he gets it. He's not one of his followers. Enough.

Unfortunately, the conversation around toxic masculinity is starting to derail because so many males, my sons included, switch off once you mention the 't' word. They take it personally. I get it, but they're missing the point. We're not criticizing men. We're critiquing a system, a structure, a culture. Anyway, 'toxic' doesn't quite cover it.

During my interview with author Rob Delaney, he used a word that I think captures both the rigidity of the Man Box and the male fragility that puts everyone on edge. I asked him about his concerns around masculinity in general.

Rob said: 'I suppose I just hope it can adapt and that I can do my little part to help it adapt. Men are great and necessary but they're also brittle (collectively) and resist change more than women (again, collectively). So I just hope, and work for, a world where men and boys realize there are an infinite number of ways to be a man.'

Brittle masculinity. Rough, harsh, flimsy and at breaking point.

Brittle masculinity is Tate puffing on a cigar and claiming trillions in the bank. It's Elon Musk buying Twitter on a whim, haggling over eight-dollar verifications, insisting on free speech, then banning any account that parodies him. It's Trump every time he opens his mouth. It's the spectre of Putin with his eye on Ukraine and his thumb hovering over World War Three. Brittle masculinity is the ultimate tough guy with the broken core.

'Enough with tough guys,' Paul Kivel tells me.

The tougher our kids are, the more likely they are to end up in trouble, either wounded or hurt[ing] someone else. Toughness doesn't protect anybody; it promotes more violence. Also, it isolates our boys. It's a disaster for boys to be tough. It's not who they are and it's not what they want or need. The people who survive best are not those who are tough, but those who are flexible, resilient, who have skills to adapt and be in different kinds of relationships and situations. Those are true survival skills.

A few days after our conversation about Tate, my sons announce that Tate's been banned from Instagram and Facebook.

'Interesting,' I say.

Ezra shakes his head. He thinks it doesn't make sense for them to ban him since he doesn't post on those channels, and anyway, it's only going to make him more popular. People will start seeking out his content in other ways. Also, if they're banning Tate, they should ban Drew Afualo too.

I tell him that Instagram has banned influencers I know for much less (apparently, the shadow of a nipple is more controversial than racism or misogyny). Meanwhile it took years for Twitter to kick out Donald Trump. Ultimately, social-media companies care most about the bottom line.

Ezra says that at least he and his brother are self-aware enough not to get sucked into Tate's universe. He reckons it's over for some of Jed's peer group, the new Year Nines who've spent summer bingeing on Tate and Sneako.

'Who the hell is Sneako?'

Jed face palms. 'Look, Mum.'

He shows me a video of a guy raging about women being gold-diggers. Clearly, this man is hurting on some deep, psychological level. Sneako's videos rack up hundreds of thousands of views. His angry, hectic style reminds me of the videos my boys have spent hours watching. Your kids might watch them too. YouTubers who talk through video games or post reaction videos to music and other media. It's an entire subculture built mostly by young men and boys, aimed mostly at young men and boys, and for the most part, it's innocuous. But this style is being co-opted by people who have more dangerous ideas to spread.

Left to me, social media would be illegal for children under eighteen. I'm not anti social media; after all, I'm a content creator myself. However, the internet is the Wild West and social media is its final frontier.

Sometimes I joke with my sister about how modern life and everything that's coming is too much for us. We'll retreat to our village in Onitsha or somewhere more remote; live off-grid. Our cousin Nnenna invites me to bunk off with her to the farm she's planning to buy with her partner. I could learn to milk cows and grow carrots. My husband's ex-girlfriend from university moved with her family to the Outer Hebrides. I fantasize about some such existence, far from the madding trolls, free from the clicks and bytes and dopamine rush of teeny hearts on a screen. Realistically, though, we can't all avoid the modern world, or ban our children from technology. The trick is to stay tuned in to what they're watching and reading; teach them to be conscious consumers; check in with them regularly. Suggest alternative role models. Remember not to lecture them (but give yourself grace if you do). Set time frames around social media, draw up a family media contract if it helps. Find ways to show them that, no matter how seductive the World Wide Web might be, there's a whole wide world out there that's far more interesting to explore.

In a couple of years, my eldest will be off to university, where his room will inevitably contain a laptop and gaming console. He'll be free to play or watch whatever he wants without feeling my or his dad's eyes on his back. He'll be an adult by then; no more parental controls or filters online or in real life.

All we can hope is that we've done enough to keep the attention vampires at bay. That he remembers to listen to that still, small voice inside, reminding him to check himself and to question everything. A voice that sounds a little like his mother's and his father's perhaps, but mostly like his own.

Conversation and Reflection Prompts

How do you respond to sexist jokes from family members?

How can you teach your child to shut down sexist comments?

How does 'I'm a feminist but . . .' make you reflect on internalized sexism?

Who carries the load at home? Does it feel fair? How can you make it fairer? Discuss steps with your household.

What did you learn from the discussion about Andrew Tate? Have you discussed Tate with your child? What about Drew Afualo?

Do you prefer 'toxic masculinity' or 'brittle masculinity'? How do these terms make your boy feel?

What boundaries do you set around social-media use? Would a family media contract be helpful?

FAMILY GAME NIGHT

Have a go at playing 'What's More Macho?'. Discuss what you learn about gender expectations. Talk about things your child can do to push back against stereotypes, like carrying the purple lunchbox if he likes it!

LESSONS FROM OUR FATHERS

It's one thing to be cancelled on social media. It's quite another to be erased in conversation by a stranger, only a few days after your father has died. Nearly two decades have passed since we buried my dad, so my memory of the events is hazy. Even then, the days smudged into each other: a messy collage of pained looks, suffocating hugs, containers crammed with food and snacks, outpourings of sympathy. *Ndo nne:* Sorry for your loss. Try and hold yourself together. Be strong for your mother, OK? *Jisike.*

I never met the stranger in question, but I can picture him. Let's give him a squat build, a smug grin and tight trousers. He's the kind of man who wears expensive watches and tips like he's short for change. That guy who's always the loudest whether he's talking over you, laughing at his own jokes, or picking food from his teeth with his tongue.

The exchange happened shortly after my cousin Ngozi had welcomed the man into our home to join the assembly of mourners.

'What a shame, what a pity,' he said to her.

'Honestly,' my cousin replied. 'We're all so sad. Although the past few years have been quite difficult. We thank God that Ajie went peacefully.'

'Indeed. But the real tragedy is that after all these years, he only managed to have one child.'

My cousin corrected him. 'Actually, Ajie had three children – Obi, Nkiru and Uju.'

The man smirked. 'Yes, but only one of them was a son.'

In Igbo culture, the man is the head of the household. When it's time to eat, his wife will serve him first. There's a common notion among Igbo people that we have no official king, but every man is king of his domain.

In truth, there are several Igbo communities with monarchs. My family can trace our lineage to the first kings of Onitsha, which is my father's hometown. My dad was honoured with a traditional title, the Ajie of Onitsha, putting him second in line to the Obi (king) of Onitsha. The Ajie is a member of the king's cabinet, also known as the Ndi Ichie, who are considered immortal beings.

Growing up, nobody but the Ajie was supposed to sit on my dad's special chair. At our childhood home in eastern Nigeria, his seat was adorned with beads and regalia, a ceremonial fan and an air of mystique.

As young kids, we would dare each other to perch on it. I can still recall my heart hammering and butt cheeks tingling with defiance as I leaned back in what I'd come to think of as my father's throne.

However, you don't need a high-ranking title as an Igbo male. Entitlement comes with the territory. As an Igbo man, if your brother passes away, you are entitled to take his wife as your own. If your parents die, you inherit everything, and your sisters are left to fight for whatever scraps you throw their way. In traditional Igbo society, if you have no sons, you are considered irrelevant.

When my cousin told us what this man said to her, my sister Nkiru and I stared at each other with our mouths open. Then we started laughing. I was incensed, of course, but I couldn't hold back the giggles. We imagined how our father would have reacted to the news of our non-existence. Dad had one of those throaty, irrepressible laughs that would rumble out from deep within his being. Sometimes I thought he might choke from guffawing so hard. He would have laughed that man out of the room.

There's a photo of me as a young girl on my father's shoulder, laughing like I'm on top of the world. My dad is laughing too, that familiar smile breaking his face wide open. He's looking up at me as if I'm something much more precious than any trophy. In my father's arms, I could do anything. I felt safe and celebrated. I knew I was special because he told me in so many ways. Like how he'd whistle out the syllables of my name – O-bia-n-uju – so I could come and get a piece of meat he'd saved for me on his plate. Now, I realize this makes me sound more like his puppy than his actual daughter, but these were some of the times I felt most treasured by my dad.

Yes, I was a daddy's girl. The apple of his eye, the crayfish in his bitterleaf soup. Nkiru still gets indignant when she recalls our dad coming back from a trip abroad with a gift for me: a thin chain with a trinket that said 'Daddy's Number 1'.

'I mean, talk about favouritism.'

But she was his favourite too. The beauty of my father was that he made everybody feel special. All my cousins and older relatives described having a personal relationship with him. When we buried my dad, each one had a memory to share about how he had championed their cause, lifted them at a low moment, taught them lessons they'd never forget, made them feel like they could conquer anything.

On a sweltering afternoon in 1977, my parents had gone to support my brother and sister at their first UK sports day, Mum in a cropped Afro and Jackie O sunglasses, Dad's pot belly straining his shirt as he blew pipe smoke to the wind. They gathered with other parents to watch the hundred-metre race. From the start, there was one clear winner, a whirr of skinny brown arms and legs bursting past the finish line.

One of the other dads turned to my father: 'My goodness, your son runs like lightning!'

My dad took a puff of his pipe and smiled.

'Actually, that's my daughter.'

There was nothing my dad enjoyed more than seeing us win, and especially seeing my sister beat the boys, year after year. If I had called my dad a feminist, though, he might have been bemused. Dad came from a culture and a generation that made clear distinctions between men and women. He was cool with Grace Jones and Boy George, they could sit at his table, for sure, although he might have had a few questions to ask them! I imagine that when he thought of a feminist, what popped into his mind was the stereotype of an unshaven bra-burner who wanted to turn society upside down.

Despite this, he married a staunch feminist. In her day, my mum was radical for an Igbo woman. She wore whatever she liked, dyed her hair frequently, smoked cigarettes and drank whisky. She could leave grown men quaking in their boots with a single look. Mum was also fiercely traditional and would argue with us over the slim-fit portions of food we served our dad after he got ill. 'Don't you know he's a titled man?'

They were well matched because Dad was both traditional and radical too. In fact, the feminist ideals we grew up with were inspired by him as much as by our mother. Dad brought us up to be critical thinkers and to challenge the status quo; to claim our space unapologetically in a White man's world. He told us we could marry whoever we pleased, and that marriage was certainly not the end goal. I was raised to believe that no boy was better than me and that, no matter what I wanted in life, it was there for the taking if I put my mind to it.

Despite his claims of being a whizz in the kitchen, Dad wasn't exactly a domestic role model. However, his feminism came through in other ways. I think of his soft nature, his willingness to be tender and vulnerable at a time when this wasn't valued in a man. We would watch sad movies together and sob. One afternoon, a visitor popped round to find me, my dad and my sister in floods of tears. The visitor was aghast, wondering who had died. It took us a while between sniffles to explain that we'd just finished watching *The Champ*. Have you seen it? That film will knock you out emotionally.

My father taught us manhood isn't about titles or status or your ability to keep a dry eye through a Hollywood weepy. True manhood is pliable. Strong when it needs to be, soft when it counts.

The very first lessons we learn about maleness come directly (or indirectly) from our fathers and father figures. This has been the way throughout history and across global societies. Traditionally, the father was the founder, protector, teacher and provider. He went out to earn the bread, catch the fish, hunt with the pack, bring that bacon home. He spent more time out of the house than at home with his family. Yet he was the one your kids looked up to and in whose footsteps your sons would walk one day.

The word patriarchy means 'the rule of the father'. Originally, it referred to how a father governed a household but over time it came to mean societies dominated by men. One modern example of patriarchal rule is Logan Roy, the head of the Roy dynasty in the brilliant TV series, *Succession*. Logan has built a multi-billion-dollar global empire largely by stoking social divisions and saying 'fuck off' to anyone in his path. His kids are afraid of him, yet desperate for his approval. Logan represents toxic masculinity at its most intoxicating. Everyone around him is drunk on his power even though it's destroying them.

When people toss around slogans like 'damn the man' and 'smash the patriarchy', they're talking about men like Logan Roy, who is both a personal and an institutional figurehead for White male supremacy. At the end of the day, Logan is just another old-school dad who thinks his parental duty amounts to putting a roof over his kids' heads and toughening them up for the brutal road of life. When you look at their relationships, what stands out is what's missing: empathy, care, connection. Logan's shadow looms over them but there's a spot at the head of the family table marked empty, because he's just not there.

In the 1980s, a generation of us grew up with Bill Cosby as our TV dad. It creeps me out now, since the name Cosby is synonymous with crimes of sexual assault. But I gained so much from Mr Huxtable, the funny, occasionally stern (but with a twinkle in his eye), patient, wise, loving and ultra-cool father we spent an evening with every week. He was a successful African–American man who cared and provided for his family and always found time for each of his children.

Above all, he loved his wife to bits. Relationship experts often describe how important it is for children to witness a loving partnership between their parents. This is what many of us learned watching Cliff and Claire Huxtable model family values, mutual respect, good-natured ribbing and an easy chemistry on screen.

Sometimes I think about how many children, and specifically Black families, got their fix of fatherly attention and advice through those half-hour episodes. My boys grew up watching reruns of *The Fresh Prince of Bel-Air,* another classic show that gives us a different vision of fatherhood: Uncle Phil managing his spoilt rich kids and the rascally nephew he takes under his wing.

One of the most emotional scenes is when Uncle Phil calls out Will's dad Lou for abandoning his son. Lou has promised Will a father-and-son trip, then ditches him at the last moment. At first, Will puts a brave face on but then the bravado cracks and Will cries: 'How come he don't want me, man?'

Uncle Phil doesn't say anything, doesn't try to offer advice or platitudes, he just hugs him so hard that Will's baseball cap falls off.

It never fails to leave me in tears, not just because of the breathtaking acting from both Will Smith and James Avery, but because it's true to life for so many abandoned kids worldwide.

Under a YouTube clip of this scene, a comment by a Nathan Jordan that has more than eighty thousand likes reads, 'Uncle Phil's the dad we all wanted. Lou is the dad too many of us got.'

My father was more of an Uncle Phil than a Lou. He couldn't have been less like Logan Roy. Yet when I look back objectively, a great deal of our relationship was defined by his absence. I think of all the years that I spent at boarding school in another country. The trips he'd take alone, leaving my mum with her sisters and dozens of cousins all crashing at our home, or when he'd shut himself away in his study for quiet time, letting us run wild outdoors. Then there was the long 'cold war' before his illness, when my parents' marriage nearly came to breaking point.

One of the lessons I learned as a child was that a mother stuck around, sometimes through gritted teeth, but a father could come and go. For so many of us, our memories of growing up are marked by a father's absence. This physical (or emotional) disappearing act can be particularly difficult for sons looking to their fathers to learn how to be a man.

In an article for *Psych Alive* magazine, clinical psychologist Dr Deryl Goldenberg examines male longing and what he calls the 'father–son wound'. He quotes one of his patients who felt his father's emotional absence sorely: 'He didn't tell me what kinds of problems he wrestled with, what he felt, or what it meant to him to be a man. I've had to make it all up for myself, and I'm never sure I got it right.'[3]

Dr Goldenberg writes about being raised by an emotionally absent father himself, and, subsequently, having trouble connecting fully with his son. Moved by the vulnerability in his article, I got in touch with Dr Goldenberg and he spoke with me from his practice in Santa Monica, California.

'I hated my father most of my life,' he said. 'I felt at war with him. He didn't know how to be a father. Coming out of that 1950s and 1960s era when I was growing up, a lot of men still had that John Wayne mentality. Spare the rod, spoil the child. Things get tough, the tough get going. You're going to learn how to be a man, how to tough it out. That starts with the way I was disciplined as a child.'[4]

In his article, Dr Goldenberg references writer Franz Kafka's *Letter to the Father*. This is an extremely personal and moving document that gives an insight into the *Metamorphosis* author's difficult upbringing and how it affected him as a man and a writer. Kafka talks of being saddled with self-contempt and self-loathing because his father was so critical.[5]

Dr Goldenberg said: 'I had a lot of that, but it was buried. I didn't realize how turned I was against myself. When we're excessively punished and mistreated, we shut down emotionally, it's too much for the child, they're overwhelmed.'

This type of overwhelm from abuse or maltreatment is known as 'toxic stress' and it can have devastating long-term effects on a young person. Studies have linked it to changes in brain structure, as well as impairment of the developing nervous and immune systems. It is like living your daily life in a state of emergency. When a child grows up like this, they're at a higher risk as an adult for a range of physical, mental and behavioural problems ranging from eating disorders to substance abuse.

When I was growing up, many adults I knew would beat children with belts or canes or even cricket bats, and this was seen as a positive way to keep naughty kids in check. However, research has shown how corporal punishment can be a form of toxic stress, especially when it's done by a parent. For a child can't turn to their parent for comfort if their parent is the source of their pain. Boys in particular were meant to tough it out and weather the pain rather than act soft by seeking comfort after a thrashing.

Dr Goldenberg recalls being strapped by his father, a high-school dropout, for bringing home less than stellar school report cards. As a teenager, their relationship became more fractious and disagreements would escalate quickly. 'At twenty-three, I told him if he hit me again, I would hit him back. So he stopped. But it didn't improve our relationship. I wasn't so afraid of him but I had no real feelings of care or respect. I turned into a tough, mouthy kid.'

Dr Goldenberg's experience is a cautionary tale of how the toxic elements of masculinity get passed from generation to generation:

through rigid ideas, hard words, closed fists. He said he was set on having a better relationship with his own son but found himself in a similar pattern of pain, shame and disapproval.

Sadly, Freud is so right: the compulsion to recreate the past on the present is in all of us. Even with therapy and a lot of resources, I couldn't curb my attitude to my son. I wasn't striking him or punishing him as often or as hard, but my attitude was critical and harsh. He felt very hurt. It took years before we started to be friendly again.

Listening to Dr Goldenberg brought to mind something I heard in the thought-provoking documentary *Beyond Men and Masculinity*, which examines boyhood, masculine identity and the links between shame and male violence. Family therapist and author Terry Real said: 'Family pathology rolls from generation to generation like a fire in the woods, taking down everything in its path, until one person in one generation has the courage to turn and face the flames.' It takes so much courage to be the one who turns, but it can change everything.

One of the things that helped Dr Goldenberg, apart from therapy, was forming men's support groups while studying in Israel and during his first years after graduation, in Vancouver. 'I found it especially beneficial that men could provide each other with what we never got, emotional nourishment from our fathers.'

For me, the word 'nourishment' here is crucial. The emotional care and connection we seek from our parents is as vital as food. We need it to thrive. For Dr Goldenberg, it was a surprise to realize that at one point he had looked to his dad for love.

'Only in therapy did I realize that I had a memory from [when I was] a very young baby of wanting my father to love me. Before that, I had no memory of ever wanting anything from my father. Because if you don't want anything from someone cruel, you're safe.'

It pains me to picture that little baby crying for his dad and that father who had no real idea how to answer his son's call. One of the challenges of being a dad is being caught between grandiose expectations of what fathers are supposed to do and the low standards of what society will accept from a sperm provider.

It's a weird set-up, especially when dads are so necessary. Not so much to 'protect and provide', as the patriarchy insists, but on a basic human level. You only need to watch a dad and his child playing together to see this.

It might sound like a cliché, but across mammalian species, male infants are more likely to engage in roughhouse play than their female counterparts. When a human father gets down on all fours and wrestles with his kids or chucks them onto his shoulders and runs around, it's not just fun. It's teaching them a bunch of psycho-social tricks: how to use your physicality without causing actual harm; how to self-regulate; how to test your limits safely; how to work off excess energy creatively; how to think your way out of situations; how to reach for the moon without losing sight of solid ground.

There's a meme that shows three images of a dad throwing his child in the air. The first photo is captioned 'What dad sees'; the second photo, 'What baby sees', shows the baby soaring higher. The third photo, 'What mum sees', shows the dad tossing his child so high you'd better hope that child grows wings.

It's a funny take on how parenting, much like life, is about perspective, and why mums need to let dads do their thing. I know that, having carried them in my body for nine months, like packages marked 'Fragile: Do Not Break', I could get a little precious with my babies. But I had to learn to trust that their dad was in control of a situation, even when it looked like he was blasting them to no-man's-land.

Jed asked me once if his dad had ever told people that 'we were pregnant'. I do remember this happening a couple of times, and personally, though I get the sentiment, I still think it's an annoying expression. If you've suffered through the swollen ankles, emotional ups and downs, or the indignity of trying to pee into a cup when you can't see below your bump, it might strike you that, no, your other half is not also pregnant. You are going through this solo.

Yet a strange thing happens to a new hands-on father. He experiences a drop in testosterone levels as he assumes a nurturing role. He also experiences a rise in prolactin, the breast-milk hormone that's associated with feelings of attachment. No, he's not about to start breastfeeding, although there have been rare cases recorded of lactation in cisgendered males, not just trans and non-binary parents. The benefits for dads who stick around to change nappies, do late-night feeds and sing lullabies include a closer bond with their baby and an enhanced feeling of wellbeing.

And for the baby, having an involved father is one of the key markers of a happier, healthier life. It's not the be all and end all, of course. There are single mothers, same-gender parents and grandparents bringing up thriving families worldwide. Some of my favourite male role models, like Trevor Noah and Barack Obama, were famously raised by their mamas.

Still, a dad can play an essential role in a child's sense of self. Kids might look to the adult men in their lives for an understanding of how they want to be or who they want to partner with when they grow up. When a child lacks a decent father figure, it can show up through acting out at school, lacking healthy boundaries, excessively risky behaviours, and poorer educational outcomes. That's why it's important to model the kind of man that you want your child to know, or to seek out that model if there's no dad at home.

Crucially, though, there is no one definition of a dad, and fatherhood can mean so many things to so many different people. I asked Elliott Rae, author and founder of website *Music Football Fatherhood* about what the word 'father' evoked for him.

I'm thinking about the conversations we have with dads who didn't have dads in their lives, dads with children with additional needs, dads who aren't with their partners, dads who are feeling pressure to provide but also feeling they're not giving enough at home, dads in interracial relationships. It means different things to different people, but, ultimately, it's about growth, reflection and learning,

patience with your children, family and yourself. Grace. Forgiveness. The ability to forgive ourselves for our past mistakes is really important.[12]

Grace is one of my favourite concepts. In Christian terms, grace means benevolence or the unmerited favour of God. For me, grace is where our spirituality meets our humanity. It's not about overlooking evil or wrong deeds. Rather, it's making room for human imperfection. Extending a hand when someone slips up. Choosing to be kinder in the way we see and treat others and ourselves.

This idea of grace and forgiveness is echoed by Street Feast founder Dominic Cools-Lartigue, who grew up without a father and didn't speak to his dad for around twenty years.

After his mum nearly died in hospital in January 2021, Dominic decided to reach out. Recalling the experience, he said, 'I thought it would be weird if I got a phone call saying your dad's dead, without ever knowing him as an adult. So I tracked his number down through the internet. I probably had it for a year before I called it.'[13]

Things didn't go smoothly.

'He proceeded to talk at me for an hour. He didn't ask me one question about myself. I was like, do you know what? I've got to know loads of old people that I truly love, but I didn't need another one talking at me. I've got two half-brothers who don't know I exist. It's weird.'

However, even though he doesn't understand it completely, Dominic has made some peace with things since becoming a dad himself.

'I've softened my view of my dad from having Remy. I will never condone it, abandoning your child. However, being a parent, being a father, I know how hard it is. So I can imagine why someone given certain circumstances might think *I can't take this on,* especially when they're really young and a new parent. It's easy to think you can't do this. But you do it because you love that being so much.'

I found it incredibly moving speaking with some of these fathers like Dominic, who's in his forties, and Dr Goldenberg, now in his seventies, who are still grappling with the father–son wound and figuring out what they'd like to do better. I get a sense of how hard men can be on themselves, yet there's so much room for forgiveness, for grace, for the emotional nourishment that can end damaging cycles.

I think of my boys and how their entire beings would light up as soon as their dad came home. The way that as babies their heads would turn towards the baritone voice they'd been hearing since the womb. I can still see Abiye now, a pudgy baby Ezra nestled in the crook of his elbow, showing him the world from our windowsill; Abiye's softened tones beckoning a shiny-faced Jed to take the next steps.

Sometimes it's easy to focus on what's missing. But these small, everyday moments of connection stack up, no matter how mundane they seem. It's only when we step back and really look at the whole picture that we can see what we have built together with our loved ones, piece by piece.

Aside from that photo of me on my dad's shoulders, I have no clear memory or evidence of physical play with my father as a little girl. I do remember clambering onto the sofa to hug him, cushioning my head against his soft, round belly. Reaching curiously to tug at his goatee. The smell of Old Spice, bitter black coffee, book jackets and pipe smoke. Despite his many absences, my father never felt remote.

Inevitably, it's the in-between times that I remember most. Watching Westerns together. My siblings and I cracking up when he tried to sing opera. The sight of Dad's head lolling back, seconds before the thunder of his snoring. How, after his first stroke, he remembered that he liked to wear his hair in a side parting.

Several months before he died, I had returned to Abuja after years living in the US. It had been ages since I'd seen my dad. The last time was in a nursing home in London. It was after his second stroke, the one that stole his language and his sense of time and place. I had wept then to see him glassy-eyed and fragile, surrounded by strangers. My mother had fought the doctors to get him back to Nigeria. Being on native soil turned out to be good for him. After a spell in hospital, he was strong enough to be taken care of at home.

I hugged my dad, cradling his head between my hands, kissing his forehead. He gripped my hand and shook it vigorously, a slight frown over the grin on his face. He was admonishing me for being gone for so long. I could hear it in his eyes although I couldn't quite make out what he was saying. Then, surprisingly, clear speech came out:

'What of your sons?'

'What?' I leaned in closer.

'What of your sons?' he repeated.

'It's me, Daddy, it's Uju. I don't have any sons,' I replied quietly, smiling.

But I knew he wasn't confused about who I was. To this day, I believe he was talking about Ezra and Jed. The sons I would have eventually, whom he would never get to meet, but who would carry his eyes, his grace, his humour and the many lessons from my father that still live in me.

Conversation and Reflection Prompts

What does the word 'father' mean to you?

What is or was your relationship with your father?

How do you think this relationship affects the way you raise your son?

How does the patriarchy hold fathers hostage and how can they break free?

What kind of father or father figure do you want to be?

What lessons did you learn from your father (positive or negative)?

What steps can you take to repair any father–son (or father–child) wounds?

EXERCISE

Write a letter to your father from your ten-year-old self, being as open as you can be. Write a letter from the present day. Explore any lessons you've learned about your childhood and about the parenting journey so far. Invite your son to write a letter to his father or father figure too.

HOW TO TRAIN YOUR DRAGONS

n a standard monster movie, the hero comes out swinging, slays the beast, gets the girl and saves mankind, all in a matter of 180 minutes. But *How to Train Your Dragon* is not a typical blockbuster. And Hiccup is no ordinary hero.

My youngest was only one when the first film in the trilogy came out, so we didn't get to see it in the cinema. The boys and I watched it a few years later on DVD, snuggled up under blankets with popcorn bowls, all wide-eyed as the story unfolded. I fell hard for the big-hearted epic about Vikings and wild beasts and a hapless kid who becomes the saviour of his tribe, though not as anybody expects. My kids loved it too and we watched it again soon after. And again, and again.

I wouldn't say it's our favourite animated film. However, as a parent of boys, it's one that's stuck with me. Long before discussions around toxic masculinity became mainstream, the Dreamworks movie pulled manliness apart and showed us a different model. It explores courage, empathy, what it means to be a boy, what it means to be human.

If you haven't seen it, here's the story in a nutshell (spoilers ahead): Hiccup is the son of Viking chief Stoick the Vast, although he looks and acts nothing like his big and brawny dad. Hiccup is slender, sensitive and would rather tinker away as a blacksmith's apprentice than pick up a sword. He's a lover, not a fighter, much to his dad's despair. As a mark of coming of age, Hiccup and his Viking peers are sent to kill a dragon. Hiccup sees a Night Fury, one of the fiercest dragons, and manages to wound it but finds himself unable to kill it. Instead, he befriends the Night Fury and makes it his mission to show his tribe that man and dragon can live together peacefully. Of course, this goes against everything the Vikings believe in and only adds to Hiccup's sense of being an outlier, until a real dragon threat looms and, when sheer force doesn't chase it away, it's up to Hiccup to find another solution.

In a love story, the point at which the two leads connect for the first time (whether physically or emotionally) is known as a 'meet-cute'. This trope is also seen in bromance and odd-couple movies, and *How to Train Your Dragon* incorporates both genres. When Hiccup and his Night Fury friend Toothless become pals, it's through a beautiful sequence that closes with one of the most iconic images in modern animation.

Hiccup has managed to win the dragon's trust by helping to fix his tail after shooting him down. The dragon tries to repay him by feeding him. My boys giggled watching Hiccup take disgusted bites of raw fish just to please the beast. Hiccup reaches out to pet the dragon's nose and the creature snarls and flinches. Taking a beat, Hiccup tries again. This time he puts his hand out, palm side facing the dragon, and closes his eyes. It's a moment of heightened tension and vulnerability. We don't know if the dragon will respond or fly away. He might even bite his hand off. Then, slowly, Toothless leans in and touches his snout against Hiccup's palm.

You'd have to be made of dragon hide not to melt inside. Of course, the stunning animation, character build-up and soundtrack add to the emotional high. But it's the message that's so powerful. There have been many times over the years, while parenting my two wildlings, that I remember that scene. I remember that I can't force them to respond exactly how and when I want. Sometimes you just have to be a loving presence. Stay patient and stay open and they will come of their own accord.

Hiccup is the voice and eyes of this movie, a fourteen-year-old boy on the cusp of manhood. In many ways, he's a typical teenage boy. Awkward and unsure but doing his best to act like he's got a handle on things. However, the character that reminds me most of the boys I've known is Toothless, the blue dragon: sparky and playful, shy, reckless, tender, loyal and brave. When Hiccup is sent to slay the dragon, he winds up finding a soulmate. He can't kill him because he notices the creature is just as frightened as he is. He says: 'I looked at the dragon and I saw myself.'

Canadian actor Jay Baruchel was the voice of Hiccup from the first film and TV spin-offs, up until the film trilogy wrapped in 2019. Hiccup's dad Stoick is played by proto-action man Gerard Butler. By contrast, Baruchel is a slim-fit, nerdy-looking, self-professed 'square peg'.

In a media interview, Baruchel said: 'Hiccup is a great emblem for anyone who is wired differently. He's still all Viking, even though he's the least Viking of them all. So he's loyal. But I had a dad whose sole ambition for me was that I play hockey and live exactly the same life that he did. And that was never going to be an option.'

For Baruchel, *How to Train Your Dragon* is a film that's made for the 'square pegs', the oddballs and the misfits.

'Hiccup tells these kids that the things you've been told are failings can actually be virtues, and will be, if you give them time.'

As Baruchel reiterates, the story is really about the importance of believing not just in yourself but in something bigger than yourself and having the courage to challenge the status quo. That becomes the true test of growing up.

How to Train Your Dragon is a metaphor about people who dare to break the mould. It's also symbolic of why traditional masculinity sets so many children up for failure. Take Stoick, a proper Viking's Viking, who's embarrassed by his weedy son. His character reflects so many fathers who wind up in a stand-off with their boys when they dare to colour outside the lines.

Educator and author Naz Ahsun remembers her son, now in his twenties, having some difficulties with his father growing up. She describes her boy as 'one of the misfits' and a homebody, whereas his father went to boarding school from the age of seven.

'They had a totally different upbringing. He wanted them to become more independent, which I'm not saying was a bad thing. I do think I'm very overprotective, but his father was an ex-army officer, so there were some clashes in expectations.'[2]

For the younger generation of boys, what she would like to see is for them to be able to freely express themselves. She says: 'It's almost like men can only express themselves through violence, rather than through their vulnerability. I would like to see more of them embrace that sensitivity that is already a part of them.'

It's painful to witness the gulf that can appear between a father and a son when communication breaks down. Following the Man Box code, they might resort to barked commands, harsh words, slammed doors, silent treatment or outright eviction. This happened in our home when my stepson Isaac came to live with us aged seventeen to nineteen. Isaac was flailing in his studies, seemed disaffected in general and soon he was at loggerheads with his dad. Often, I felt caught in the middle. It took a couple of years after Isaac moved out for them to start to repair the rifts. These days, Abiye bursts with pride talking about his eldest, and they are super-close not just as father and son but as genuine friends who enjoy each other's company.

For Hiccup, he's banished by his own father for befriending dragons, and it takes a threat to the village for Stoick to come to his senses. Sometimes what's difficult for a father to reckon with is how alien his child seems. Sometimes the hardest thing is that he recognizes his own character traits in his son; traits that he's been trying to shun or quash. The soft, vulnerable inner child that he's spent so long hiding away because 'that's what men do'. But you can't keep hiding when those qualities show up in your kid. *I looked at him and I saw myself.*

Several men I've spoken with have expressed how they've grappled with masculinity and its rigid constructs. Of the people I interviewed for this book, the one I can picture as a teenage Hiccup is *Guardian* writer Tom Lamont. He told me: 'I didn't have a troubled childhood or anything. The parts that stand out as difficult were more about fitting in with other masculine alpha boys. So I bring a lot more baggage to raising a boy based on my experiences as a rather timid kid.'

In an interesting twist, Tom has ended up parenting a son who sounds more like Stoick than Hiccup.

He loves noise, charging around and getting into scrapes. He's a leader of the pack. At the moment, he goes into school with his hair in a top knot and there's an instinct in me that's like, 'Oh, you'll get teased.' That's the voice of the 1980s child in me, which every part of my conventional adult brain wants to break down. But there are certain things that are hard-wired.

The wiring can feel almost impossible to untangle. Gender campaigner Abi Wright, who runs Festival of the Girl, shared an incident that happened at home with her other half.

He had a DIY accident where he fell, and it was very dramatic and worrying. Luckily, he only needed a few stitches. But he was crying from the shock of it all. My two daughters were there. Later, one said to him, 'Remember when you cried,' and he said, 'No, I didn't,' and I said, 'Nick, you did!' I could see in him that need to defend his masculinity. It's a stereotype that even the most gentle, sensitive man I know would still say he didn't cry. We thought he'd broken both his legs; of course he cried!

She credits her partner for his bravery in admitting, just before their second daughter was born, that if it were a boy, he might struggle to cope with him showing traditionally feminine behaviour. 'He said he would find it harder bringing up a boy if he wanted to go out wearing a dress or make-up. It was much easier to get his girls playing football. My brother is also sensitive, but that masculinity is really deep-rooted in all of them.'

You can be a parent who embraces every type of dragon until your kid shows up as a unicorn. Many of us have felt that prickle of self-consciousness when our child goes against the grain. Picture-book author Scott Stuart shares video clips and anecdotes about coming to terms with his son dressing as Elsa from *Frozen*. At first, watching his son dance around in a princess outfit poked giant holes in Stuart's sense of manliness, until one day he looked at him – properly looked at his boy – and all he could see was his joy. Everything else faded away.

We have to keep picking at these knots. Like a lot of boys, Jed has eyelashes to kill for – seriously, he could sell them on the black market. On holiday recently, my niece Mayowa offered to pay him a tenner so she could spend the evening curling his lashes and applying eye make-up. Jed shrugged. Why not? Easy money. I was smiling but I felt that prickle behind my ears. What if he went out in public like that? What might people say? I'm embarrassed to even admit this in writing, but sometimes those protective or regressive instincts can override your conscious beliefs.

'These things are challenging, and we shouldn't gloss over that,' says Kirstie Beaven, editor of *Sonshine* magazine. 'My kids are quite close in age, and my son thought his sister was the best thing he'd ever seen. They're quite close in size and there was a long period from about eighteen months to about three when he could choose his own clothes and he often chose to wear one of her dresses or skirts.'

Kirstie's family live in east London, where she notes that her kids are growing up with a range of expressive possibilities. 'No one really bats an eyelid if your hair is long, or your clothes are not stereotypically boyish or if you want to come to World Book Day dressed as a female character.'

However, she admits that she felt uncomfortable about her son's wardrobe choices. 'I had to check myself and ask: why do I feel uncomfortable? Why is it bad that people might think my son is a daughter? What am I afraid of? It's all tied in with misogyny and homophobia. Even if you think you've done the work, you can find out you need to do more.'

Her son is older now, and no longer wears girl's clothing, which she says is down to peer pressure.

Even though we live in an area where there are men wearing skirts and dresses from all cultures and backgrounds, including men in kilts and guys in salwar kameez on their way to mosque, he has learned he is not to wear a dress. It's sad, really.

My husband' and sons' traditional Kalabari outfits involve a long skirt for men. Abiye wore one on our wedding day and never felt so cool. Across Nigeria, it's common for men to wear a wrapper, a style of sarong skirt. In Fiji, men wear a skirt called sulu. Males from the nomadic Wodaabe tribe (found in Chad, Mali, Niger and Nigeria) are famous for dressing up elaborately and wearing colourful make-up in fertility ceremonies to attract female suitors. If your boy wants to wear a skirt or dress, long hair or nail polish, it doesn't make him any more or less masculine than David Bowie in thigh boots, Billy Porter in a gown at the Met Ball or that youth in Dalston at the corner store. Imagine we all just chilled out a little more about stuff like how an individual expresses their gender identity. Imagine how much more relaxing life could be.

Kirstie's partner works in animation, and she nods to the creative industries in general as a safer space for men who are a little quirkier, who have more of a sense of humour about themselves. She says she hasn't seen *How to Train Your Dragon*, although she's read the book.

I was interested in the main character, who is the heir to the throne of Hooligans but is approaching it in a non-stereotypical way. I think that resonated with my son. He's very slim and he's not ever going to be the strongest kid. Genetically he doesn't have that. He's not going to be the one who wins the wrestling matches, and I think the fact that you could use your brain and empathy to be a new kind of hero is a great message for all kids.

The movies are based on the novel series *How to Train Your Dragon* by bestselling children's author Cressida Cowell. Although Dreamworks took plenty of liberties with the plot and character development, some of the core themes are explored in the book. It's a hilarious and heartwarming underdog (underdragon?) tale that pits ancient values of grit and brawn against a more visionary outlook. In a talk with his granddad, Old Wrinkly, Hiccup learns what he will need to help his tribe. Old Wrinkly tells him that victory can no longer rely on 'overdeveloped muscles'. What's required for the Hero of the Future is something much more special and yet available to humans of all descriptions: imagination.

It will be Hiccup's imagination – his ability to dream, to think on his feet, to see things from a different perspective – that wins in the end. This is good news for all the boys who don't fit the model that's been built up for generations. It's a clarion call to our future artists and dreamers, poets and weirdos, carers and storytellers, scientists and educators, musicians and homemakers, tinkerers and late bloomers. If you dare to imagine more for yourself and for the world around you, if you can inspire imagination in others, you can achieve anything.

Cowell has talked about how the books were inspired by her childhood, spent partly on a remote island in Scotland. She had the freedom to wander in and out of caves and mountains and she'd invent tales of fiery creatures that lived on the island. Her dad encouraged her and would tell her more fables at bedtime. He lit the spark, and she birthed a universe of dragons. I can't help thinking about how, in a different era, he might have forbidden her from roaming so freely, for girls were supposed to sit neatly, and only boys could have adventures. Some girls weren't allowed to learn or write. The boys, even the quiet ones, were forced out to the mines or the frontlines to toughen them up. The girls with fierce eyes and big imaginations scribbled their stories in the dark.

We've come a long way, some might say leaps and bounds. Yet we have aeons to go when girls and boys in so many countries across the globe face gender restrictions.

Astrid, the female lead in the dragon franchise, plays the counterfoil to Hiccup. Where he's knock-kneed, she's sure and steady. Where he's hesitant, she rushes in. Astrid comes from strong female Viking stock – they give as good as they get. It's smart of the filmmakers to make Astrid the more 'masculine' out of the two leads. Their relationship shows how masculine and feminine energy can come in any gender, and how they can work together with less resistance, more flow. This message bucks against the divisive narratives that boys and girls can pick up from a young age.

As *Dear Patriarchy* podcaster and author Jen Audrie observes: 'The patriarchy pits males and females against each other, when we actually are programmed not by society but innately to work well together.'

I've come to think of the patriarchy as a giant fist, the invisible hand of a mythical god with a stranglehold on the world. Our work here is to pull those fingers open and let go; to transform it from controlling fist to Hiccup's open hand, waiting patiently for love to come in.

What gives me hope is the rise of soft power. A phrase coined by academics, soft power is often described as an alternative to the traditional physical and fossil-fuel economy. Instead, it's about intellectual property, the rapid advancements of technology and creative industry. As AI and driverless cars become the norm, it's our creativity and curiosity – the things that make us most human – that will stand out. Imagination. That's what our heroes of the future need.

The words 'soft' and 'power' are an unlikely combination. That's because throughout history, we've equated power with manhood and softness with femininity. *How to Train Your Dragon* reminds us that not only can we have both, in truth it's the only way forward for our survival. We've lived to see the geeks inherit the earth. Now it's time to raise a generation that can imagine something better, freer and more equitable for all people. A generation fuelled by soft power.

Abi Wright says: 'I like to think I've brought my kids up in a fairly gender-neutral environment, but at the end of the day, me and my partner were brought up to act like a girl and a boy, so it's still there.'

One way they try to counter this is by staying aware of the media their children are consuming.

When I feel overwhelmed about gender stereotyping, I come back to what I can do with my kids, which is sit and talk about it. Question what we see and what they're watching. Books and TV are really useful tools. It's something that feels a bit less daunting for parents if they're having discussions based on what their child is already engaging with.

Paul Kivel, one of the pioneers of the Act Like a Man Box, agrees. He says:

It starts with simple conversations, reading books and watching movies, questioning the roles and characters that

you see and what they notice. It's about providing them with the tools so they can decide how they want to be and how to treat others and how to be part of the community.

How can you teach soft power to a young boy? Show him the scene in which Toothless puts his face against Hiccup's hand. Ask him what he thinks it means, how it makes him feel. Talk about how brave Hiccup had to be, and also Toothless, to trust a being they didn't know; a creature that had sought to hurt them previously. Ask what they might do in Hiccup's place? What if they were Toothless, the Night Fury? Would they put their defences down and lean in? Has there ever been a situation in real life that reminded them of this moment?

Talk about how strong you have to be inside to face your fears and try something outside the norm. Discuss how one of the most courageous things you can do is to open your heart to somebody new, especially someone who isn't anything like you. Describe a moment from your past or present where you've tried to be as brave as Hiccup and Toothless. Talk about the times you've failed and why you're willing to try again, just like Hiccup. If your son is too young for a big discussion, you could just play this scene. It packs an emotional punch at any age. It's soft power in action.

One of my favourite lines in the film trilogy comes in the final instalment, when Hiccup meets his mother. Having grown up without a mum, Hiccup discovers Valka living in a dragon sanctuary. Hiccup remarks: 'It's not every day you find out your mother is some kind of . . . crazy, feral, vigilante dragon lady.'

We watched the third movie in the cinema, and this line got a big laugh from the crowd. I cackled because, like many boy mums (and, as I'm discovering, mums in general), I identify as a mother of dragons. I've watched them fight and roar and soar through the air and break and burn things. I've sat with the patience of a saint until that saint said, 'Fuck it,' and let my fire rage. Some days, I wanted to open the windows or, heck, the roof, and toss them out with a cheerful: 'Go forth and

Godspeed.' Yet if anyone came for one of my babies, I was ready to cut them with my claws.

Crazy, feral and vigilante is about right.

In the book *How to Train Your Dragon*, Hiccup goes searching for answers on how to keep his dragon Toothless in check. Following the advice of his elders, he seeks out the number-one book on dragon training by Professor Yobbish, only to find that the entire content of the book is one chapter with a mind-blowing insight on dragon training: 'Yell at it. (The louder the better).'

It's funny and a clever dig at the authoritarian model of control favoured in many societies and groups: from schools to the military. Parents can be guilty too of the 'yell your child into submission' approach to discipline. We can't help ourselves sometimes, but we know it doesn't actually work.

Even with everything I know, I still get to the point with my kids where I lose it. The expression 'seeing red' is spot on, because it feels like flames are taking over your vision. You lose sight of what you are trying to achieve, and all your senses go into overdrive. These are generational chains that we have to break, even though they have a grip on us that defies time and space. I've heard my mother's voice yelling at my kids through my own throat. I'm not proud of the times I was brought to my knees by a creature who hadn't learned to wipe his own behind properly.

A more conscious parenting style has grown over the past few decades, focusing on a relationship-centred approach. Its core message: choose connection before correction. The best way to reach somebody – your child, your partner, your student – isn't to yell or manipulate or bludgeon or burst into flames. You don't have to constantly correct (or keep proving why you're correct). Seek connection instead and watch your relationship transform.

We see Hiccup choosing connection with Toothless and their relationship blossoms. It boosts his self-esteem and it's infectious, spreading a sense of unity between man and dragon across the village. Their bond becomes a source of strength and self-acceptance.

Ultimately, the pair are an example of balanced masculinity: the hectic, action-packed version and the quieter, more creative side, and how they can come together to create more whole and more free identities.

Psychologist and masculinity specialist Dr Deryl Goldenberg says we all need to have courage for the changing times and, more than that, we need new definitions of courage.

Masculinity can mean so many different things to so many people. Men need to ask themselves what other courage there is besides standing up for your country, defending honour, running up a football field. There's a new kind of courage that has to be acknowledged by men, and that's psychological courage. It takes courage to go in and face your inadequacy and your insecurity. It's really vital that a boy or a man can say, 'That hurts my feelings.' Men are used to thinking of that as sissy behaviour, which is bullshit. It takes courage to be vulnerable.

In that initial scene when he encounters Toothless, we hear Hiccup talking himself into killing the dragon, cutting out its heart and taking it to his father as a trophy. He cries: 'I'm a Viking. I'm a VIKING!'

Instead, he cuts the dragon loose from the ropes he'd caught him with in the first place, and in so doing, Hiccup sets himself free too.

We have been weighed down for centuries by false ideals of what it means to be strong, bold, loyal, commanding, courageous. What qualities to look for in a leader and who gets to call themselves a real man. It's time to cut loose and set everybody free. Let every dragon fly.

Conversation and Reflection Prompts

Have you and your boy watched the film How to Train Your Dragon, or read the book? What are your thoughts?

Is your boy a Hiccup, Toothless, Stoick, Astrid, someone else or somewhere in between?

Discuss what it means to be a Hero of the Future.

Talk about when your boy last felt brave; helpless; afraid; powerful. What can he do when those feelings come up?

Discuss what it feels like to be a misfit and why we need to celebrate difference in all its forms.

Talk about friendship. Does your boy have any friendships as close as Hiccup and Toothless?

What does soft power mean to you? Explore this with your boy.

FAMILY MOVIE NIGHT

Watch the How to Train Your Dragon movies and talk about the different themes that come up. Look for other films, TV shows and animations that challenge the Man Box codes. Keep picking those codes apart.

PART 2

GRO

VING
UP

WHAT BOYS LEARN AND HOW IT'S TAUGHT

Before Ezra took his exams last summer, he asked me what I got for my GCSEs. When I told him, he called me a 'bang out'. I turned the phrase on him when his results came through and he beat my score. It's revealing, that term 'bang out', meaning somebody who works or studies too much. A try-hard. A swot. In Nigeria, the expression 'banging out' means quite the opposite, referring to someone failing their exams.

'Ah, he banged out of school o!' In other words, he's a loser. A dropout.

Funnily enough, I wasn't really a swot. Or at least, I wasn't when I left my birth country. Up until the age of seven, I was fiercely competitive at school. My first year of primary school was spent in Nigeria, where I was top of the class – or rather, I would have been if it weren't for two other students who were constantly jostling for my top spot. I remember coming home with a paper graded 99 out of 100 and showing it to my dad. As he praised my result, he assured me I could get full marks next time.

'I know, I will,' I replied, and I did. I must have been insufferable.

Starting at boarding school in the UK, it wasn't long before I was beating the other kids in my year. I wrote to my parents expressing my surprise. Weren't *oyinbo* (White) children supposed to be better educated? Within that first year, however, I had quickly learned that being the brightest spark in the room doesn't always light people up. I was already struggling with fitting in as one of the few Black kids in a crowd of White faces. The last thing I wanted to do was stand out for being a nerd. So I dumbed down ever so slightly; not enough to make my parents question the effort they'd spent making sure I had a top-notch education, but just enough to keep me hovering around third place. A sharp tack, but not a clever clogs.

My interest in boys was developing, and I would have a series of crushes and romances through primary and secondary school. My teen journals were like Mills & Boon fan fiction, brimming with desire and self-doubt. To be honest, I probably loved books more than I loved boys. Nevertheless, I couldn't shake off the idea that being brainy wasn't a good look for girls. It was a subtext running through the books, TV, films and glossy magazines that I consumed. They portrayed a world in which nobody cared about the smart girl until she took off her glasses and revealed herself to be a beauty in disguise.

At exam time, I was able to get away with last-minute cramming sessions. I would watch my more organized friends with their colour-coded folders and flash cards and giggle nervously in a silent panic. The night before a test would find me and a couple of other deadline-surfers up late, knocking back Pro Plus tablets to stay awake. I managed to ace my GCSEs, but I got two Ds because it turns out that you can't wing it with maths or biology – you're either right or wrong. I passed maths on a retake, but, like around 64 per cent of girls, I'd already internalized the belief that I was crap with numbers.

The stories we tell ourselves can make all the difference. Studies have shown that if you tell a female student that boys are better at maths before she takes a maths test, she'll actually do worse in that exam (and possibly other exam subjects too). This is a phenomenon known as a 'stereotype threat'.

We're not sure who they inherited it from (Abiye's no maths whizz either), but our kids have always excelled in maths. Ezra is studying it for A levels. As a toddler, Jed would count every door number on the street, astonishing passers-by as he counted into the hundreds. I envisioned him winning awards as a future Cambridge mathlete or, at the very least, as a guest on *Countdown*.

Jed and Ezra are often amused by my inability to add, divide or subtract without using my fingers or a calculator. It's possible I have dyscalculia, described as 'a specific and persistent difficulty in understanding numbers which can lead to a diverse range of difficulties with mathematics'. Dyscalculia is said to affect up to 20 per cent of students with attention deficit disorder symptoms and I'm certainly on the ADHD spectrum. It's also possible that, as a girl, I had it drummed into my subconscious that maths and science weren't for me. I'm also assuming that it wasn't too helpful having a maths teacher in primary school who would chuck things at our heads when we got a question wrong.

It's all too common for a child to write themselves off, regardless of their interest or potential, based on something a teacher, a parent or the wider society tells them. I remember being quietly (oh, OK, loudly) thrilled when Ezra decided to study drama for GCSEs. He's a natural performer; a bit stage-shy, but a proper clown at home, with a talent for impersonations. Mostly, I was excited to see him stretch himself beyond science and PE (the two more 'obvious' subjects that he chose).

As the years progressed, though, he started to lose interest. Drama was 'dead' and 'for girls', he told his younger brother. I pulled him up on this, and he said his teacher had always favoured the girls over the boys.

'She told me and another boy that we were mansplaining something to her. I lost interest after that.'

I bristled at this, because, although I've rolled my eyes as my husband and sons 'mansplained' stuff to me, it's not the kind of language I expect a teacher to use with their students. It feels belittling and inappropriate, almost like a male teacher calling a female pupil a 'feminazi'.

Ironically, the British education system is built on a long tradition of White men mansplaining. At school, we studied history as the battle hymn of the European man, marching across time, conquering one nation after another. We learned about White Men Who Did Things: invented machines, cured diseases, planted flags on the moon. Even subjects considered more 'feminine', like English literature, were taught from a male perspective.

Speaking with author and podcaster Lisa Lynn of the *Dear Patriarchy* podcast, she told me that it was the same growing up in middle America.

You get tricked into believing that the world exists only through the lens of a cis-het White man and anything else is niche. I acknowledge my privilege as a White woman, but if only someone would have said to me that all these books were written by White men and there are other options. I think that is a luxury we can give to our children, showing them there's a world out there and a history with so much culture and richness and beauty.

Things have improved somewhat since we were kids. However, we're a long way from true equity and representation in education. In fact, with the recent educational bans (mostly against books and materials about race, feminist and LGBTQ+ issues) spreading across conservative US states, you might say things are moving backwards in some areas. In the UK, a Pearson school study of 2000 teachers over 2019–20 showed that four in five teachers (80 per cent) believe that more can be done in UK education to celebrate diverse people, cultures and experiences. That's why no matter the gender of the child in your care, you need to get more involved in their learning if you want your child to see the world beyond a White male lens.

Throughout history and in various modern societies, teaching boys was our number-one priority. Girls stayed at home or learned 'womanly arts' like music and needlework. Since the industrial revolution, more girls started school as more women joined the workforce. Then, decade after decade, female students began to pull ahead.

Recent figures show a national attainment gap between girls and boys of 13 per cent in Early Years, 7 per cent at Year One phonics check and 8 per cent at KS1 and KS2 SATs. From pre-school to tertiary education, girls are leaving boys in the shade. In 2022, for the first time ever, UK girl pupils outperformed boys at every stage, in every subject, including maths at both A level and GCSE. This trend can be seen not only in the UK, but in Australia and New Zealand, Europe and North America. Even in Sweden, the country heralded for its progressive schooling system and ranking first in the EU's Gender Equality Index, the widening gap between girls and boys has experts scratching their heads.

What is going on? Academics and psychologists have been wringing their hands over this issue for years. Some point to things levelling out after so many decades of gender inequality. Others claim schools are not set up for how boys learn. Occasionally, you'll hear a rumour about girls being smarter than boys. Ignore this nonsense.

The answer fluctuates between a number of factors and theories, some of which remain controversial. One hypothesis is that boys are at a disadvantage from the start. Although there's no clear-cut evidence of a 'boy brain' or a 'girl brain' – it's worth noting that the latest science seems to show that there's more brain variation *within* genders than between genders – there's also mountains of research that suggests boys process information differently and that they develop later than girls in many areas.

The average boy enters nursery already behind on language development. This delay begins from babyhood and, without intervention, can continue well into puberty. A typical boy entering primary school might feel slightly less confident about reading and writing than a girl. He might have less fine-motor precision and wonkier handwriting. He might have an easier time understanding 3D reasoning, which helps with maths and logic questions. He's probably more tuned in to solving number puzzles and figuring out how to break things apart and put them together again.

According to several studies, one reason boys start to fall behind is down to us mums (sure, blame the mothers again). Apparently, parents, and mums in particular, are less likely to talk, sing and use a bigger vocabulary with baby boys than with baby girls. One theory why is that baby girls make more eye contact and are better at 'joint attention', (a shared focus of two individuals on an object).

I can't say this was my experience. My Nigerian relatives accused me of 'speaking grammar' with my babies. Ezra was so precocious with his speech that he would leave strangers open-mouthed when they asked how old he was and he'd state clearly: 'Eighteen months'.

Still, the more I read about the male brain, the more it started to make sense. So baby boys are slower than baby girls because of different brain structures and hormones? Of course, I thought, gazing sympathetically at my sons as they wrestled on the carpet. According to one study, female brains mature on average ten times faster than male brains because, from as early as age ten, female brains learn to 'prune' information to focus on what is important. For male brains, this can take until around ages fifteen to twenty. Not surprising, I mused, storing this tidbit to whip out next time my husband refers to himself as a 'genius'.

One article claimed that a baby girl can hear ten times better than a boy, and this only increases with age. If it's a softly spoken female speaking, the writer stated confidently, then some boys can only hear every third word. 'Aha!' I whisper-shouted to myself. No wonder nobody in my house listens to a word I say. Their brains can't handle it. My voice must be like brown noise to them – soothing, but unintelligible.

However, the more I looked into theories on gender and brain development, the more I flip-flopped between certainty and confusion. That's because the jury's still out on the research, neuroscientists often disagree, and what any of this means remains open to interpretation. In recent years, much of the neuroscience has been challenged or debunked (and I could find no solid data to back up that article's claims about girls hearing better than boys). New brain imaging reveals that implied gender differences have been overegged. Moreover, the field of neuroplasticity explores how our brains are malleable and can adapt to changing circumstances.

Parenting coach and author Elaine Halligan has done a ton of research in this area too, owing to her experiences raising a son who is neurodiverse. She says: 'some of these differences are down to nature, but many differences arise because of how adults treat boys and girls: how we speak to them, how we touch them, what activities we do with them, how we dress them, what toys we give them to play with, what our expectations are of them.'

While we can't ignore the impact of gender, we can't overlook how our brains, bodies and behaviours adapt to the culture that surrounds us. Anecdotally, educators I've spoken with do observe a gender difference in class. As a general rule, boys tend to be more easily distracted, prefer to learn in shorter bursts and to take breaks for physical activity. Most likely, this is down to a cocktail of brain activity, hormones and socio-cultural expectations.

Before he applied to secondary school, Ezra and I visited a local boys' school. Afterwards, I mentioned how their results were especially impressive since girls' schools typically outperformed boys' schools.

'That's sexist,' he replied.

'I'm not being sexist, these are stats.'

'You're basically saying girls are smarter than boys.'

'No, that's not what I'm saying,' I went on to expand on a popular theory about why schools are better suited to girls. 'Boys are sometimes quite restless in the classroom. Girls tend to be better at sitting still, paying attention, doing what they're told.'

Ezra was shaking his head vigorously as I pontificated. 'You must not know the girls in my class,' he replied. 'They're the complete opposite of what you're talking about. Those girls are like caged animals!'

It made me laugh, and it was a reminder that we each bring our preconceptions into any given situation. If we want to challenge the status quo, we also need to check our assumptions on a regular basis. For instance, given the strong performance of some girls' schools on academic league tables, I had an inkling that single-sex schools might be more successful for both boys and girls. However, the research on single-sex education is inconclusive, with studies outlining as many pros as cons.

Sonshine magazine founder Kirstie Beaven points out that most of us are subject to confirmation bias.

If you think boys are more boisterous and that girls need less time to run around, or aren't so interested in engineering toys, then the expectations that you have for them are completely different. What happens if your child doesn't fit those stereotypes? Some are happy to explain it as a quirk rather than acknowledging that humans are on a wide spectrum.

She feels that, by prioritizing gender so much, we can miss out on other potentially more illuminating things about ourselves and our kids.

My son could hold a pencil from a very young age, and I was so surprised because my daughter liked colouring and painting, but my son had a talent for it. It's something that

he really loves. If I had bought into the idea that boys can't develop their fine motor skills until aged seven, I might have missed that. But I never thought, boys can't do that. I thought, this individual can do it.

In school, gender definitions can become more rigid as kids pull away from their parents to form their own identities. They also feel immense pressure to conform to their peer groups. A 2015 review by Cambridge Assessment discovered that boys across the globe spent less time than girls doing homework and had more negative attitudes to school. This was partly attributed to boys spending more hours playing video games than girls (which eats into their homework time). In terms of attitudes, 16 per cent of boys said that 'school has been a waste of time', compared to 8 per cent of girls.

One reason girls are said to outperform boys is that it's not seen as 'cool' or 'manly' to care about your grades. Many boys who are above average would rather toe the midline than get called names like 'bang out' and 'geek'.

Kirstie says that our obsession with gender and labels can leave a bad taste in the mouth.

It's adults that have decided that gender is such an important marker; it's not that important for very young children. Yet it's the only thing we constantly divide them by. We tell them every single day. At school, they're called girls and boys. You would never do that by any other external trait. You'd never say: 'Come on, children with brown hair, we're all going to the park now.'

More recently, some educational settings encourage teachers to welcome a class with 'Hello, everyone,' instead of 'Hello, boys and girls.' The aim is to increase interplay between boys and girls and decrease stereotyping around what each gender can do. It's also more inclusive for those children who don't fit within the gender binary. These micro-interventions (the opposite of microaggressions) are key, because gender biases can set in at such a young age.

Teenagers Cormac Harris and Alan O'Sullivan, both sixteen, won a Young Scientist contest for a project called 'A statistical investigation into the prevalence of gender stereotyping in five- to seven-year-olds, and the development of an initiative to combat gender bias'. They held workshops with 376 kids aged between five and seven, from a variety of schools, taking them through tasks such as choosing between gender-specific and gender-neutral toys, drawing and naming an engineer, and rating male and female competency at a number of gender-specific roles. Apparently, 96 per cent of the boys drew a male engineer, while just over 50 per cent of girls drew a female engineer. This result aligns with other studies that show how gender stereotypes are especially strong among young boys.

Kids are tiny little sponges. They might ascribe qualities to themselves based on what they absorb from society, such as the idea that girls are supposed to be neat and tidy, or that boys are supposed to be outdoors climbing trees. Then, their brains make the necessary connections, and they act accordingly. By the time a boy arrives in school, this subliminal training might have already formed a huge part of his identity. However, by creating more awareness around gender coding, challenging biases and being prepared to break a few rules, both parents and educators can help overcome limitations. Please note that this isn't about stamping the boyishness out of your boy. It's about expanding the possibilities for all our kids, because not every boy or girl fits the same mould.

For every boy who likes to rampage around the playground, there are others who'd rather be colouring or playing dress-up. Quite often, it's the same boy who might express himself differently depending on his mood or his playmates. Author and podcaster Lisa Lynn bemoans the challenge of raising a gentle boy against a system that's determined to knock that gentleness out of him.

Within our house, we do really well. We learned about existing outside the gender binary and painting our nails

and dressing up however we want, and knowing that boys and girls are equal and that we don't play rough. Then all of that influence that I'd worked really hard to build around him got stripped away when he went to proper school, because he was around other kids. I constantly felt the tug and pull of society as it expects boys to behave and look and act. He's in Year One and that's a really hard battle to fight.

How does she manage it? 'Every day, I say "What happened today? What did you hear today that we need to question or understand?" Because he's so young, we talk about stories being true or not true. "Does that feel like a true story?" "Does that feel kind?" It's a lot of checking in with their emotions.'

Podcaster and educator Zahara Chowdhury also describes her son as being in many ways atypical to the stereotype of what a boy is expected to be. I asked her about her specific concerns as an educator around how boys are being taught.

'How long do you have?!'

Zahara points to issues such as the lower-achievement statistics for White working-class, Gypsy, Roma and Traveller, and Black British boys of Caribbean heritage, as well as teachers who perpetuate toxic narratives such as 'boys will be boys'.

She says, 'I think so much more needs to be done with ongoing CPD (continuing professional development) to overcome the stereotypes and bias. Teachers need serious culture and behaviour training – and so do parents – on how to navigate hormonal changes; how to equitably raise boys and girls to achieve and aim high, whatever that may be.'

Zahara also referred to the research that shows boys don't read as much as girls and are more likely to be school refusers. Some experts see the lack of focus on getting more boys to read as a glaring gender imbalance. There has been much energy and money poured into the under-representation of girls in science, technology, engineering and maths (STEM). However, comparatively boys have been short-changed when it comes to improving their language and literacy. In 2020, the National Literacy Trust (NLT) and Puffin released a report on how boys had fallen further behind girls at reading for pleasure during the UK lockdown.

Author and educator Naz Ahsun emphasizes the significance of the reading gap. 'Boys aren't reading enough in general. When you think about GCSEs and exams, it's all reading, no matter what subject you're doing. If you cannot understand what you are reading, and also writing, because reading informs your writing, then you are going to struggle.'

She has a quick tip for encouraging the digital generation to get back into books:

More boys and men are listening to podcasts. I say to their parents, get them to listen to an audiobook and they can follow along in the actual book. If they do ten to fifteen minutes a day, that's all they need. That will support their reading level, and also develop stamina as well.

Indeed, the NLT report says more schools should host 'audio libraries' to get boys reading. The report also recommends seeking out male role models, whether that's dad or granddad cuddling up with a book at bedtime, or schools inviting father figures in for reading sessions. We need more investment and support for our local libraries too. Libraries are a godsend for new parents and lower-income families. Reading helps with so many facets of learning, including basic communication, writing, foreign languages, everyday comprehension, revision and critical reasoning. Reading literature is shown to increase empathy, open-mindedness, self-awareness and mental wellbeing. Quite simply, books build better humans.

The expert advice is that, rather than trying to force Dostoyevsky onto an unwilling boy, let him read whatever he likes. So long as it's a story with words, it's all part of his reading practice. If your sons are like mine, brace yourself for an era of *Beast Quest, Diary of A Wimpy Kid, Tom Gates* and *Jamie Johnson*. When my boys were younger, they'd read anything. Then they got to an age where they only wanted to read books about 'boy' things like football or . . . well, football. The last book I bought Jed was a book about an African–American mermaid. I'm still hoping he'll crack it open one day.

One question I keep asking myself as I write this book is whether the males in my life will read it. Statistically, men are not reading books by women. I'm pouring my heart into writing about the issues that affect boys and men, but I wonder if it has to come from a man for the message to get across?

Lisa Lynn gave me her thoughts on this.

> **It shows you how deep the roots of patriarchy run when you're having to ask your children to make an allowance to read a book by a woman. Jen and I wrote Chapter Two in our book [Dear Patriarchy] for men, and we don't know if any men will read it. But who better to teach men about the system of oppression that they are enacting but the people who are oppressed by them?**

The patriarchy does indeed run deep. Unfortunately, sexism is rampant in many schools. From reception, boys and girls split along gender lines, and by secondary this split becomes a chasm. Tackling sexism in school is an ongoing process, not just for students but for staff.

One teacher told me:

> **Some of the male staff at our school, not all of them, but some, are typical White middle-class male chauvinists. It's how they've been enculturated but it's highly irritating. One teacher says the most outrageous things, and we'll clap back 'Don't be so bloody sexist.' I wish teachers had more training, because it needs to be addressed.**

Naz Ahsun says sexism was rife at some of the state schools she's taught at previously. 'You really have to hold your ground with that kind of aggressive behaviour. Particularly for young female teachers, you have to put on a persona almost. If you don't have boundaries in place, you are totally screwed.'

The real problem is that sexism remains systemic, and the schooling system is a microcosm of society. Teaching attracts more women than men, some say because it's deemed a 'nurturing' and 'caring' profession. In other words, it's not a job for real blokes. Another issue is that the pay's not that great and, as we know, the man code insists that men should earn more, and also be providers. New research from the Institute for Social and Economic Research (ISER) at the University of Essex showed that male staff in schools had fallen to a record low. This can affect how boys behave in school, and also what they can see themselves becoming.

The same research revealed a stark gap in teachers from Black or global majority (formerly referred to as ethnic minority) backgrounds, with almost nine in ten English state-funded schools (87.8 per cent) not having a global-majority teacher in their senior leadership team. About 60 per cent of state-funded schools do not have a single global-majority classroom teacher (in the north-east and south-west, it's 81 per cent and 80 per cent respectively). The overwhelming Whiteness of education is failing our kids, particularly our Black sons. If boys face a gender gap in attainment, Black boys are falling off the map.

Systemic racism, racist bullying, unconscious bias, microaggressions and colourism (prejudice against darker skins) are some of the greatest barriers for Black male students. One study used eye-tracking technology to show how pre-school teachers scanned for misbehaviour among Black students and honed in on Black boys. A Black boy with darker skin is more likely to be seen as rowdy or aggressive in class, and subsequently punished or excluded. The really worrying side of this is the domino effect that can lead from detention to permanent exclusion, pupil referral units to dropping out of society and, eventually, to jail. In the UK, as in the US, it's become known as the school-to-prison pipeline.

My sons enjoy some 'lighter-skin privilege'. They come from a stable home and have always been model students. Yet I still remain vigilant.

I've seen first-hand what happens when a Black boy gets labelled 'difficult', and the knock-on consequences it can have. If you are parenting a Black or Brown boy, or a child from Gypsy, Roma and Traveller communities (groups who are also facing high levels of exclusion), you have to stay fully engaged with the school and your child to make sure they don't get left behind. It can be unbearable pressure for families already feeling the crush of a racist society.

The current UK government has refused to acknowledge the need for widespread anti-racism and diversity training across the education system. Race literacy is severely lacking among both students and staff, and many schools are ill-equipped to handle racist incidents or attitudes.

Street Feast founder and entrepreneur Dominic Cools-Lartigue shared his experience of being plucked from a state school and earning a scholarship to a private school.

I can remember sitting around this big wooden table with people talking about my potential. What they didn't realize is that there's no point saying that to a child without giving them the tools. There were only two Black kids in my year, and the teachers were not interested in me or him. We were left behind and left to languish. It was so stressful, I got an ulcer in my early teens.

It's a common activist refrain to demand 'a seat at the table' and yet Dominic is right: if you aren't properly equipped, then that table becomes just another barrier.

Dominic describes his own son Remy as 'super-smart, always top of the class'. After a difficult time in primary school, he's settled into a secondary school with a diverse group of friends. Every now and then, though, racism or machoism rear their heads. 'He's gotten into fights about it. I remember this time last year, someone in his crew fronted him up in the playground and Remy refused to engage. So, word goes round, "Remy's a pussy." Someone says that to him and he knocks the kid.'

Dominic had a word with his boy, although, as a dad, he understood the impulse.

It's not ideal, but he needed to stand up for himself. We had a brief chat, and he knows fighting isn't the answer. I told him, you're smart, try to pause and work out the best response. Remy was never very sporty, and you know football is social currency in the playground, so it affected him. But his super-power was that he was smart. I always say the biggest muscle you have is your brain. I try to reinforce what's good, because if you focus on the negative, that's what they believe.

As a parent, you have to be your boy's number-one champion and advocate throughout their schooling years. You also have to be ready to shake the system. This might sound daunting, but you don't need to go it alone. Parenting is meant to be done in community, and when your boy starts school it's an opportunity to expand your network. Look for like-minded parents, find parenting support groups and get professional help if you need it.

Remember that sometimes mainstream isn't the answer. There's a huge movement towards home-schooling and unschooling, particularly for parents of Black children and parents of neurodiverse children who feel let down by traditional education.

Elaine Halligan wrote her book *My Child's Different* and launched her business The Parent Practice based on the long, painful, but ultimately rewarding journey she had with her son Sam. She describes him as a 'gleaming diamond' who was naturally impulsive, sensitive and intense.

'He got into lots of trouble at nursery and every day we were presented a report card. "He's not listening, doesn't share and can't stand in line. Circle time is a nightmare, he just can't focus and needs constant attention." Our sweet Sam soon became labelled as "the naughty one".' By the age of seven, Sam had been expelled from three schools. A friend of Elaine's who worked at the Local Educational Authority called to check in, having noticed that Sam was on the list of children missing from education. By this stage Sam had been misdiagnosed with a host of conditions, from autistic spectrum disorder (ASD) to pathological demand avoidance (PDA).

At her wits' end, Elaine and her husband sought help from a parenting coach that transformed their relationship with their son. She learned new skills about psychology and behaviour and motivation. 'When we understood that Sam's main issue was severe dyslexia and ADHD, we started to realize all behaviour has a cause. All behaviour is a form of communication, and we began to have more empathy.'

Working together to build his self-esteem, validate his differences, encourage him to be more self-reliant, and find the right school setting for him, they saw huge improvements.

'Today, reading and writing continue to be a struggle for Sam – yet this struggle never holds him back. He wears his dyslexic badge with PRIDE! He is honest and open about it. Dyslexia has turned out to be his super-power.'

As a society, we need to find ways to accommodate each child's individual learning journey, regardless of gender, race or ability. Above all, we need to stop stigmatizing difference.

One thing I appreciated about my sons' primary school was its diversity. There weren't many other Black kids in their years. However, there were kids from all backgrounds: Turkish, Caribbean, Somali, Polish, Thai, Bangladeshi, Italian, English. It was a far cry from the all-White school I landed in when I first came to Britain. Their classrooms included children with special needs ranging from cerebral palsy to Down's Syndrome. My sons' besties had two mums. One of the first openly transgender kids we got to know was one of Ezra's classmates. None of this was a big deal to the kids, and that's the beauty of it. When we talk about diversity in abstract, it sounds like a massive puzzle to solve, another huge box waiting to be ticked. Yet, close up, it feels ordinary, necessary, liberating. It's what real life is supposed to look like.

Conversation and Reflection Prompts

How do you think we can bridge the gender attainment gap?

Are you worried about your boy falling behind academically?

How can you support or expand your boy's learning at home? Have you considered home schooling or unschooling?

Has your boy been affected by gender stereotypes since he started school?

Is your boy a reader and how can you encourage this?

Has your child experienced unique challenges because of race, gender, disability, neurodiversity or something else? How are you working through this?

Are you willing to share your story to help somebody else?

READING CHALLENGE

Set a reading challenge for your boy, e.g. with monthly themes, such as Books by Female Authors, Books about Real People, Books by Black or Asian Authors, Books about Food and so on. See if he can expand his tastes and build a habit. Offer incentives to make it more fun, such as a family outing for a certain number of books read. If he's a reluctant reader, encourage audiobooks, comics, magazines and graphic novels, and make the best use of your local library.

HOW TO RAISE A GOOD SPORT

Athis first sports-day race, my son refus~~ed~~ super-pumped ahead of the event, wea~~ring~~ pride and happy to miss a morning of s~~chool~~ join his classmates at the starting line, he shook h~~is~~

'Come on, it will be fun,' we pleaded. His da~~d~~ morning at work to be there. Our camera phones were ready.

Ezra was resolute. The pressure of putting himself on display for a bunch of screaming parents had got to our four-year-old. I held his hand, and we watched from the side-lines, cheering on his friends instead.

The following year, Ezra decided that he was brave enough to join the line-up. It was more of a horde of kids from both classes, scrambling together and stepping on each other's toes. Yet there he was, flashing a nervous grin at us before the starting pistol went off. I don't remember where he placed, somewhere in the middle; what mattered was that he ran. He was flushed with pride as he jogged up to us afterwards, panting.

'Did you see me?'

We told him how brilliant he was for taking part.

That first sports day was a first for me too, as a mother. I was disappointed that Ezra didn't run, though I tried not to show it. I had been a sprinter back in my schooldays, one of the fastest in my year. I remember getting up at the crack of dawn, puffing out wintry breath as we trudged down to early morning relay practice; the agony of defeat to a runner at another school who I had underestimated because, for once, she was smaller than me. Afterwards, I kicked myself. People had always underestimated me too.

I remember the look on my parents' faces as I claimed first place, following in the family footsteps. My sister Nkiru had broken school records in the hundred-metre and two-hundred-metre races, and my cousin Nini would smash them, going on to become an inter-county athletics champion. I was never at that level, but I was fast. I can still feel my stomach bottoming out at the call of *on your marks, get set . . . go!* Heart pounding in sync with bare feet on the track, running like the grass was on fire, like I was a streak of light, a comet from another planet. Running was when I felt most free.

ird sports day came in Year One. He told me, 'I'm going to win
.e.' He'd been bragging all week about winning races in the
ground. Often, he was neck-and-neck with Burke, his closest
ntender. 'I'm going to beat him, Mum.' I gave him a reassuring smile,
not taking him seriously.

I stood with the other parents at the finish line, camera phone poised. We have a running joke in our family about my crappy recording skills at sports day. I get so caught up that I forget to switch on the video, or I wind up filming the grass.

The video from that Year One race captured sky, grass and my voice screeching until I was hoarse. Ezra didn't just win – he beat his classmates by several yards. Other kids and parents had rushed to slap him on the back and squeeze his shoulders before I could get to my boy and give him a massive hug. They crowded round me too.

'You must be so proud.'

I was bursting.

'I told you I would win,' Ezra said, joy beaming out of him. Later that day, he came home with his first gold medal. When he won gold again after the 2012 Games, he bit the medal like he'd seen the Olympic champions do.

For the rest of his time at primary school, Ezra won the sprint every single time. He was unbeatable.

As someone raised in the UK but born in Nigeria, competition isn't part of my sensibility, but it's in my blood. We have an expression, 'Naija no dey carry last': in other words, Nigerians don't accept anything less than first place.

My cousin Mary once asked a taxi driver in Lagos what the essence of being a Nigerian was. He told her: 'We no see mountain.'

'I just loved that,' she said, 'it really sums up our drive and determination to succeed, against all odds.'

The Nigerian urge to achieve, to hustle, to overcome all barriers is one of our biggest selling points. It's also what many of my country people believe holds us back as a nation. Perhaps we don't see the mountain because we're too busy looking for a shortcut. Maybe we could actually move mountains if we worked as a team, rather than every man for himself.

In Ezra's Year Two race, the boys and girls ran together in a jumble. Parents got mad because it was unfair for the girls. Ezra won convincingly, beating the fastest girl in the school. She was in tears, claiming an injury had ruined her chances. As her dad carried her off in sobs, he told me conspiratorially: 'She's just not used to losing.' Simone was a gifted athlete who played multiple sports and went on to win Junior Sports Person of the borough. I was pleased that Ezra had won his race, but silently I'd been rooting for Simone.

I have been afraid of competition many times in my life. For girls, competition can be an ugly word. We are supposed to toe the line, not blaze across it with our fists in the air and gold medals in our sightlines. Competition is seen as unwomanly. We are allowed to compete, so long as we don't do it better than the men.

Yet every time I've stepped out to compete, it has taught me something about myself. I have grown a little from the inside. Win or lose, I have reaffirmed what the writer Albert Camus called 'an invincible summer' within me.

When our youngest lined up for his first ever race in nursery, we had lowered expectations. It was a surprise and delight to watch him fly. 'Wow,' other parents exclaimed, 'you've got another sprinter on your hands'. You can guess what was on my camera phone that morning. Grass, sky and screaming. I remain thankful to the parents with steady hands who have successfully recorded my boys over the years.

Jed didn't go on to win every school race like Ezra. By Year Four, he was no longer the fastest, and in Year Six he didn't make it through the heats. We clapped together as other mums and dads shouted their kids to victory.

I remember after he won his race at nursery, Jed said: 'Mum, I felt angry because I wanted to win.'

We laughed because we understood what he was trying to express. That he had a fire in his belly. A determination that felt like anger, but that could also be fuel to push you through to your ultimate goal.

There are some families who model composure and compassion during every sporting interaction. The mother lets her toddler win, so she can see the smile break across his face. The dad grins modestly as the eldest son takes the prize. The kids and parents split into evenly balanced teams where there's no cheating or heckling and, at the end of the day, everyone's a winner. This is not our family.

We are obnoxious when we win, disgraceful when we lose. Each of us is competitive in a different way, but it all comes down to petty with a capital P. Card games get messy and board games are carnage. There's Abiye, barely playing unless he can guarantee success. Ezra and that unbearable grin, hip shake and moonwalk when he comes out on top. Jed, smug as anything or else whining about whatever mighty obstacle stopped him from winning. And me, smiling graciously but quietly plotting how to take each one of those suckers down.

The first time I played Wii Tennis, the instructions warned me to be aware of my surroundings. 'Get on with it!' I cried. Two minutes later, I had whacked my toddler off his feet as I tried to ace a serve with the Wii controller. Oops. I also remember watching in fascination as Ezra, just three years old, showed his Nana Helen how to play Wii Boxing, only for her to rain punches on his avatar like she was Mike Tyson, then celebrating as if she'd won an actual title belt. 'I see where you get it from,' I told Abiye, laughing.

Competition is human nature. If you ask that guy Darwin, it's pretty much the driving force of our evolution. Personally, I have a theory about football and sperm. Something about tiny little shooters chasing after an ovum. You get the idea. It's not scientific, but I'm convinced that's what has men so obsessed with the beautiful game. If women ran the world, maybe we'd have come up with something less one-track-minded.

In macho terms, sport is something that guys do, and men talk about. It's the great stereotypical leveller, the dude icebreaker: 'Did you see the match?' 'What team do you support?' For parents of boys, there's often an automatic assumption that your offspring is going to be out on the field, living out your glory days. It's telling that, in American sitcoms, the dads call their sons 'sport' and 'champ'. Several studies have shown that many mothers talk about male babies in the womb as if they're getting ready to sign them up for the Premier League: 'Oh, you should feel this little guy in here, he's got a left foot like David Beckham.'

I'll admit that I was one of those mums. However, I take no credit for the fact that my sons seem to have been born with balls attached to their feet. Literally the first thing Jed did as soon as he was able to toddle across our carpet was kick a ball with such force that he toppled over. When Jed was barely two, I signed both boys up to a soccer group for pre-schoolers. It was the sweetest thing to watch their determined little legs pursuing the ball from one end to the other. It was clear they had a talent for it.

'They'll play for Arsenal one day,' their group leader would say, giving them high fives. Deep down, I think we all believed him.

When Jed dropped out of his football club in Year Nine, a part of me felt gutted. Ezra had quit his club just before GCSEs. This might be the end of an era. Jed's still passionate about football, giving blow-by-blow accounts of the latest signings and transfers and keeping up a Fantasy Football league with his mates. But he's more into basketball now and was pleased to make the school basketball team. After their first game, he came home with a rueful smile.

'We got pasted,' he said. 'But I got the second most rebounds and coach said I did well.' He gets an extra lift from these comments since he's one of the shortest on the court.

I'm most impressed by how he handles loss these days. My sons have learned a lot about winning and losing over the years. From the jeering, accusations or complete meltdowns that would follow Ezra beating Jed at Hungry Hippos, or Jed winning yet another round of Memory – the boy is clearly an elephant, not a hippo – to the stoic support of a seven-a-side team hunched together like brothers in arms, while their coach assured them that they could make a comeback. I saw Ezra's evolution from a ball-hogger who only wanted to dribble and score goals, to a timid forward in his first team and, the following year, the Players' Player of the Season. I've watched Jed transform from the sorest loser to a trophy-holder and a kid who's learning to take life on the chin.

What's fascinating is seeing how much playing sport reveals about your child's personality. Ezra looks and occasionally acts like a natural striker (that is, self-centred and laser-focused). However, he plays best on the wing. Running through defenders, switching gear easily, picking his options for a pass, shooting from both feet. He's a showman who's at his peak when the spotlight isn't centred directly on him; the kind of kid who could lead from the front but would rather carve his own path, at his own pace.

On the pitch, Jed is a steady presence with a light touch. He's got the skills to dribble through players, but he's more likely to find the perfect pass. When he scores a goal, he'll jog calmly back to position with a bashful smile on his face. One of the mums who used to coach his team at primary school told me how much she loved his style of play. 'He's a natural CAM (central attacking midfielder),' she said. 'He's so great at hold-up play, his mind is two steps ahead and he has so much composure.'

She might have felt differently about his composure if she could see Jed whingeing over a Scrabble game or on the point of tears about his team on FIFA. But that's the thing about competition. It can bring out our best qualities, but it can bring out the worst in us too.

I remember going with Ezra for a football trial when he wanted to join a local under-nines team. He was nervous, as he didn't know any of the other boys, and I was apprehensive about the other parents.

I stood to one side, observing a group of dads egging their kids on, or rather, yelling at them. They seemed to be in turbo-lad mode and, as a newcomer, my heart sank. I envisioned future tournaments, standing on the side of a muddy pitch and watching my boy get ripped to shreds by hectic tackles and boorish spectators. In fact, my experience couldn't have been more different. Over the next few weeks, months, and years, I discovered that there were as many mums as dads invested in taking their kids to training, matches and even overseas tournaments. We became a makeshift family, holding each other through the highs and lows, marvelling as our sons transformed from gangly youths into strapping young men still finding their feet.

I had a similar experience with Jed's first grass-roots football club. We were a friendly group of parents who prided ourselves on singing loudly and drowning out the competition. They were a scrappy team, and we wanted to make sure the boys knew we had their backs. For the most part, it was all good fun. However, there have been times when I've seen or heard things get out of hand.

One dad described being at a match with his son when he heard a spectator yelling, 'Kill them!'

'Kill them?' he said, 'Please remember my child is on that pitch!'

I've been at tournaments where I've spotted the type of dads I worried about, drenched in beer and testosterone. The kind of father who screams insults at his son throughout the match, and then loudly picks his game apart as they walk home. In one league our sons played in, a dad got into a physical fight with a referee, and his kid's team got banned for the season. I've heard coaches who put all the blame for defeat on their young players' shoulders or fill their heads with toxic, coded messages about masculinity. *Shake it off. Grow a pair. Take one for the team. Isn't it time you cut your hair? Toughen up. Man up.*

Author and activist Elliott Rae is the founder of the website *Music, Football, Fatherhood*. He leads seminars and workshops on gender equality and positive masculinity. His organization works with Premier League football clubs bringing together men in the community for honest and open conversations on issues ranging from single fatherhood to domestic violence. After a big football game, male violence climbs and often skyrockets in international tournaments. The match-day combination of excess drinking and intense, unregulated emotion can be especially dangerous for women and children. Data from the University of Lancaster showed a 38 per cent rise in domestic-abuse cases when England loses a football match, and a 26 per cent rise even if it's a win or a draw.

Elliot's organization offers a rare space where fathers, husbands, grandfathers and sons can speak from the heart.

I'm so interested in sport and masculinity, particularly football. A football stadium can be the most emotional place in the world for a man. When England get knocked out of the World Cup, there are shots of men weeping and no one bats an eyelid at that. I find it fascinating. The good thing is that it's a safe place to be emotional. But on the negative side, sometimes at a football game you'll see a guy getting very angry at a player for giving away a corner. You know that it's probably because he's frustrated at work, or has money worries or difficulties with his relationship. He just doesn't have anywhere else to express the anger and that's sad.

It is sad that a football ground is one of the few places where men feel free to express their feelings, to show tenderness to each other, even physical affection. When the ball hits the back of the net, all inhibitions vanish. Strangers in the stands will embrace, while men on the pitch will kiss each other on the cheeks, pat each other's backsides, come in for bracing group hugs. The flip side of this is that the combative atmosphere can breed aggression, both on and off the pitch, not only at Premier League games but at youth matches.

And it's not just the men. Up and down the nation, and in various countries, soccer moms are also screaming blue murder and getting into heated confrontations. I don't know what it is about football that gets the blood boiling over. Although, it's the same with American football, Little League baseball, ice hockey. Parents bring their aspirations and frustrations and dump them on their child like a stack of balls he's not allowed to drop.

What are we modelling for our kids? At every youth league, there are signs put up to remind parents that this is just a game; that they should treat themselves and others with respect and that the kids should be allowed to enjoy themselves. How can our children take this to heart when it's not the message they receive from wider society?

The entire system is set up to push the 'winners' to the top and weed out failure. It might be simplistic to blame capitalism, but you can certainly point the finger at the patriarchy. Traits that are seen as feminine, like sensitivity, cooperation and caring for your fellow human, are shoved aside in favour of grinding and dominating. Prime Minister's Questions is a show of one-upmanship where scoring cheap points seems more important than having something of substance to say. I picture Parliament, and frankly any male-dominated institution, as one big locker room full of brattish men and a few women biting their tongues.

When Donald Trump boasted about grabbing women by the pussies, it was laughed off in some circles as locker-room talk. For a certain type of man, the locker room is a hallowed space where they can truly be themselves. Except the locker room isn't really a safe space, it's another arena, where strong arms rule and the feeble are fed to the lions. It's in locker rooms that boys use humour to mask fear, where they body-shame each other, and in some cases, a place where there's physical and sexual violence. In the book *To Raise a Boy,* author Emma Brown shares disturbing tales of boys who are raped by teammates using objects like wooden broom handles. It's a reminder that sexual violence is never really about sex. It's about power.

Hopefully, you will never have to carry your child to hospital with sexual injuries after a match or training. However, as a parent or caregiver or coach, you will have to cope with a barrage of programming from society (and sometimes from within your own home) about how a boy should compete. This will happen whether or not your son shows any interest in playing for a team. Sports and masculinity are so inextricably linked that it can take a lot of untangling for a boy to feel like it's OK to bow out.

That being said, I don't think you should teach your son not to join in. If he's not sporty, encourage him to take part anyway. This is not about proving his manhood or any such rubbish, but rather, it's about having a go and finding out what happens next. Lead with curiosity. Let him try a variety of sports and see if anything sticks. I've seen boys who are the tiniest, thickest or skinniest in their class grow in confidence almost overnight from discovering they've got a talent for bending the football, or running long distance, or making a clean dive into the pool, or spinning on their head in a hip-hop class. It's not just good for their sense of self, it's important for all kids to see people of all abilities taking part.

When Jed joined an after-school football practice in primary school, there was a kid in his year called Bertie (name changed) who joined too. Bertie was shorter than the rest and wobblier on his feet owing to his disabilities. The other boys made space for him as he took his time working the ball around the cones. They were extra careful to pass the ball with him if they were matched in pairs. They whooped and cheered whenever Bertie scored a goal.

One afternoon, Bertie had a little accident in the middle of the hall. Their coach Danny kept his cool, carried Bertie to one side, got a mop to wipe up the mess, helped Bertie into a clean pair of trousers, and the boys went on with the session. I loved to see how sensitive the other players were to Bertie in the moment, with nobody pointing or staring or teasing him. I was also impressed by how Danny kept smiley and chatty throughout and didn't make a fuss. He wasn't even a parent himself at the time. But he realised that what Bertie needed in that moment was to be treated with care and dignity and to carry on playing. I know the boys present learned a lot about sportsmanship that day.

That same term, Bertie passed away and the school community was invited to his memorial. There were songs and speeches and people sharing tearful, funny stories. What I remembered most was Bertie's giddy little face as he raced up and down the school hall, cheered on by his classmates.

Sports can provoke our lesser instincts, but also our most human qualities. We laugh or grimace as a flasher streaks across the pitch. Yet all of us are naked out there, in one way or another, when the whistle blows and everything's on the line. Our emotions rise to the surface, every muscle taut with anticipation, whether you're a player or a fan. Not everyone is equipped to play in a team, but everyone can be inspired by competition.

One of my life mottos is 'Raise Your Game': it's the founding theme of my blog. It's a manifesto for giving it your best shot, being a team player, having fun, going outside your comfort zone and redefining success on your own terms. It's about learning how to win and to lose with grace and a sense of humour. These are essential lessons to teach our boys, especially about how to fail. A boy who never learns to lose might grow into a man whose ego cannot take a knock; the type of man who competes with everyone he meets. A man who talks in barbs or fists.

'Raise Your Game' works in a relationship too, particularly in marriage, which, like sport, can bring out the best and worst in you. When you learn that you are not actually going to win anything until you realize you are on the same team, then you can choose to handle conflict and life's hurdles as one unit rather than a constant, bitter competition. You can focus on playing fair, having fun and growing to new heights.

There was a time at our kids' primary school when they didn't give out any medals or trophies. Apparently, everyone was a winner. In other words, nobody was. I guess I understood it to an extent. But I thought it was unfair to those kids who excel at sports. Not every child is academic, so they should have opportunities where they also feel like they're smashing it, whether that's at sports day or in an art or music or poetry contest.

Competition is good for the body, the heart and the soul. Sport has so many wellbeing benefits. It's great for boys who are restless or struggle with ADHD. It can be a prescription against mental-health challenges like depression and anxiety. If you are a parent of more than one child, healthy competition can help with stuff like tidying a room (try setting a timer to see who can pick up the most in the shortest time); eating their vegetables (who gets a 'peas power up'?); and even getting them to bed on time (who can fall asleep the fastest?). Honestly, it worked like a charm for me on several occasions. The flipside was when Jed's birthday came along, two weeks after Ezra's, and they'd start measuring contests over who got better gifts!

Encourage your kids to compete, not necessarily against each other but in whatever way competition works for them. It doesn't have to be on a court or pool or playing field. It can be a 5k charity walk, or a challenge to see who can grow the tallest sunflower at school, a LEGO challenge, an academic test, a tyre race, a knitting competition, an art show, a tug of war, a cup-sorting or yoyo record, a rare Guinness World Record, a talent contest, a bake-off, a marble rally, a backyard sports day, a conkers tournament, a pet parade, a card game, a go-karting track, a disco marathon, a bubble-blowing challenge, a spelling bee, a fancy-dress contest.

Show them your competitive streak too, especially if you are a woman. Talk to them about age-old beliefs about boys and girls, and who can play what sports. Model healthy competition through fair play, encouragement and a growth mindset. In other words, don't obsess over the end result; praise their efforts instead. Teach them that your number-one competitor is always yourself. Remind them to root for themselves as much as for anybody else.

I'm definitely the least sporty in my household, although I do challenge myself. I've learned hula-hoop tricks and samba steps off YouTube. During lockdown, the boys taught me football kick-ups in the garden. I've wobbled around on skates in our kitchen, or what Abiye calls the world's smallest roller disco. As a family, we enjoy watching sports documentaries and movies. The familiar tale of a ragtag group of no-hopers defeating the odds (and logic) to come out on top, or at least discover what they're made of. As formulaic as these movies are, I applaud the message.

Years later, I look at a photo of Ezra crossing the finish line, paces ahead of his teammates, and I fill with pride because I know how long it took him to muster up the courage to compete. You see, those sports-movie clichés are true. In the end, it's less about the victories or the losses or whether anybody else was there to capture it because your mum forgot to press record. What really matters is the distance you travelled and how much you grew along the way.

Conversation and Reflection Prompts

Is your boy sporty? How does he feel about this?

What role does sport and competition play in your family life?

Do you encourage your child to compete? Are you inspired to do so after reading this chapter?

What does good sportsmanship look like? Discuss with your boy.

Who are your son's sporting role models? Can you think of anyone who doesn't fit the traditional definition of an athlete?

Has your boy expressed any gender stereotypes about sport, e.g. 'throwing like a girl'? How do you challenge this?

What does 'Raise Your Game' mean to you?

BE A GOOD SPORT

Commit to trying a new sport, game or activity with your son (and/or other family members). Look for something that will inspire healthy competition, learning new tricks, challenging yourself, having fun and lots of bonding moments!

BOYS AND BODIES

never had my bra pinged by the boys at school. You might call this a win for feminism, but that wasn't on my mind back then. I was just a girl, standing in front of a mirror, waiting for her boobs to arrive. I would smile sympathetically at the girls who came to school after summer holidays, clasping self-conscious arms around their chests; the girls who blushed and hissed at the boys snapping their bras in class. Secretly, though, I wondered what it would be like to attract that kind of attention.

The flat-chested ones among us would giggle as we flung our arms in and out, chanting: 'I must, I must, I must increase my bust!' à la Judy Blume's *Are You There God, It's Me, Margaret.* Silently, I was hoping for an overnight transformation.

I didn't start wearing a bra until I was thirteen and attending a girls' secondary school. It was a size 34AA that I bought at Marks & Spencer, my cheeks burning as I paid at the counter with the pocket money I'd been saving up. Although my period had arrived a year earlier, the rest of me was slow to catch up. I often think that being a late bloomer, like being an outsider, has served me well in life, but as a schoolkid, it kept me up at night.

Despite having nothing up top worth covering, even as a pre-pubescent girl I wouldn't take my shirt off like the boys did in summer. I envied their freedom sometimes, but I had no desire to be mistaken for one of them.

So, it was with a surprised 'Oh!' coupled with 'Go, girl' pride that I spotted Sally, one of my son's classmates, in a park one summer, shirtless and free as the breeze. Back in the day, they would have called Sally a tomboy, mainly because she was seriously into sports. Unlike several of her friends, she didn't need a bra yet, and this didn't seem to bother her in the slightest.

It was refreshing to see her run about with her friends, boys and girls alike, none of them batting an eye about her lack of a top. I wondered whether this was down to her confidence, their innocence, or perhaps an evolving acceptance of different body types. I hoped it was a combination of all three.

In some areas, girls are forbidden from going topless in public even before they've hit puberty. It may sound ridiculous, but I've heard of a baby girl as young as eighteen months being cautioned by a lifeguard on the beach. Apparently, her swim nappies didn't provide enough coverage. One mum was astounded at a water park when another parent told her it was 'inappropriate' to let her daughter splash around topless like her older brother. Her daughter was three.

Adults can be so quick to sexualize bodies rather than letting kids express and grow into themselves at their own pace. I realized that my initial surprise at Sally's freeness had more to do with my own adolescent experiences and projecting some of those insecurities onto her.

Typically, the rules are different for boys. Whether it's a six-year-old or a builder with a penchant for beer, there are generally no penalties for a lad who wants to go bare-chested in a public space. Since 2012, 'Free the Nipple' activists both online and offline have been advocating for the right for women to go topless too. The slogan is inspired by actor/director Lina Ecco's documentary of the same name. The Free the Nipple movement aims to challenge the gendered double standard and to spark a wider conversation around body image, censorship and the male gaze. Now a global hashtag with its own Instagram account, Free the Nipple has been championed by everyone from celebrities to breastfeeding mums. For some amusing and provocative takes on nipple liberation, follow #FreetheNipple on social media.

Sometimes it amuses me that, for all my self-consciousness as a young person, I am now the parent of a teenager who refuses to wear a shirt. It has become something of a family joke. On the day of his final GCSE exam, the front door opened and I heard him hurtling up the stairs while removing his school uniform for the last time. By the top stair, his shirt was unbuttoned to the waist. He cast it to the ground.

'I'm done,' he announced.

I wasn't sure if he meant done with exams or done with being dressed. On a video call from Toronto, his cousin Mayowa shook her head, amused.

'Is Ezra allergic to clothes?'

I said that perhaps he was turning into Axel, the older brother in US family sitcom *The Middle,* who spends much of the series wandering around in boxers, eating cereal and groaning at everything his mother tells him to do. In fact, he's more like his Uncle Alex, who's famed for taking off his shirt in nightclubs and dancing on tables while pouring champagne over his pecs.

Abiye claims Ezra's body is more like his, lean and sinewy, while Jed has my family's body type. In truth, they are both a mix. Jed is naturally heavier than Ezra, and I sigh inwardly when people refer to him as 'solid' or call him 'big man'. I know that for boys as well as girls, these seemingly innocuous comments can chip away at their self-image.

Both Ezra and Jed were nine-pounders at birth. Within their first few months, each baby was on the ninety-eighth percentile in height and weight. Their height evened out over the first few months, but their heftiness persisted. Even as a slim and active five-year-old, Ezra was heavier than he looked.

I got letters home from primary school, cautioning me about my sons' weight and suggesting an after-school weight-management club. I chucked both letters in the bin. Although Jed was rounder and thicker than Ezra, neither of my sons was obese, as the letter declared. For years, Black and Brown campaigners have pushed for the BMI index to be updated as it doesn't reflect ethnic diversity. In fact, it was created by a White man, based on a so-called average White male. Research shows that, overall, people of African descent tend to have greater bone density and muscle mass.

This isn't to say that you should ignore medical advice about your child, especially if you are concerned about their weight. Do seek support and take advantage of the free after-school clubs available. All that being said, you know your child best, and if they are generally well and active, it's better to focus on Health at Every Size or HAES (a growing movement, championed by influencers like Stephanie Yeboah, Riccardo Onorato @GuyOverboard, Molly Forbes, Kelvin Davis, Megan Jayne Crabbe @BodyPosiPanda, Dr Joshua Wolrich, Anna Sweeney @DietitianAnna and author Linda Bacon), rather than honing in on their weight when they're still so young and potentially setting them up for a cycle of self-consciousness, dieting and shame.

When they were babies, my boys were deliciously chunky. I could have munched on their fat cheeks and dimpled thighs. I craved their fleshiness as much as I swooned at the smell of their newborn heads. Isn't it strange how we can delight in every ounce of the bodies that come through us while denouncing so many parts of our own?

For many women, the changes you go through in pregnancy can put a dent in your self-esteem. For me, it was liberating. Pregnancy didn't cure me of my insecurities or self-consciousness completely; I still prefer getting dressed in private and making love with the lights low, but motherhood flipped a switch that let me see myself with new eyes. Through the magical, discombobulating process of growing and nurturing two humans, I became less hung up on my inadequacies. I started to appreciate my body more for what it could do and what it had experienced.

If I could go back and tell Uju at thirteen that she would breastfeed both her sons for eighteen months, she would probably giggle nervously and think me a liar. She didn't know yet that you don't need a Pam Grier bustline to satisfy a hungry baby.

I look at my thirteen-year-old son and try to imagine a future version of Jed returning to the present. What would he tell himself? Perhaps that he should eat a few less sweets because his teeth will thank him later. Maybe also that he doesn't need to drink quite so much milk. Jed has always been a milk monster, but whenever I open the fridge these days, there's another empty bottle with a dribble of milk at the bottom; barely enough for a cup of tea. Why is he drinking so much? Is he part-cow now? And why on earth doesn't he just throw the bottle away? As I grumble, Ezra smiles. 'I did the same thing when I was his age,' he says. 'He's trying to grow taller.'

In Year Nine, Jed is still the shortest of his friend group, a fact they remind him of loudly and often. When he's out with his mates, Jed wears the relaxed smile of someone who's used to being ribbed for his height, yet confident in his other qualities. He was thrilled to make the school basketball team.

Ezra was also one of the shortest in his class. In 2020, he would measure himself against me daily to see if he was growing. One morning, he stood in socks with his shoulder against mine and we gazed in the mirror. Undoubtedly, he was a breadth of an inch taller. Ezra whooped loudly and did a knee slide across the floor.

Three years later, he's towering over me at five feet eleven. He reassures Jed that he'll catch up with his peers, although of course he doesn't want his little brother to be as tall as him.

Abiye says he didn't start growing until he was fifteen. It slowed down his blossoming school career as a rugby player. To make up for it, he developed a super-thick skin and a tongue like a blade.

As a fellow smallie, I'm sympathetic to Jed's cause. I peaked at five feet four and (a very important) half inches by around age fifteen. This is above the average of five feet three for a British woman, but I still feel short. It's different for girls, though. My height isn't seen to diminish me as a woman. In fact, petite is a preference for a lot of men.

Some of this can be put down to the macho notion of cis-het males as physical 'protectors and providers'. However, it's not just men who think this way. One study revealed that women are happiest when their male partner is eight inches taller. Men in the study showed a preference for at least a three-inch height gap. Around 13.5 per cent of guys only liked dating women who were shorter than them. For women, it was around half (48.5 per cent) who said they preferred a taller partner. No wonder some shorter guys feel like the odds are stacked against them.

According to what some economists describe as the 'height premium', the taller you are, the more successful you become. Tall men seem to strut through life as the ultimate alphas, winning in every competition from the job market to the dating game. This might sound old-school, yet such ideas are prevalent, even among the TikTok generation.

My husband recalls reading about how American presidents are becoming taller, election after election, with Donald Trump clocking in at six feet two inches. This is according to Trump's 2012 driving licence, although the man who likes to do everything 'huuuge' and 'bigly' claims to be six foot three, giving himself an extra inch.

Recently, following the release of the HBO documentary *The Princess,* Twitter was aflurry with old images of Prince Charles and Princess Diana that had either been staged or doctored to look like he was taller than her. In truth, they were the exact same height. And that was when she wasn't wearing heels.

For your average, gender-rigid guy, wearing heels is not an option. Some boys get a lift from the bubbles in their trainers, but unless you're comfortable stepping out like the artist Prince, who wore four-inch heels most days, it can be brutal out here on these streets.

Scott is one of a number of men who have taken desperate measures to get the height they feel they deserve. I came across his story in a *BuzzFeed* article about leg-lengthening surgery. He was 5 foot 7 inches and felt inadequate as well as victimized by the type of guys who body-shame short men on TikTok. In many ways, I could be empathetic to his struggles. However, I was disturbed by what he put his body through to gain a maximum of three inches. The article described an agonizing process of slicing through skin, breaking and resetting the bone, inserting a titanium rod and months of healing, with a potential for infection or opioid addiction.

For people with achondroplasia (the most common form of dwarfism), limb-lengthening surgery can be a life-changing medical intervention. However, it remains controversial amongst members of that community who prefer to embrace their unique stature. My niece Mayowa was born with severe hip dysplasia, a congenital dislocation of the hip that can limit motion and lead to osteoarthritis. At age fourteen, she went through agonizing bone surgery (a periacetabular osteotomy) and had to use a wheelchair for months. She told me she was gobsmacked that anybody would put themselves through something similar for cosmetic purposes.

I felt the same dismay years ago watching a young man get painful, bloody calf implants on MTV. Wouldn't it be easier and less devastating to wear knee socks with some kind of padding than to go under the knife?

It sends a shiver down my spine. But the culture of 'never enough' has all of us by the throat. We might not all be experimenting with penis-enlargement ointments or travelling overseas to get a Brazilian butt lift; we might not be desperate to the point of self-mutilation, yet each one of us can place ourselves along a spectrum of trimming, concealing, dieting, plucking, tightening, filling, colouring, airbrushing or repackaging our appearances into something different; trying to fix up whatever we think will give us a couple more inches of self-worth.

I often thank my stars that I didn't grow up with social media. I can't imagine what the constant comparison would have done to my teenage self-esteem. It was hard enough being raised on women's magazines. I came of age with the 1980s supermodel: Naomi, Christie, Linda, Cyndi, Kate.

The supermodels didn't make me feel bad about myself. They were iconic, untouchable, otherworldly beings; totally out of our reach, although we knew them by their first names. It was the everyday girls with pink cheeks, tousled hair and teeny waists that graced the pages of *Jackie* and *Cosmopolitan* that got to me. I would scan their images, knowing that my dark skin, thick thighs and tight Afro curls would never quite cut it. Reading magazines like *Ebony* and *Essence* was self-affirming, as they featured Black women of all shapes and sizes. There was still a preference for models with lighter skin and straighter hair, so colourism remained an issue, but at least I felt seen.

At school, I knew girls who dieted constantly and compulsively measured the gap between their thighs; girls whose hair fell out in chunks and whose breath was always sour. They'd be in the bathrooms after breakfast, lunch and dinner, vomiting up their insides until they had nothing left to give. By the time I left secondary school, at least two students had been hospitalized with eating disorders. One didn't make it to her twenties.

Growing up, I never met a guy who counted calories or who even knew what a calorie was. Today, eating disorders and body dysmorphia are on the rise across genders. While young girls might aspire to the cartoonish proportions of Nikki Minaj or Kim Kardashian, young boys are drawn to the 'gym bro' prototype. Back in the 1980s, the likes of Hulk Hogan and Conan the Destroyer were clearly fantasy figures. Nowadays, you'll find regular men with more preposterous muscle definition bursting out of your children's tiny screens. Worse still are the guys who push products supposedly guaranteed to pump you up and give you bulges in all the right places.

I remember walking into a Holland and Barrett health store and watching in amazement as my then-six and nine-year-olds ran towards the giant bottles of protein powders on the front shelves. The bottles were so absurdly large and heavy they couldn't even lift them, though they were doing a good job trying.

'Mum, can we buy these?'

The lady behind the counter smiled.

'Sorry, boys, those are for adults.'

I was baffled as to how they had figured out what these bottles contained before reading the labelling. Then it struck me: WWE. They were obsessed with wrestling and would watch it on YouTube. The ads that popped up must be full of protein shakes and steroids. Seductive promises targeting an audience that includes pre-adolescent boys. Eat me. Drink me. Transform yourself from Bruce Banner to The Incredible Hulk.

By the age of six, boys have a set idea of what real men are supposed to look like: big and strong (note that research shows kids as young as three expressing body image issues). The superhero costumes that my sons played in, and in some cases slept in, came with built-in muscles. I remember squeezing their foam biceps and pretending to be impressed. I thought they looked adorable, and I enjoyed seeing how pumped they got wearing Spiderman and Batman and Hulk outfits. I wasn't thinking about how they might feel once those costumes came off.

In truth, I don't think it was an issue at the time. Those were the days when they'd jump in the bath together or dash through the house without their pyjama bottoms on. They wanted to be big and strong so they could smack down fantasy opponents. This was still child's play. It wasn't a lifestyle choice.

As a parent, though, it's hard to predict or notice the shift from body free to body conscious. One minute your little boy is joyfully running around, balls akimbo. The next, he's locking the door and yelling 'Mum, get out!' when you walk in on him changing.

It's normal for a growing boy to want more privacy or to start taking more interest in the way he looks. As a tween or teen, your boy might ask you about skincare. He might get into dyeing his locks or slathering them in hair gel. If you're lucky, he'll even use deodorant. His focus on personal grooming might extend to fashion (or 'drip' as my boys call it) and trainers ('kicks'). Boys around this age start to see being fit less as something they do but as something they become. He might ask for a gym membership or start going with his mates to the school gym after lessons.

Ezra informs me that in sixth form he's going to be in the gym daily. It's all part of what he quips about as 'max prestige, light-skin rizz' (urban slang for the irresistible appeal of an attractive, light-skinned Black man). This includes growing out his hair and spending a lot of time holding his camera phone above his face, narrowing his eyes, and licking his lips suggestively. The latter is a joke between him and his mates, a send-up of what some guys do on social media. I remind him not to spend too much time lifting weights and to be mindful of safety measures. He responds by flexing his muscles, Schwarzenegger style.

A fitness programme can be fun and healthy for your son and even better if it inspires the whole family to get involved. You don't need to put on gym shorts and start tailing your son on his workouts, but do stay on track of his habits. Talk to him to try and ascertain how he feels about his body. This is the age range (tween to teen) when boys' banter turns from silly ('You look like a banana') to more targeted. My sons are quick with the comebacks. Sometimes, it's funny ('Your hairline is a mountain range.' 'Your balls are the size of the equator.'). But when it gets mean I intervene, because things can easily spiral out of control.

Manorexia is the non-medical name for a combination of male eating disorders that might include anorexia nervosa, bulimia, excessive working out and muscle dysmorphia. Also termed 'bigorexia', muscle dysmorphia is when a person who's been hooked on gaining muscle mass still sees a puny wimp in the mirror. They spend all their time and money at the gym or with a personal trainer. They fill themselves with harmful supplements and steroids, leaving them and those around them susceptible to wild, angry moods, also known as ''roid rage'. Other dangerous side effects of steroids include high blood pressure, organ damage, heart failure, fertility problems and dementia.

Unfortunately, owing to the male code of silence and self-reliance, a boy or young man suffering from any of these conditions is also less likely to get help.

Since so few male sufferers seek advice, it's hard to find accurate figures, but the general estimate is that around 10 per cent of people with eating disorders nationally are male (some estimates go up to 25 per cent). Males experience similar triggers to female sufferers, including emotional challenges, personal upheavals, bullying, social influence and media images of manliness.

The warning signs of eating disorders include dramatic mood swings, skin and hair changes, hiding your body under baggy clothes, sudden or excessive weight gain or weight loss, spending inordinate amounts of time working out, buying weight-loss or muscle-mass supplements and scrolling through endless videos by 'fit fam' influencers. Look out for other flags too: perfectionism, self-effacing comments, controlling tendencies. Contact your GP for advice and links to support groups if you suspect your son has an eating disorder, as these conditions require a multi-pronged approach to treatment.

Eating disorders have plagued boys as young as five to men in their fifties and older. Back in 2008, former MP John Prescott was praised for opening up about his struggles with bulimia. He became the face of a campaign aimed at raising awareness for male sufferers. In 2013, *Hunger Games* actor Sam Claflin spoke out about his own manorexic tendencies and how he had wished for a 'Ryan Gosling six-pack'.

Society expects men to take it on the chin. Casual jokes about dad bods and moobs (man boobs) fly thick and fast, especially on social media. We forget that our boys are watching. We forget that they can be affected as deeply as girls. Often, it just looks different.

A girl might hold her belly in. A boy might puff his chest out. Either way, neither of them can breathe freely.

'Why are you gassed?'

I hear this from my boys all the time. It's slang for 'why are you feeling so pumped?'

This time, it's Jed talking to Ezra as we walk along the street in Montego Bay, Jamaica. We're in the part of town known as the Hip Strip, a touristy and buzzy line-up of restaurants, bars and gift shops. Ezra strolls ahead of Jed, with Abiye and I making up the rear.

Abiye has just observed: 'Ezra, you've really grown since we've been on holiday. I reckon you're taller than Isaac now.'

I agree.

Jed says, 'I can see him smiling from behind.'

I can see Ezra's cheeks curving too, as his shoulders square out.

'Why are you so gassed, Ezra?' Jed says and another round of affectionate teasing begins.

I think about that expression 'gassed' and how ultimately all the chat about height and size and gyms and six-packs amounts to little more than hot air.

My nephew Seyi is six feet, four inches tall with size thirteen feet. His dad is six feet five, and had to get his shoes specially made. I point out to Ezra and Jed that being extra tall isn't always ideal. Besides, height does not make the man. I've dated guys of various sizes. There are advantages to being smaller. The tallest boyfriend I had was six feet four, and kissing him was a strain.

'Mum! TMI.'

Realistically, I know that I can bang on about how height makes no difference. However, the main thing that will change the way a person feels about themselves is life experience and their evolving internal story.

As a parent, you can try to influence this through the way you treat your child at any size. Loving words and affirmations, positive reinforcement through the stories you watch and read, and the images you surround yourselves with too. Focus on what you love, not what they lack. Show them role models, athletes and sex symbols who don't fit the Man Box mould. Celebrate true diversity in body types and abilities and what beauty and strength look like in different parts of the world. If they're on social media, encourage them to follow body-positivity influencers. Visit museums and galleries where they can see a range of human forms.

Help your child track some of their features along their family lineage or their cultural roots. Years ago, a Yoruba British friend told me I had such 'strong Igbo looks'. Anxiously, I ran through a mental checklist of my stature, my complexion, the swell of my forehead, the 'yams' (musculature) of my calves and thighs. Then he added, 'It's really beautiful to see', and my whole body glowed.

I show Ezra a photo to see how much he resembles my late father. It's in those famous Asika eyes. Jed is clearly a descendant of Dele Cole, his paternal granddad. As a baby, when he'd perch on his granddad's knee, wearing the same style hat, they were two peas in a pod.

Speak kindly to yourself too, because your kids are listening. Do your best to model what it looks like to be comfortable in your own skin. It's not easy to model this when you haven't cracked the code as a grown-up. But you can make a start along the path to self-acceptance, and parenthood is a great point to begin.

There's a popular saying that 'every body is a beach body'. It's a statement against the magazines and media that try to cut us down to size every summer. It makes most sense when you're actually on the beach, surrounded by bodies of all shapes and descriptions. Elderly ladies in sun hats and swim skirts. Middle-aged men with gloating bellies and teeny Speedos. Women in burkinis. Waifish girls in triangle tops. Babies in waterproof nappies, boys in swim shorts and rash vests. Dimpled, wobbly, sturdy, slender, pink, brown, glossy, or crêpy like papier mâché. The sunshine welcomes us all. Take off what you need to take off. Release the pressure. Breathe.

As our kids grow, I hope there are more spaces where bodies of all ages and genders can breathe freely. I also want to see more inclusive beaches where, if you are in a wheelchair, or blind, or living with another disability, you can come out in your swimmers and enjoy the sun with ease. Every body is a beach body.

On our last evening in Montego Bay, walking back to our hotel, Abiye and I decided to go for a moonlit swim in the sea. The boys refused to come in, complaining about getting sand in their trainers again. They sloped off to their room whilst Abiye and I stripped off to our swimwear and waded into the inky waters. A tiny part of me was high-fiving my younger selves. Uju back in the day would have talked herself out of it, but here I was, middle-aged in a bikini, floating under the moon in paradise.

Later, Ezra asked: 'You and Dad weren't skinny-dipping, were you?'

'Of course not.'

'I swear down.' His forehead smoothed with relief.

'Didn't you see us go in?'

'Yeah, I mean I just turned, and I saw you guys' heads in the water and I thought, *what?!* These man weren't wearing swimming costumes!'

I'm highly amused by Ezra's horror imagining his forty- and fifty-something-year-old parents tossing caution, and our clothing, to the wind. I'm also impressed that he thinks we have it in us to skinny-dip at 9 p.m. on a public beach.

In Jamaica, we spend all day in the water. Ezra lifts me up in the pool and threatens to dunk me. His dad once told him the measure of a man is when he can lift his mother and turn her upside down. Abiye recalls doing this to his own mum in his late teens. I've warned my boys against it, but I see that glint in their eyes from time to time.

In the pool, it's irresistible. Ezra carries me easily. When we're in the sea later, he carries me again. He climbs and rides on my back then Jed leaps on too and our trio collapses, laughing. I lift each boy onto one hip as I did when they were babies. Ezra shouts: 'Mum's hench!' and that sets us off laughing again. For an instant, it's like I'm holding past and present in both hands. And there's nothing bigger and stronger than this feeling.

Conversation and Reflection Prompts

How do you feel about your body? Has parenthood/adulthood
changed this for the better or worse?

What does your boy like best about his body? When does he feel
happiest in his skin?

Has your boy expressed any thoughts about his body that
concern you?

How has social media affected the way your boy sees himself?
How about you?

Who are the role models your boy looks up to? What are their
bodies like? Do their bodies define how he thinks about them?

What body-positive steps can you take as a family, e.g. ditching
the scales, exercising for fun, eating for pleasure, dressing to
accentuate and not hide your physique?

How can you encourage your boy (and your whole family) to
embrace Health at Every Size?

SELF-PORTRAITS

Ask your boy to draw a portrait of his whole body (you and your
other kids can draw one too). Place your portraits side by side
and notice their similarities and also what he might have missed.
Focus on the things you love about your boy, e.g. his cheeky
smile, his caring hands. Try this exercise again and again, as you
work on your body positivity as a family. See how the portraits
change over time.

HOW TO TALK ABOUT PRIVILEGE

When my sons were little, taking them to the park was a daily exercise. One afternoon, I was sitting on a bench, watching them chase each other on scooters. Around us, mothers helped toddlers mount slides, towelled off children after splash fountains, wiped the last grains of sandpit off their babies' feet.

A tall, rather attractive man in his thirties arrived, pushing a double buggy. I watched as he put the pushchair brakes on, leaned down and lifted one baby into a swing seat. The other baby had her hands outstretched as her father scooped her out and placed her in a swing beside her sister. The muscles in his forearms rippled as he began to push both girls, one after the other, as they shrieked with delight. I couldn't take my eyes off them. What a gorgeous sight.

'Awww,' I thought. 'Bless.'

It was only afterwards when discussing this reaction with a friend that the blinkers fell from my eyes. Why the heck was I so impressed by some dude pushing his children on a swing? Sure, he had twins to contend with, and that was no mean feat for anyone. But I had two kids under five, and that involved bicep-building double-swing episodes too. Also, it wasn't as if I'd never seen a mum pushing her twins around. In that case, my first thought wasn't 'How gorgeous' but rather 'Damn, she looks knackered'.

I realized I had been guilty of perpetuating that age-old trope of praising dads for what mums do every day, despite being a mum myself. Shame on me.

If you want to get a look at male privilege in action, pop down to your local park and watch Awesome Dad out with his children. He's walking tall, king of the jungle, mane flapping in the breeze, baby carrier strapped to his chest like a badge of honour. Stopping balls in front of a tiny goal with the showmanship of a world-class keeper. Building mini dens that would make Bear Grylls proud. Spinning his laughing kids so fast on the roundabout, you worry they might fly off, until he saves the day with a wink and a smile, as his World's Greatest Dad medallion glints in the sunlight and everybody cheers.

I'm exaggerating, perhaps. Most dads today are just putting in their park shift like any parent – that is, one eye on the kids, two thumbs on the mobile phone. Nonetheless, average dads are treated like heroes compared to mums doing the same job. Male privilege means that, as a father, you can do the bare minimum and still face less judgement or outright hostility than a mother trying her best. Carrying the baby? What a star. Changing nappies? Utter legend. Taking the morning off work to attend a school event? We will never forget your sacrifice, sir.

Now let's follow Awesome Dad out of the park to a nearby cafe. Despite being a pitstop for parents, the cafe only has one baby-changing table and that's inside the women's toilets. The dad feels icky about whipping out a changing mat and placing it on the sticky floor of the gents. The cafe owner is kind enough to let dad sneak into the ladies' for a few minutes. However, as his daughters grow, Awesome Dad is going to find it far trickier to take them out in public. He can't watch them when he's using the urinals, and he has to lurk outside the women's toilets while his girls go in alone. He's grateful for more gender-neutral toilets, but finding truly inclusive spaces for a father and his kids is harder than he anticipated.

Some other hurdles he might come up against: being the only male in the parent and baby group; being overlooked when the school mums' WhatsApp group make social plans; not getting enough parental leave; feeling like the secondary caregiver; being asked if he's babysitting his own children; knowing he'll have a fight on his hands if he ever needs to challenge for custody in a paternity suit.

Privilege is about the benefits we enjoy, but it's also about the barriers we don't face; in many cases the barriers we don't even recognize. Yet the most privileged among us can also face unseen barriers. There are no single stories. That's why any conversation about privilege must be intersectional. In other words, we must look past the icing to consider the many colours and flavours that make up our individual layer cakes.

I use the layer-cake metaphor to break down intersectionality for kids in a visual they can understand; how each layer of who you are – your race, your age, your gender, your abilities, your education, your social background – might also act as a barrier in different circumstances. An intersectional approach means that we appreciate the fact that every one of us has many layers, that our disadvantages often stack on top of each other and that our privilege is multi-layered too.

The word 'privilege' tends to stoke defensive reactions. Nobody wants to look like they got ahead without deserving it, or like their life is jammier than the next person's. The term 'White privilege' has got people so worked up that a UK parliamentary enquiry claimed it was harmful to White working-class children who were falling behind in school, as if social inequity, austerity policies and budget cuts had nothing to do with it.

Jen Audrie of the *Dear Patriarchy* podcast has no patience for the fragility around talking about White privilege.

I really think that the light that is being shone on the White cisgender heterosexual male is well deserved. I don't feel defensive, like, 'Oh, my White boy, he's not like that.' I think both Lisa and I have very real conversations with our boys and our partners, because we need to have a balanced society. I mean, in the US it's a nightmare. The defensiveness and the White supremacy and everything that's coming through right now is despicable, and it's killing people.

Several US states have banned schools from discussing White privilege, and teachers have been fired for bringing it up in class. In the UK, I've been accused by the right-wing media of pushing a 'woke agenda' for advising parents to talk to their young kids about White privilege.

Let me explain myself here. I'm not suggesting you sit your two-year-old down and drum words like 'privilege' or 'intersectionality' into his sweet little head. You could try it, but I don't recommend it. However, you can talk about what's fair and why. Explain that, if you have more than others, it's good to share. Also, if you notice that someone has less than you or is being treated unfairly, it's kind to help in any way you can. Make it relatable with some examples that illustrate your point.

In my book, *Bringing Up Race*, I used the example of crayons and how countries as varied as the UK, South Africa, Japan, and India referred to pink or cream tone crayons as 'flesh coloured'. This shows how White skin has been pictured as the norm, while people with dark skin are portrayed as something other.

To demonstrate White privilege to a White child, you could ask if they can identify crayons, colouring pencils or craft paper that reflect them, and whether they can find the same amount to represent people with different complexions. Ask them why they think this is, how it might make someone who is Black or Brown feel, and what we could do to change this.

You can also examine the books on your shelf or at the local library, the textbooks used in class, the TV shows and adverts they see every day. Who is featured most? Who is missing? Who is controlling how this story gets told and why?

Since 2020, UK TV and newspaper adverts have been awash with Black, Asian and mixed-heritage people. It's like they suddenly discovered we exist. Not everyone is thrilled to see us everywhere, however. A Sainsbury's Christmas advert in 2020 showed a Black family celebrating Christmas dinner like regular folk. It nearly broke the internet with viewer complaints. Comments like: 'Am I living in England or Jamaica?' or 'I thought it was meant to be a White Christmas!'

I'll admit, I've sighed heavily on occasion when yet another Black man eating a burger or a Black woman shouting 'bingo' comes dancing across the screen. And yes, they're often dancing or rapping for extra cringe factor. It feels as if the ad company is yelling, 'Hey, check out our cool ethnic credentials!' I remain sceptical about how many actual Black or Brown executives are in the room where the decisions get made. Representation matters, but it's merely tokenism when it's not backed up by real change.

Yet I don't dismiss it out of hand because slow progress is still progress. It's easy to take for granted how common it's becoming to see an Asian, Black or mixed-heritage family on mainstream TV. I remember when we were such an oddity that I got compared to pretty much any Black person on telly. 'Look Uju, it's you!' my White schoolfriends would crow as Floella Benjamin appeared on screen with her big wide smile and beaded fringe. At the time, I had my hair braided with beads too, but I didn't want to be Floella. I wanted to be me.

What I didn't know at the time was that Baroness Floella Benjamin would pave the way for the next wave of presenters from marginalized backgrounds across mainstream programming, and ultimately all these new ads that sometimes irk me will contribute to shifting the narrative around what Britain looks like and who deserves to be seen.

One of the first signs that you have privilege is feeling triggered when things don't go your way. It's a sign of how comfortable you've been until something tipped you out of your cosy chair. As the oft-quoted saying goes, 'To those accustomed to privilege, equality can feel like oppression.' For those who are used to seeing themselves reflected in movies, TV, books, billboards, magazines or the job market, making room for others can feel like being squeezed out. However, we can all learn to make room.

Privilege can come in many forms, but I would argue that male privilege sits – nay, manspreads – in pole position. Regardless of race, caste, wealth or status, being a man gives you a certain amount of power from birth. From households to workplaces, healthcare, sports, courthouses and religious institutions, the arts and media, ice-cream vans and bin men – where are all the bin women at? – masculinity dominates.

Of course, certain industries like publishing or fashion are full of women climbing through the ranks and cracking glass ceilings. However, if you look at who's running things behind the scenes, you'll find a man in almost every nation, and almost every single time.

Male privilege hit me hardest when I became a mum. My husband and I went from partying all weekend, having conversations until dawn and going to bed whenever we pleased, to a life of stark contrasts. By all accounts, he was a hands-on dad. But since neither of our children ever took to bottle feeding, I was the one left holding the babies. He'd step out when it suited him while I stewed in resentment and breast milk.

Recently, I read Emily Ratajkowski's essay in which a new-mum friend of hers complained about lying awake next to her snoring husband. She said: 'There is nothing worse than the undisturbed sleep of a White man in a patriarchal world.'[3] I can assure you that the untroubled sleep of a Black man is almost equally nerve-pinching, especially when you're experiencing that rare form of sleep torture known as new motherhood.

To date, my husband giggles in his sleep. Sometimes I find it cute. Other times, I want to put a pillow over his head. One night, on a recent family holiday, I was sleeping peacefully when the sound of my husband stumbling into our room woke me around 3 a.m. He'd stayed out to explore Montego Bay after hours. As usual the following day, he'd regale us with tales of how he'd made friends with a seventy-something-year-old named Rambo who had promised to take him snorkelling. But that night, he was half-cut, wriggling out of bed to use the toilet, then attempting to walk out of the hotel room stark naked.

'Babe, where are you going?'

I steered him back to bed. We were in a room with two beds, and it was with relief I watched him stagger over to the unslept-in bed, leaving me alone in mine. At last, I could get some sleep. A couple of minutes went by and . . . wait, is he giggling? Please no. Then . . . oh my God, he's humming now? I could just about make out the melody to the Bob Marley protest song, 'Them Belly Full (But We Hungry)'. His humming got louder and I lay there, teeth gritted, contemplating whether to get up and kick him out of his bed. Until, still fast asleep, he belted out the chorus: 'OH, WHAT A TRIBULATION!'

I wanted to cry and laugh at the same time.

'You should have been the one singing that,' my sister said when I reported him later.

Abiye was highly amused by himself the next morning, and it's gone into family lore. It's the kind of thing I love about him that also irritates the crap out of me. Not the sleep-singing so much, but the unwitting freedom he enjoys being able to go wandering off into the night on a strange island. Sure, there's some risk involved. But there's also adventure and fun and snorkelling with guys named Rambo. There's liberty beyond my imagination. Beyond most women's dreams.

And no matter how much I try to explain it, he'll never really get it on a visceral level. He'll never understand just how much larger his world feels sometimes, just by virtue of being male. Nor will he ever lie awake at night mentally packing the kids' suitcases while I'm chuckling in my sleep.

If the man you live with, your best friend and soul mate, the closest thing you have to a male ally, cannot fully recognize his privilege, how can you have a useful conversation about it? Furthermore, how can you raise it with other males in your life: boss or co-worker, uncle or father-in-law, GP or mechanic, teacher or student? Your own son?

One of the trickiest things about privilege is getting someone who has it to notice it. That's why I encourage you to start these conversations young. How do you explain the concept of privilege to a boy? Make sure he understands that privilege doesn't mean you are wealthy or posh or living without other disadvantages. Male privilege doesn't require you to own a sports car or a designer watch. It's the gentleman's club where sometimes all you need is a pair of balls and a strong handshake. However, don't let this become a lopsided conversation. You can talk about how everyone benefits from some form of privilege, and how each of us also has disadvantages to overcome. This is the human condition.

Here's a definition that's simple enough for a young child to grasp: privilege means you don't have to worry about something that affects somebody else every single day. So, White privilege means you don't face the microaggressions, biases and systemic racism that people of colour are up against daily. For instance, you can apply for a job without worrying that your 'foreign-sounding' name will hold you back. You can travel Europe without concerns about how the locals will treat you. You can have a police encounter without fearing for your life.

Male privilege is about the ability to move through life without the pressures that weigh on female and non-binary people. You can have a baby without worrying if it will affect your chances of a promotion. You can go topless without experiencing harassment. You can walk home late at night without fearing for your life.

If you are White and male, it might seem like you've hit the privilege jackpot. Except there are no single stories, and your version of privilege might intersect with a working-class upbringing, a mental-health condition, a physical disability, trauma or a personal history of grief. It's important to bear this in mind, although that doesn't mean that you shouldn't use your influence as a White male to challenge racism and sexism wherever you see it – including in yourself.

Lisa Lynn says:

What you have to be saying to your boys, and White boys in particular, is, you're not the gatekeepers of excellence. Just because you look and see yourself everywhere, that doesn't mean the world is built around you and that's how it should be. It's been built around you for a purpose. If you see a world that looks like you, there's inequity. So you have to be making a big stink about it.

When you talk to a boy about male privilege, talk about how they can show up as an ally. This can include anything from speaking up for female rights and needs, especially in an all-male space, to creating more opportunities for girls and women to speak for themselves. Teach your son to be a breaker of chains; in other words, to disrupt those patterns of thought and behaviour that allow racism, sexism and other injustice to persist.

Tell him you don't need Thor's hammer to break a chain. He can do this by interrupting a racist or sexist or ableist comment, asking a question that makes people reflect, choosing not to engage in hate speech disguised as banter, sticking up for a friend or for his own values, or simply choosing to walk away if a situation gets out of hand and someone is spoiling for a fight. Smash that macho chain right there.

As a parent, you can break chains too. One way to do this is through simple wordplay. Try reading a fairytale to your son, and swapping out all the gendered pronouns to show how the messages of who has the power – typically the prince/rescuer – and who needs protecting – the princess/damsel in distress – can be subverted.

In September 2022, comedian Sarah Silverman shared a video on Instagram about a language experiment where you switch out any word or phrase that is traditionally masculine (e.g. 'doorman', a 'bunch of guys', 'may the best man win', etc.) and change it to something feminine. For instance, 'womankind' or 'may the best woman win'. She invites boys and men to try it so they can get a sense of how the English language centres males and conditions people of all genders to see the world through a masculine lens. She emphasized that it's a lesson about exclusion, so the game isn't directed at or for non-binary people, since they already understand what it's like to be excluded.[4]

You can try a similar language experiment by comparing words that empower Whiteness and diminish Blackness. Typically, white is seen as pure, good or innocent, e.g. lily-white, white flag, white as snow, etc. Whereas black often denotes something wrong, bad or outright evil, e.g. blackballed, black heart, black sheep . . . the list goes on. In April 2020, the UK's National Cyber Security Centre made a conscious decision to use the terms 'allow list' and 'deny list' instead of 'whitelist' and 'blacklist'. I couldn't help but smile at their website statement:

I hope that if you're seeking to make this, or similar changes in your own organization, this blog post helps you to convince people around you that it's worth doing. And finally, a word from the NCSC's Technical Director, Ian Levy (supported by the full NCSC Management Board): 'If you're thinking about getting in touch saying this is political correctness gone mad, don't bother.'

When I wrote *Bringing Up Race*, I was deliberate about using the racial term 'White' in upper case, because I wanted to draw attention to Whiteness as a racial characteristic. At first, referencing 'White' people so often was uncomfortable. I found myself wanting to write 'white man', or even just 'man', instead of 'White man' because like so many of us I had been conditioned to see Whiteness as the default. I had to strengthen that muscle. Now, writing 'White' is second nature.

Becoming mindful of the privileges we enjoy, or the disadvantages we face, can put us in an uncomfortable state. It forces us to re-examine everything we are and everything we know. However, we need to talk about privilege because it's a first step towards accountability. When you can own your part in an unfair system, you can start to think about how to make things fairer. Opening up these conversations can create a consciousness shift in which a boy moves from passive observer to active changemaker.

Privilege isn't necessarily a bad thing, either. I've read talk about 'dismantling privilege', but it's the systems themselves that need dismantling. Once you understand how your privilege gives you an advantage, you can use that to help others who don't enjoy the same benefits. Like Spiderman said, with great power comes great responsibility. And ultimately, true power comes from empowering those around you.

Too often, privilege looks like hoarding power and opportunities. We can counter this by raising children with abundant mindsets. The more you give, the more we gain. Imagine raising a generation of men who believe in sharing power and not hoarding it. It could transform the future of our planet.

They look like they're dancing, but it's called a Privilege Walk. This social experiment has been carried out by schools, clubs and organizations around the world. If you want to see a version of it, head to YouTube and watch a video titled 'What Is Privilege?' by BuzzFeed (As/Is).

The idea is simple: get a diverse group of people and ask them to stand in a line. It's more powerful if they stand together holding hands at first. Ask them a series of questions, and with each response the participants either take a step forwards, backwards or remain in position. Questions explore various privileges and disadvantages that reflect racial and socio-economic differences, as well as age, gender, ability, cultural background or even world-view.

It's an eye-opening exercise. Everyone starts in one place and then, owing to factors mostly outside their control, they end up separated. Some wind up at the front, others way at the back. In the exercises I've watched, race and gender play an obvious part in determining who lands where, although it's not always so clear-cut.

BuzzFeed shares the questions it asked participants so that you can try this at home or with a group. Sample questions include:

If your parents worked nights and weekends to support your family, take one step back.

If you are able to move through the world without fear of sexual assault, take one step forward.

If you can show affection for your romantic partner in public without fear of ridicule or violence, take one step forward.

If you have ever been diagnosed as having a physical or mental illness/disability, take one step back.

If the primary language spoken in your household growing up was not English, take one step back.

If you can go anywhere in the country, and easily find the kinds of hair products you need and/or cosmetics that match your skin colour, take one step forward.

I did the 'walk' on my own and it was interesting to see how, despite my obvious racial and gender 'drawbacks' as a Black woman, I was able to move forward thanks to my education, social class, sexual identity and cultural capital. I took more steps forward than back, although for many of the questions on this list, I stayed stuck and reckon I would end up somewhere in the middle of most line-ups.

A viewer left a poignant comment on the video about the fact that the participants begin standing together, only to end up separated, in some cases by yards: 'To see them slowly let go of each other's hands is insanely heartbreaking.'

Watching the Privilege Walk, this awkward line-dance towards recognizing and owning the perks and challenges you and those around you have experienced, I thought about how unpacking topics like these is like learning new steps. At first it's clumsy and you stumble on the beat and possibly step on somebody's shoes. But with practice you can find your rhythm and meet your fellow dancers in sync.

It's worth doing a Privilege Walk with your son, perhaps including more specific questions around boyhood and masculinity. To widen the scope, you might suggest to your child's teacher that they try something similar in school. This exercise can provoke many difficult feelings, however, so it must be handled sensitively.

What else can you do? If you are reading this book, then you have a certain amount of privilege. The privilege of literacy. The power to open a book and discover the world anew. This is an incredible gift to pass on to a boy. Reading is a powerful tool to cultivate empathy. Sharing stories can help shape a child's understanding of what things are like for people who don't live or sound or look like you.

Another way to broaden his perspective is to encourage your boy to join you in acts of service. Whether that's starting a petition, donating to a cause, or volunteering in your local community. Take him to help you at a food bank or homeless shelter or get him to join in with putting together packages for gifting to children in need. Share creative ideas about how you can support someone who's sick or destitute. Tell him about times you or a family member struggled and how you made it through.

Kids can be excessively 'me-centric', and you can counter this by building gratitude into your daily life. There have been numerous studies around how simply listing three things you're grateful for every day can transform your wellbeing. These days, I'm all about appreciation. It captures so much in one word. It means recognizing the worth of something or somebody; being or feeling grateful; enjoying an experience or quality; or the act of noticing or being aware. To appreciate also means to increase in value. In other words, it's an opportunity to grow.

How about beginning an appreciation practice with your son? When I think about asking my teenagers to join me in an 'appreciation practice',

I can already see the raised eyebrows and gagging gestures. If yours are anything like mine, maybe don't tell them upfront. Just start it anyway.

Appreciate the little things. Lean in when your kid tugs your hand and says, 'See!' What are they seeing? Isn't it amazing? Tune in fully when your child bids for your attention and wants to share the most incredible (or incredibly mundane) thing about their day. *Wow, did that really happen?* Listen closely to their likes and dislikes and surprise them with a piece of insight that blows their tiny mind.

Or just sit and look at your child, really look at their face, their fingers, their funny little expressions, and be filled again with a sense of utter wonder that this complete human being is sharing part of their life journey with you.

If there's one thing being a parent can teach you, it's awe. That spine-tingling feeling that knocks you for six when you experience something you don't have the language to explain. Picture Keanu Reeves saying 'woah' a million times over. I'm not going to pretend that parenting is awesome 24/7; most days it's sheer drudgery. But there are those moments when the sight of your son strolling through the school gates, or the clasp of your baby's fist around your finger simply take your breath away.

Over the past fifteen years, social scientists have become somewhat obsessed with studying awe and its benefits. Obviously, visiting the Pyramids or the Taj Mahal are great contenders for getting the goosebumps popping. However, awe can also come from watching a David Attenborough video, listening to Prince (or whatever music makes your heart sing) or looking at old family photos.

Apparently, people who experience awe regularly report better relationships, more creativity, and an overall greater sense of wellbeing. It can also shift your perspective dramatically. In one experimental group, participants drew themselves smaller after having an awe-filled experience. This effect is called 'unselfing', a quality that not only helps decrease your mental chatter but also increases your desire to connect with and support others. Awe experiences help break down walls. Studies show that a person who feels awe is more likely to describe themself as 'a human being' or 'an inhabitant of the earth'. It inspires humility, the antidote to entitlement.

Sometimes I feel caught between wanting my boys to be full of themselves, to be overflowing with the essence of who they are, and the fear of raising another set of entitled men who think they can do whatever they damn well please. It's a delicate balance. My immediate plan is to practise appreciation and at the same time keep looking for ways to nudge them out of their comfort zones. Encourage them to try new things, whether it's a different route to school or an unfamiliar flavour. Show them stuff that makes them question what they think they know, and what they imagine is possible.

I believe you can knock the entitlement right out of a boy or man when you take them beyond the scope of what they can imagine. There is no manspreading at the top of the mountain. There can only be awe.

Experts say that taking an 'awe walk' – that is, going outside your regular environment to appreciate your surroundings – can reduce stress, heighten perception and increase feelings of connectedness. As you stroll around taking note of things you might have rushed past earlier, you are engaging in a different kind of Privilege Walk. A reminder that being alive is a privilege. That we are all inhabitants of the earth. So, if we look closer, if we ask the right questions, we can learn this dance together. Two steps forward, one step back, reaching for each other's hands to close the gaps.

Conversation and Reflection Prompts

When did you first become aware of your own privilege?

Discuss with your boy what he understands about privilege and how it shows up in his life.

How does White privilege affect you or your boy? Discuss.

How does male privilege affect you or your boy? Discuss.

What does your boy's (and your own) intersectional layer cake look like?

Ask your boy how he can use his privilege as a force for change?

How can you do this as a family?

PRIVILEGE WALK

Try a Privilege Walk with your boy (invite friends, family, classmates and so on, if they're open to it). You can look at examples online, borrow their questions or come up with your own. Make space for any difficult reflections and feelings that arise. Discuss what you've learned and how it might inspire you to do more for those who have less.

RAISING BLACK BOYS

My eldest was about nine years old when he perfected the Black boy strut. It's hard to describe this on paper, but when you see it, you know it. That combination of swagger and stroll, a sloping and a leaning and a dragging of the feet. A tilt to the head that says, 'Watch me now, but don't come too close.' Sometimes, it's less slink, more bounce, as if they're walking to a beat only other brothers can hear.

At nine, Ezra could pull off different versions of the strut so accurately and so humorously that he'd leave me creasing with laughter. I captured him on video once and you can see the camera shaking as I try to hold in my giggles. Now he's seventeen and, while he doesn't exaggerate his steps for comic effect, even in low lighting you can tell it's a Black boy coming down the street.

My youngest walks like a strange mix of toddler and old man. When he was little, he was often slightly off balance. He would wobble and keel over easily, run and bump his head into the nearest sharp edge. Despite being injury prone, Jed was always leaping and racing and spinning. He had flair too, a natural finesse on the dance floor. I miss those days when he lacked any self-consciousness and yet took himself so seriously. Jed the professional break-dancer (at least in his head). These days, he treads with eyes low and shoulders hunched, as if he's carrying the weight of the world in the oversized schoolbag on his back.

If he was approaching you in a balaclava, you might not guess Jed's race, although maybe you would. Maybe you'd recognize those taut shoulders, the heaviness in his shuffle. Black males walk with added weight, like something's pushing them down or bigging them up. No matter what, as soon as that mask came off, he'd meet the same prejudices faced by Black boys, whether in Camden or Cape Town, Copenhagen or Connecticut.

If raising boys is a challenge, then raising Black boys is an extreme sport. Even without the stats to hand, I can reel off a litany of disadvantages for Black males in Western society. Black boys fare worse in social care, education, criminal justice, health outcomes, mental health, the workplace, housing, the media. The only place where they might seem to have an unfair advantage is in sports. Even then, they're relegated to the playing fields where they become fair game for fans and critics. Black officiators such as linesmen, referees, managers and club owners are few and far between.

On top of this, Black boys have to cope with a barrage of ideas, not just about manhood, but also what it means to be a Black man. How to handle yourself, how to talk to girls, how to treat your women, how to navigate the system, how to uphold the race, how to flash your cash, how to protect your ends, how to make ends meet, how to walk down the street. Don't show weakness. Don't allow yourself to be vulnerable. When I think of being Black in this world, I think of pressure and Black manhood as a pressure cooker that could overflow at any moment.

Except, of course, that's not the whole story of Black men, and not even half the story of my boys.

My youngest was born into a world where the most powerful man on the planet shared his complexion. For eight years, all he knew was a Black American president. No matter how distant the Obamas might seem to a young kid growing up in Britain, their presence created huge ripples here and around the globe. If you can see it, you can be it.

On election night 2008, I was seven months pregnant and glued to the TV screen, my heart fluttering each time another round of votes was called. Obama was ahead but I couldn't relax after the 'hanging chads' catastrophe that gave George Bush a second term. When the win was announced on a giant ticker across the screen, I fell to my knees, weeping. I never imagined that I would see it in my lifetime: a Black man with a 'foreign-sounding' name leading his beautiful family into the White House. I placed my hands over my belly, Jed turning peacefully inside, and I said a prayer of gratitude and protection. Please, God, keep him safe from those who want to see us fall whenever we rise.

When I went upstairs, I found my two-year-old awake in bed. He reached out for me to lift him up, rubbing his eyes and grinning.

'Yes, we can!' Ezra shouted and I hugged him tightly. For all I know, he had been dreaming of Bob the Builder, not Obama's campaign slogan, but it felt like synchronicity; like the start of something unimaginably wonderful.

However, the Obama era didn't make life much easier for Black boys and men. If anything, things got more heated. Between 2009 and 2017, the rate of stops, arrests and killings gave rise to the Black Lives Matter movement. Here in London, the unexplained death of Mark Duggan in police custody sent the UK into a state of emergency. Some are quick to point out that the 2011 riots weren't just about police violence, nor was it just Black boys burning shit up, yet most of us recognized what had been unleashed, ready to rip at society's throat. The monster that White supremacy created. The self-fulfilled prophecy of racist, doom-mongering tabloids. Every hateful headline, every grainy image of a Black male accused of a crime, had come back to haunt us.

We are all subject to these twisted fairytales. When you're spun the same story over and over, it creeps into your bones. I have grown up with Black men as family. Yet sometimes, walking past a cluster of unknown Black males, my stomach tightens like a White woman clutching her purse.

To be honest, the feeling is tied more to my sex than my race. Perhaps it is the cell memory of men who have hurt me. Black men are more likely to take note of me than White men, because the truth is that most unwanted male attention, and gender-based assaults, are directed at females of the same race. Since the dawn of White dominant culture, the media has painted a picture of the Black male savage who preys on innocent White women. From the racist allegory of King Kong climbing a tower with his blonde victim to the horrific lynching of Emmett Till, it's an image that has caused devastating harm. Yet the stats don't add up. If you are a White female, your biggest threat is a White man.

Ezra comes home and tells me how, while running for a bus with a schoolmate, they had almost frightened the wits out of a White woman coming in the other direction.

'Mum, you should have seen the look on her face, she was terrified!'

He's half-laughing, still a little shocked himself. I caution him to be more careful, for I have empathy for any female who sees two, now quite tall, male figures rushing towards her. At the same time, there's a niggling sense of annoyance, because I know part of the reason that woman felt afraid was because of the colour of my son's skin. Choosing my allegiance as a Black person and a woman is never easy. Intersectionality means we shouldn't have to choose.

When my sons were little, they were prone to getting lost. One time, we were in a gadget shop in Stratford. I wandered down one aisle with Jed in his pushchair. Ezra went to the next aisle to play with a touchscreen. In the blink of an eye, he was gone.

'Did you see my son?' I asked the security guard, who looked confused, having just observed the little boy with the twisty Afro minutes earlier. I checked at the counter, asked several attendants, circled the shop in a frenzy. *Please, please, please.* With my heart between my teeth, I headed to the exit. Where the hell was my son?

Right outside, I saw my sheepish-looking four-year-old being escorted towards me by a man in police uniform.

'Is this your boy? He told me he was lost.'

Grabbing Ezra in a hug while telling him off for leaving the store, I felt liquid with relief. At least he had followed my previous advice. I used to tell my children that if they ever lost sight of me in a public place, they should look for a police officer or for another mother with young kids. Those seemed like the safest options.

However, as Black boys grow, a police officer is not usually the safest choice. Also, if they approached a White woman, even one with kids of her own, I couldn't guarantee that she would help. In the age of Karens, she's just as likely to call the police on them herself.

Editor Kirstie Beaven, who is of mixed Asian and White heritage, has had tough chats with her kids about the police force in Britain. 'We've spoken about some of the stuff that's come out about the Met Police internally, such as the racism and the sexism and not just what happened with Sarah Everard's murder but the number of women of colour that have not been adequately protected.'

For Kirstie, as for other Black and Brown people, the difficulty comes in reconciling the public image of the police with their history of brutality and abuse. Being the parent of a daughter who looks more Asian (with darker skin and hair) and a son who presents as White (with fair hair and blue eyes), Kirstie's discussions with her children have to engage with the intersection of race, gender and power. She recalls cycling with her kids in the park when her daughter mentioned that a friend of hers had told her the police were racist.

I said, 'Yeah, that is true' and we had a conversation that it's not all police officers but the institution. My son was only six, and piped up, 'I thought the police were there to help you.' I had to acknowledge that it's tricky, possibly they might help him. Under this system, my son might get preferential treatment. Like, that's shit.

We need more allies, particularly those of us who are parenting in the margins. Educator and podcaster Zahara Chowdhury shared with me some of her deepest fears as a mother. 'I am absolutely petrified of racism and Islamophobia. It scares me into wanting to keep my children at home with me all the time, or to move to a more diverse country.'

Zahara lives in London, one of the world's most diverse cities. Yet for UK families of colour, the rise in bigotry surrounding Brexit and the toxic media spin about refugees and immigrants can be hard to bear.

'I am so scared of my child having to account for his identity. I think the trauma associated with being a mother of colour is hugely underestimated, especially in a Western, White world. It makes me so angry.'

We need more allies, truly. One thing that perks me up is knowing how many people (of diverse racial backgrounds) are familiar with my sons and ready to come to their aid. My boys have grown up and been schooled in the same area since Ezra was one. Where we live is one of those London village-style communities where you often run into friends you've known since your babies were at stay-and-play together. Almost every week, another parent, a former teacher or someone who taught them football as toddlers will tell me they spotted one of my boys out and about. It's an informal neighbourhood watch. We can sleep a little easier as parents because we have eyes everywhere.

That's not to say bringing up Black boys, especially in London, won't keep you up many nights. Now that they're old enough to wander around town alone, there are times when I can't stop checking my phone for that next alert, a message to say they're on their way home. Between the muggings and the knifings and the drug busts and the postcode beefs and the stop-and-search and the false accusations and arrests, it's almost more than an anxious mind can bear.

Author Chine McDonald is parenting a new baby and a toddler, both of Black mixed heritage. She says: 'My worry is that by the time my babies become teenagers, they'll be stereotyped as dangerous or inferior in some way because they are Brown boys. I worry about their physical safety. I also worry about the microaggressions that might make them feel less than they are.'

Personally, I worry about the invisible shield a Black boy has to wear to feel safe. The weapons he might carry to feel invincible. The act he has to put on in order to feel seen.

So much of Black masculinity in the West is an ongoing performance, and so many Black men are living with performance anxiety. It's a dazzling, dizzying high-wire act that blends talent, strength, wit, speed, agility, resourcefulness, resilience, bravado, grit, poise, aggression, charm, sexuality, rhythm, bragging and nonchalance. Alexa: play 'Vossi Bop' by Stormzy.

My teenagers are learning how to be Black men partly from their father, granddad and uncles, but mostly, it would seem, from their peers and the influencers they follow on YouTube and TikTok. It's fascinating to see the Black-man baton passed along as each one crosses into adolescence. The need to wear your hair a certain way, to dress with 'drip', to carry yourself with attitude, to walk with a certain swagger. The need to talk 'road'. To keep up with the patter and the slang and the music.

There's a big part of me that delights in the familiarity and the audacity of the Black male performance. I love to see it, especially when so much is stacked against them. However, I wonder what they could become and how much easier life would be if they didn't feel so much pressure from the culture and from society.

When Jed was eleven, he made his first Spotify playlist. Eight hours and seven minutes of explicit hip-hop, mostly with artists whose names began with Lil. He knew every single lyric. I shared this anecdote on my social media to much amusement from friends and family, especially as I pointed out that if he dropped an F-bomb in their presence, they shouldn't blame me. They should blame Lil Tecca, or Lil TJay, or Lil Loaded, etc. The only artist I made Jed remove was an eighteen-year-old serving time for murder. I mean, come on. Otherwise, I let him express himself, because that was his thing, and I knew how important it is for an eleven-year-old kid to have something they call their own. Those lyrics made Jed taller, sharpened his hairline, popped a little more bounce in his shuffle. It was also the lockdown of 2020, so I put it down as part of his home-schooling.

I have ongoing conversations with my sons about hip-hop and its offspring, grime and drill. We discuss the attitudes, the use of the N-word, the hypermasculinity, the way they talk about women, the way women talk about themselves. How hip-hop is a movie projector that both shines a light and blows things out of proportion; how each artist is starring in their own gangster flick or X-rated romcom, their own documentary or quirky indie drama. My boys can separate braggadocio from reality.

I'm torn, though, because it feels like, just last week, when the American rapper Takeoff from hip-hop trio Migos became one of a long line of hip-hop acts shot and killed before he reached the age of thirty. Senseless murders seem to spill off the records onto the streets. Most of us recognize that it's art, but not everybody can tell the difference; sometimes not even the artist. I worry about whether I'm a bad parent for letting my sons blast trap beats in the shower or throw up gang signs for family photos.

'You're not a Crip, Jed, you're literally a Year Six child.'

This was Ezra to his younger brother one summer, and I wrote it down because it made me smile: a reminder that my kids are still my kids,

RAISING BOYS WHO DO BETTER

straight outta Islington, a long way from Compton. They may play at being roadmen in their slang and swagger, but they're regular boys who come home after school and whose lives revolve around what's for dinner.

I remember myself at fourteen, driving around with my older siblings and rapping at the top of our lungs to NWA's 'Fuck the Police' blaring from the car stereo. From LA to London to Lagos, hip-hop gave us a language we could share; a bassline that felt like home.

Still, I'm torn. As a Black woman, I can't ignore how elements of the music I grew up loving continue to stomp all over us. I am a Black mother, and I can't pretend the singular narrative of money, power and bitches has no impact on our sons or our daughters. I'm teaching my kids to read between the lines, but not every parent has so many options. We do need to hold someone accountable. Hip-hop is based on an African tradition of call and response. Except these days, it's all about the call and we see little response, while our children butcher each other for cash or reputation or the slightest of insults.

Ever since my brother came home with 'Rapper's Delight' on twelve-inch vinyl, this music has been part of my DNA. One of my favourite memories was teaching my five- and two-year-old boys to say 'a hip-hop, the hippie . . . to the bang bang boogie,' and so forth. Hip-hop is like a family member: I can criticize it, but you'd better keep your mouth shut. Listening to White middle-class commentators point fingers at 'urban' music makes me want to scream.

Besides, we know hip-hop isn't the real problem. Kanye West isn't the problem either. During Black History Month last year, I gave several talks quoting spoken-word poet Kyle "Guante" Tran Myhre, who said: 'White supremacy is not a shark, it is the water.' Kanye is a shark, and quite a small one compared to the sharks that surround him and feed off his platform. We need to look out for sharks, but we should care more about the water. Because there is so much blood in the water from people who look like me.

During my talks, I also spoke about the Euro 2020 finals. Do you remember that day? Several of us had gathered at my father-in-law's to watch the match. Like the rest of the country, we held our breaths as Marcus Rashford took a penalty. When he missed, a gong struck in my chest. Jadon Sancho stepped forward and we were all looking at each other like, could this be happening? As the shot was saved, my stomach bottomed out. Bukayo Saka walked up, and I felt sick with nerves. I was praying for a football miracle.

We all know what happened next. The hate mail; the death threats; the torrent of racial abuse on social media. What you might not know, unless you are Black, was how it felt. Right after the final whistle blew, as we sat shellshocked, our phones started going off. WhatsApp notifications from friends and family warning us not to go out, to avoid pubs and train stations, don't go in the streets. It's not safe out there for us. It's not safe to be Black when people are baying for our brothers, our sons.

I woke up with a knot in my throat. My children had to go to school, and I was afraid. Would they face racial abuse because three Black men couldn't save England's day?

We were lucky. They came home unharmed, but I heard stories from my community, of kids as young as three being racially taunted. I saw a video clip of an Asian man outside the stadium being kicked in the head. I saw another video of a Black teenager on the train being attacked because they thought he was Bukayo Saka.

Three young men put everything on the line for their team and they were punished for it, brutally. I talk about the England v. Italy match as a teachable moment. An ugly, beer-drenched, chest-thumping circus of toxic masculinity. The match also highlighted what Black people and people of colour have to deal with every day, which is not just the impact but also the anticipation of racism, and how much that screws with your peace of mind.

The England match was a study in unconscious bias, because, while Gareth Southgate is a good example of an ally, there is no Black manager who would have put three Black penalty takers up in a row: not with so much at stake.

One question I've been asked is, surely Southgate was trying to do a good thing? If those players had scored and taken England to victory, they would have been all-time heroes. I say yes, they could have been heroes. But why can't they just be human?

Racism dehumanizes all of us, especially its perpetrators. US police officers shooting an unarmed Black man, Jayland Walker, forty-six times. A British policeman killing Chris Kaba after a wrong ID. A White nursery teacher calling a Black toddler and his friends a 'gang'. A White officer kneeling on the back of a boy because he thinks he's stolen a bike. You can already guess this boy wasn't White but a brown Puerto Rican boy with Afro hair. Even after George Floyd died with a knee on his neck; even though the boy was in tears, the man kept his body weight on an innocent child.

How do we raise Black boys in a society that doesn't value Black lives? When will they see our sons as fully human?

Whenever the world outside feels heavy, we lighten up at home. This is my advice to you. Black joy is still resistance, so celebrate joy with your Black and Brown children. Fill them up with kind words, playful experiences, generous intentions, empowering stories, love upon love. Chine says: 'I tell my boys that I'm proud of them often. I go over the top with even the smallest achievements, armed with sloppy kisses and hugs!'

During lockdown 2020, Ezra and I got to watch the masterpiece *Barber Shop Chronicles* by Inua Ellams on the National Theatre's virtual stream. What Ellams told audiences in a conversation at Leeds Playhouse resonated with me:

In the last few years, images of Black bodies being brutalized by law enforcement were everywhere. On Twitter. Shared in WhatsApp groups. On prime-time news. As a prequel to think pieces, from the New York Times to the Guardian. The images and stories were trending in the US and in the UK. I can't speak about the importance of my work, that is an equation solved by an audience, but I can

speak about the psychological violence those videos and images did, and the need for them to be countered somehow. Barber Shop Chronicles does that. It shows Black men at rest. At play. Talking. Laughing. Joking. Not being statistics, targets, tragedies, spectres or spooks; just humans, breathing in a room.[10]

When I share stories of my children on social media, on my blog, in my books, I am hoping to rewrite negative scripts around how Black boys behave and think and feel. These are affirmations for my sons, for all Black and Brown children, so they can move more freely through life without the need to keep their heads down or to puff themselves up.

If life feels heavy, check out the hashtag #BlackMenFrolicking. It's the funniest, sweetest thing. For the idea of a Black male frolicking almost sounds far-fetched. Unless you've known Black boys and men intimately. Unless your daily life, like mine, shows how extremely goofy and silly and hilarious and light-hearted they can be.

We don't get to see much of this in the mainstream and that's what makes the frolicking trend so important. Like the Carefree Black Boy movement, it's a push towards seeing the people we love as regular humans who deserve to relax and take off the yoke of social expectation. To experience true liberation.

Days before the Euro 2020 finals, the England team shared a photo of a frolicking Black boy that went viral. It was Bukayo Saka in a swimming pool, riding an inflatable unicorn. The photo drew comments like: 'Bukayo Saka must be protected at all costs.' You can search up the image online for an instant mood boost. Although don't get distracted by the mythical creature floating on hot air. Look at its rider. He's laughing his head off, not a care in the world. His beautiful angular features lit with pure joy.

Conversation and Reflection Prompts

What do you understand about Black masculinity, pressure and performance anxiety? Can you or your child relate? How can you release some pressure?

If the police aren't an option, how do you think we can create more safe spaces for Black boys?

What conversations can you have with your child around music, media and its influences on the way we see each other and ourselves?

What did you learn from the racism that followed the Euro 2020 finals? How did/will you discuss it with your child?

How can you and your child be better allies?

Why is joy an act of resistance? How does Black joy show up for you?

ACTION

Start or build a collection of books, poetry, movies, TV shows, posters, art, music and stories that show Black boyhood (and girlhood too) in its complexity, vulnerability and humanity. Talk about what you see with your child. Make this an ongoing project.

PART 3

BECO

MING
MEN

RITES OF PASSAGE

After a hard day's work, my husband comes home ravenous. If I've made okra soup and eba (a traditional dish made from fried grated cassava granules boiled and stirred into a stiff, smooth dough for dipping into Nigerian casseroles), a small cry of 'Yes!' escapes him. He plates the eba, fills a deep bowl with the soup, washes his hands in preparation to eat. He sits at the table, sleeves rolled up. Sometimes he takes off his shirt. This is partly to avoid stains (the palm oil in the soup is a devil to get out), partly for the ceremony. For Abiye, eating Nigerian soup and 'swallow' (any food like eba that's made to accompany the soup) is a whole event. He comes to it like a believer comes to prayer.

I imagine that, as my husband sits bare-chested, plucking small mounds of eba and rolling them into balls for dipping into the gloopy soup, he is transported. His feet are on a London carpet, but his head is miles away at a Lagos *buka,* sun burning down, flies buzzing idly, dust in the air. A beer bottle open in front of him, the bench he's on straining with the weight of other men on their lunch break. Men from all walks of life, office workers with ties slung over their shoulders, pot-bellied drivers in vests, Okada couriers with veiny temples and forearms, their motorbikes leaning by the 'Mama Put' sign. Calls of 'Mama put more, I beg' as they wolf down cooked grains, rich stews and assorted meats with their naked hands.

'This is how you eat eba,' Abiye tells our boys. 'Don't bother with cutlery. You must eat it with your hands, or you're not doing it properly.'

This is a slight dig at me and my prissy ways. I abandoned the rule of eating Nigerian soup and swallow with my hands years ago. Throughout my youth, people told me it would taste different with cutlery. By my twenties, eating eba with a fork became, in part, a form of rebellion. It also spared my hands from the lingering smell of crayfish and iru (fermented locust beans) that makes the soup so delicious.

Jed copies his father, ably smushing the food between his fingers. That being said, Jed eats most things with his hands – chips slathered in ketchup, spaghetti wound around his fingers, picking the last grains of rice off his plate. He pops the eba in his mouth and wrinkles his nose. He's not a big fan of eba, or the sliminess of okra, preferring the softer taste of pounded yam with egusi soup.

'Try not to chew at all, the trick is to swallow the eba,' Abiye insists. 'I remember when I first ate it at your age, it was when they taught me to swallow it that I really started to appreciate this meal.'

I could point out that, while Abiye's first taste of eba was around eight years old on a visit to his father in Lagos, Jed has been eating Nigerian soups since he was a baby. But I don't say anything. I'm enjoying the spectacle, the storytelling. Ezra is trying to hide his amusement.

'What's funny?'

'Dad. He's being so extra.'

'He's just trying to get you to appreciate it the way he does.'

'By using my hands? Why? I already like eba more than Jed. He'd rather have nuggets!'

'I know, but it's good to eat soup the traditional way too.'

Ezra rolls his eyes. That word again. *Tradition.*

When Ezra turned thirteen, Abiye took him to the barbershop for his first official haircut. He bought him a steak dinner and gifted him a bottle of cologne. That month, I opened a bank account for Ezra and cut him a set of house keys. We did the same for Jed when he became a teen.

If they were growing up in another part of the world, our boys might have faced a much less cushy initiation. Across various cultures, during the time a child hits puberty, they go through a series of tests or rituals to mark their coming of age. Often, these rites aren't just about growing up, but about solidifying gender roles.

At his bar mitzvah, typically a Jewish boy makes a speech that affirms: 'Today, I am a man.' Mexican girls celebrate their quinceañera, a fifteenth birthday party that symbolizes their entrance into womanhood.

When a girl gets her first period, it's a clear sign of a new life phase, but there's no such obvious marker for boys. So, in some cultures, an adolescent male must go to extremes to prove his manhood.

A Barabaig boy from East Africa will have his head shaved and three deep horizontal cuts going ear to ear across his forehead, sometimes all the way to the skull. If that sounds unappealing, imagine wearing a glove filled with hundreds of stinging insects dubbed 'bullet ants' because their stings feel like gunshots. This is the fate of boys as young as twelve from the Satare Mawe, a remote Amazonian Indian tribe, who have to dance through the pain to show they're not wimps.

Over in the South Pacific, young males of the Vanuatu tribe go off in seclusion for weeks, building wooden towers up to a hundred feet tall. Boys as little as five years old tie a vine to the tower and to their ankles, then bungee jump to the ground below. The older they get, the further they drop. For their final jump, crowds gather below to watch them ascend to the top of the tower. Leaping at speeds of up to forty miles per hour, they attempt to get as close to the ground as possible, skimming it with shoulders and chests before landing in earth that's been tilled to cushion the impact. The crowd rushes over to check the initiate is intact and roars with approval. Afterwards, they cut off his foreskin. The boy is now a man.

You might not be surprised to learn that this ritual can result in serious injury or death. However, if the boy makes it, he'll have pleased the gods immensely, and they should provide a nice large yam crop.

Now, much as I love yam, I'm not sure I would want my sons bungeeing off one-hundred-foot towers, let alone dancing with bullet ants. However, I did understand Abiye's wish to mark their teenagedom with something significant. We wound up with steak dinners and barbershop trips but, originally, there was talk of father-and-son ceremonies and escapades in the wilds. My mother-in-law, Helen, was bemused by it all.

'I don't remember making this much of a fuss when you turned thirteen,' she told him.

Perhaps that's partly why. Growing up with a single mum, Abiye missed out on a steady male presence guiding him through adolescence. Also, he had split from his ex by the time his first son, Isaac, turned thirteen. So, creating traditions around his younger sons might have felt like a way to recapture something lost.

I often refer to the saying: 'Tradition is peer pressure from dead people', yet our traditions and rituals perform a necessary function. They help connect us from past to present, personal to social, familial to universal. Christmas, Easter, birthdays, funerals, anniversaries. There's something sacred in pausing to acknowledge the end of one phase and the beginning of the next. The word holiday stems from 'holy day'.

Rites of passage help us process difficult feelings that arise during transitions. For there is always a sense of loss; a rite of passage helps us face this loss and find acceptance. It reassures us that, after change, even after a death, we will be OK. Life, in whatever shape it takes, goes on.

Some time in the late twentieth century, archaeologists stumbled across something remarkable in the depths of a cave. An upright bear skeleton with its skull and its pelt, covered in spear wounds, lying on the ground beside it. A set of adolescent footprints formed circles around the pelt, signs of an ancient initiation rite. I envision a trembling prehistoric youth creeping in to confront his greatest fear. By the looks of it, he *bearly* made it out alive (sorry, I love a pun).

The call to a rite of passage is in our DNA. These rites date back to our earliest human ancestors. However, you might be wondering what the point is in the modern day. If you didn't go through anything similar, it perhaps all sounds a bit overblown. Why not just leave kids to get on with it like the rest of us?

As a reader, I've always been drawn to the 'coming of age' genre. If you are a storyteller, or indeed a consumer of stories, you will be familiar, at least on a subconscious level, with the hero's journey. This is the fundamental story template in which a hero leaves their ordinary world to go on a quest or mission, faces a series of challenges and returns having grown or changed. According to ethnographer and folklorist Arnold van Gennep, who's credited with defining the term, a rite of passage is also a story in three acts: separation, initiation and return.

One benefit of a formal rite of passage is to help develop your character arc. This can be especially important for children feeling their way into adulthood.

For activist and youth leader Paul Kivel, who runs the Oakland Men's Project, the communal element is key.

Having some kind of ritual recognition of transition from childhood into young adulthood is often very valuable, not just for boys but for girls and gender-nonconforming youth. To have friends and family come together and acknowledge them as people in community. It doesn't necessarily have to be a gender-reinforcing programme in which the boys go off with the men. I'm talking about something that's more universal, and community based.

Since the 1960s and 1970s, a rise in men's groups seemed to awaken a more primal need. The desire to strip off psychologically, gather tools and comrades, and run off into the forest to howl at the moon. Or rather, to have bonding sessions that focused on survival skills and emotional offloading. Wilderness therapy for men is sometimes dressed up as a macho rite to test your will, power, endurance, and handiness with a Swiss Army knife. What it really offers is a space where guys can connect openly with other guys.

The late David Adam Lertzman, a former instructor at University of Calgary, ran a wilderness retreat for many years. In his paper, *Rediscovering Rites of Passage,* he wrote: 'Without proper rites of passage, people can become disoriented and lose their way on life's journey. It is as if their life map is incomplete.'

Without these guideposts, teenagers often create their own rituals that can lead to dangerous, sometimes deadly, consequences. Statistically, adolescent boys are more susceptible to going off-track while attempting to prove themselves as men. They might take part in forms of self-initiation such as substance abuse, gang membership and hazing.

Since 2000, there have been 101 deaths recorded from hazing at American universities. Hazing, a form of abuse that's dressed up as both prank and test of mettle, has been standard practice for decades among college fraternities pledging new members. It can include humiliation, mental and physical torture. Initiates report being blindfolded, stripped naked, even branded like cattle. Apparently, one way to earn your stripes as a new pledge is to drink yourself to oblivion.

In August 2022, two members of the Pi Kappa Alpha fraternity at Bowling Green State University in Ohio received a six-week jail sentence for a hazing misdemeanour that led to the death of twenty-year-old student, Stone Foltz. After daring him to finish a one-litre bottle of alcohol in eighteen minutes, frat members dropped Foltz off at his apartment where he was later found unconscious by a roommate. Suffering from alcohol poisoning, he was put on life support and died three days later. In an NBC news interview, his parents described him as an introvert who felt the pressure to finish the bottle as fast as possible.

'And what was the point of this?' asked the interviewer.

Stone's mother shrugged, the grief etched on her face.

'It's hazing. That's what they do.'

The couple sued the university, and in January 2023 it was reported that the university had agreed to pay nearly three million dollars in compensation, described by the Foltz's family attorney as 'the largest payout by a public university in a hazing case in Ohio history'. While fraternities and sororities provide lifelong benefits for most members, they can also breed elitism and bullying. Frat culture dominates the US college system, and many of these frat boys go on to run the country. Many of their kids will pledge too.

Hazing isn't so common in UK universities. However, I recall (or rather, barely recall) Fresher's Week at uni, a free-for-all of sex, drinking and insecurity. One student got so drunk that by the end of the week he was admitted to hospital with alcohol poisoning. You only need to watch an episode of British teens living it up in 'Eye-Bee-Thah' (Ibiza) to see kids basically hazing themselves with booze and pills.

The organization StopHazing.org defines hazing as: 'any activity expected of someone joining or participating in a group that humiliates, degrades, abuses, or endangers them, regardless of a person's willingness to participate'. Hazing can happen in schools, the military, some workplaces and among street gangs. Kids as young as nine are initiated into gangs through acts like selling drugs, stealing mobile phones, knife crime or taking someone's life.

Chilling with the big boys?

Most TikTokers dancing to Goya Menor's viral hit '*Ameno Amapiano*' have no clue what he's saying. The lyrics in pidgin refer to cultism, a widespread phenomenon of gang membership in universities and on the streets of Nigeria. Some of the more brutal initiation stories – from dismemberment to human sacrifice – will give you nightmares.

Whilst any organization, from the Boy Scouts to the House of Commons, will have its share of psychopaths climbing over each other to get to the top, the majority of frats, gangs and cults are filled with anxious boys seeking the same thing: community, validation, a sense of purpose and belonging.

Sometimes I watch the boys in their hoodies cycling up and down our road, angling for a squabble, high on helium or bored out of their minds. The youths who act out on street corners or threaten Ezra and his friends in parks at night. Several of them are ex-schoolmates. It's a *Sliding Doors* vision of what could happen to my sons if they were left to figure out manhood on their own.

That youth in the bushes with his crew, drinking alcopops or stolen spirits, smoking skunk or puffing on vapes, scrolling through porn sites in the dark. Maybe what he needs is a week in the wilderness and a welcome ceremony to remind him of who he is, where he comes from and how far he can go.

According to one school of thought, modern industrial society is an adolescent culture. It's defined by aggressive growth spurts, instability and a me-centric attitude. Look at populist leaders like Trump and Boris Johnson; ideologically they act like hormonal teens (or toddlers, actually). What we describe as toxic masculinity might simply be an adolescent culture run amok.

There's an African proverb that says 'If you don't initiate the young, they will burn down the village to feel the heat'. Everywhere we look today, our village is on fire. And, for the most part, it's men and boys who are razing it to the ground. We can throw up our hands and holler like Marvin Gaye in song. Or we can take inspiration from the old ways and create new paths.

Ron Fritz is a tech CEO and father of three who instructs on the power of coming-of-age rituals. He gives an entertaining and poignant TED Talk on how we can create rites of passage for modern kids. When planning this for their children, Fritz and his partner began researching online.

'First thing that struck us is that these events are amazingly common throughout the world. Mostly they take place when a kid's around thirteen, give or take a year or two,' he tells the audience.

Which is pretty funny, if you think about it. That all these independent societies, completely not talking to each other, all figured out that you gotta get this done early. Because by the time a child is sixteen or seventeen, apparently, they know everything anyway. They don't need any help from the likes of you.

Fritz identifies a blueprint for rites of passage, built on four pillars of: ritual, community, lessons and challenge. For the community element, he assembles a 'coming of age team' made up of family members, educators, friends and mentors. He sets creative tests for his kids designed to challenge their lateral thinking and teach them life skills.

My favourite part of his method is the 'wisdom walks', during which each man in the coming-of-age team stops for five minutes to offer the boy a valuable piece of advice.

Fritz's kids are young adults now, but he says the impact of these events has increased over time. He ends his talk with a comment from one of his sons: 'It was at my coming-of-age event that I really started realizing, *hey, I gotta start thinking about becoming a man and what that means.* And I decided that day that I wanted to be a good man, modelled after the guys on my coming-of-age team.'

Have you considered creating a rite of passage for your child? Back in 2012, author Claire Potter set thirteen challenges for her thirteen-year-old son Fred to prove he was ready for independence. She wrote about it in a *Guardian* news story, sharing how she tried to make each test involve the number thirteen in some way.

Interestingly, she was inspired by her son's fascination with the first episode of the TV series *Roots*, watching Kunta Kinte undergo 'manhood training' through strength, bravery and hunting skills.

Fred Potter's tests are less extreme but equally varied, ranging from buying himself an entire outfit for £13.13, to doing thirteen household tasks, to playing a thirteen-bar blues piece on a public piano. The first challenge involved getting on a train on his own and getting off at the thirteenth stop.

Claire writes: 'I am not, of course, randomly releasing him into the wild. I have secretly micromanaged the whole thing.'

She watches with bated breath as her son climbs onto the train and it leaves the station. But she's smiling as she recalls Kunta Kinte's mother's words: 'A boy has just left, a man will return.'

I think I am stealing this idea for Jed's sixteenth birthday, because he's my baby and I know he will need a little more steering along the road to being a grown-up.

There are so many informal rites of passage in a boy's life: first birthday, first walk to school, puberty, driving lessons, graduation. The day they leave home for good.

By the time this book comes out, my eldest will be seventeen. One foot out of the door, his mind already distant. Maybe he'll take time off before university to travel or get some work experience. All I know for sure is there's not a thing I can do to stop the click-clack of time or the stomp of incoming manhood. The topics I'm exploring feel more urgent than ever. What I want to teach him, what I still need to learn as a parent, I am increasingly conscious that none of this can wait.

Creating rites of passage for our children isn't just for them but for us too. It gives us pause to reflect on the journey so far, to honour the sense that we're losing these creatures we made to a life beyond our reach. To look to what lies ahead. Because there is so much more to come.

I was struck by the words of an eighty-two-year-old Saulteaux elder, Alfred Manitopeyes, who said in an interview that traditional education is about 'the making of human beings'. It's what we can give our kids as parents, mentors, elders and community members. The stuff they don't learn in school. A rite of passage can be part of this education, but it can also be a keepsake, a way for us to hold on to a piece of them for ever, even as we're figuring out how to let go.

Perhaps the closest thing we've had recently to a formal rite of passage was Ezra's Leavers' Prom after GCSEs. I took him suit-shopping and blinked back tears as he posed, handsome as anything, in his dark-blue suit. After our sons had boarded the school bus for prom, I gathered with some fellow parents at a local pub: my own coming-of-age team. Over wine and beers, we swapped stories and photos.

Gill showed us a black-and-white shot of her son Jim's back as he exited their front door. 'That's all I got, he wouldn't let me take a picture.'

We agreed that it was still a great photo, capturing a mood that they would both look back on one day with a smile.

From the party boat that evening, Ezra sent a video to our family WhatsApp group. He was in the middle of a circle, dancing with a girl, while the crowd went wild. The clip showed his mates hyping him up before the camera wobbled and went black. Apparently, the cameraman collapsed from excitement.

Abiye responded on WhatsApp with a quip about the allure of Cole men and welcoming Ezra into the fold. Somehow, he linked it to an anecdote about losing his shirt at a bar in Bali.

The gist of his message was captured in the first line: 'Haha, and so it begins.'

No fire emojis, just a proud father passing on the torch to his son.

Conversation and Reflection Prompts

Have you created any formal rites of passage for your son? Are you inspired to do so now?

What informal rites of passage do you recall? Which one has felt most significant?

Have you experienced any rites of passage yourself?

What conversations have you had with your boy about gang membership?

What conversations have you had with your boy about hazing or self-hazing rituals, e.g. drinking games/challenges?

Who would you invite to be part of your son's coming-of-age team?

What family traditions do you hope your son passes on to his own family one day?

COMING-OF-AGE CHALLENGE

Try the Clare Potter coming-of-age exercise with your son. For instance, you could set five challenges for a five-year-old or eight challenges for an eight-year-old, etc. When he completes them, you might think about creating some type of reward ceremony with family and friends.

HOW TO TALK ABOUT SEX

What is the most teeth-clenching description of sex you've ever heard? While researching this chapter, I decided to look up examples of parents giving their children the 'birds and bees' talk. I cringed through a clip of ex-reality star Todd Chrisley's attempts to educate his kids, complete with board diagrams. When his daughter uses the term 'vagina', he yells at her: 'Don't call it that. That is your LILY!'

I giggled as Homer Simpson tries to give Bart advice by comparing a woman to a refrigerator, then to a can of beer, which inevitably leads to him getting blind drunk and passing out. The funniest scene was from a TV series called *Alternatino*, in which the dad sits his son down for a chat but the boy winds up schooling him on stuff he clearly knows nothing about, like polyamory and gender fluidity. So very Gen Z.

My favourite video was by Cut, who gathered real-life parents for unscripted chats with their pre-schoolers. It is face-palmingly, seat-squirmingly hilarious. Watch it if you haven't already (search 'The Birds and the Bees, Parents Explain by Cut' on YouTube). If anything, it will fill you with confidence that at least you can't be more awkward than the father who says: 'Mummy and Daddy took off our clothes and got under the blankets, then we did a special dance . . .'

There's one kid who shocks his dad with how much he knows about baby-making. He reels off: 'The sperm and the egg collide . . .'

Shocked, his dad asks, 'Who taught you that?'

'Nick,' the boy replies.

'Who's Nick?'

'My brother!'

Apparently, the dad was so stressed by the talk that he forgot he had another son!

These videos are brilliant because they show how uncomfortable and, frankly, nerve-racking it can be to talk about sex. It can be tricky enough with another grown-up, let alone with a child who's staring at you like they can't believe the words coming out of you. Mummy and Daddy did a special dance? Seriously, gross.

The thing is, no matter if it leaves you stammering or in a cold sweat, you shouldn't avoid the conversation. Also, you can't rely on a single talk, and it shouldn't just be about sex. It's crucial to create space for a range of discussions that will evolve as your child grows.

Like race, divorce, death or mental health, sex is one of those big life issues we can't leave children to figure out on their own. There's too much at stake, especially by the time your son is most likely walking around with a stick of dynamite in his pocket, in the shape of a mobile phone.

We're living through unprecedented times when the average child is mere clicks away from sexually explosive content. As a parent, you can put alerts, monitors and filters on every device your household owns, but you can't stop outside forces from creeping in. You can't block your child's friend who's been sneakily using their older sibling's Pornhub account and filling in their mates with the grisly details at break-time.

My boy was eleven when I caught him with porn. He'd only recently got his first mobile phone, a hand-me-down from his dad. We'd allowed it since he'd started secondary school and needed a way to keep in touch. Originally, we'd talked about getting him a 'brick phone', like the old-school Nokia models. He seemed cool with that until he realized that he couldn't use WhatsApp with his year group. We relented and, before long, he had a smartphone superglued to his hand.

I'm not one to look through my kids' phones or gadgets. Obviously, if there was a security issue, I wouldn't hesitate. But on a day-to-day basis, I feel like it's an invasion of privacy. Maybe it goes back to childhood memories of walking in to find my big sister, or worse, my mum, sitting on my bed and casually reading my secret diaries. I had padlocks on those things, damn it. So much for boundaries. Anyway, I believe in giving my children a certain amount of freedom and to trust that they're doing the right thing, even when I'm not looking.

So, my heart skipped when he handed me his phone to check something and he'd forgotten to close a browser. What shocked me almost as much as the video image that popped up was that he'd downloaded a private browser app to watch it. This seemed to make a mockery of the safety settings we'd put on his phone's Safari and Google Chrome.

'What's this? Have you been watching porn?!'

I wish I could have kept the note of horror out of my voice. The poor boy turned bright red, began stammering and, within seconds, he was in tears. He said he had only been curious and that he'd found the video by clicking an ad on a website we'd visited. Ironically, a streaming site we'd once used to watch that wholesome family sitcom, *The Wonder Years*, had been taken over by pop-ups for XXX channels. He had visited the site to stream another show and, lo and behold, he got sucked into a porn wormhole.

Once we'd wiped away the tears and I'd assured him he wasn't in trouble, we wound up having a useful discussion about porn and why it wasn't healthy for kids to see. That it gave an unrealistic impression of naked bodies and what loving, intimate sex looks like.

Studies show that children as young as seven or eight are stumbling across online porn. Research commissioned by the British Board of Film Classification in 2019 revealed that more than half (51 per cent) of eleven- to thirteen-year-olds had seen porn at some point, rising to 66 per cent among fourteen- to fifteen-year-olds. The report also highlighted the children under ten who saw porn accidentally and described feeling 'confused' and 'grossed out'.

Sex is the most searched topic on the internet, and porn sites receive more monthly traffic than Netflix, Twitter and Amazon combined. Clearly there's a very basic human desire for titillation and a fascination with sex acts. I'm not anti-erotica by any means. However, the dangers of the sex-for-entertainment industry cannot be overstated. One issue with porn is that it can normalize violence and aggressive behaviour, particularly towards women. It can teach impressionable kids that sex is something you do to someone (as opposed to with someone in a mutually consensual relationship). Watching porn can become addictive, especially for adolescent boys who are seeking stimulation but who might be hesitant around real-life sexual interactions. Porn is often used by older teens or adults to groom younger children into sexual abuse. It can also expose children to the darker side of the sex industry, involving under-age workers and sex trafficking.

I didn't go into all this detail with my eleven-year-old. However, we did speak about some of the safety concerns, such as being exposed to violent, extreme and possibly illegal acts.

I explained that most internet porn was like junk food: quick and cheap but potentially full of nasties. If he had more questions about sex, he could simply ask me or his dad or his older brother, Isaac. I'm not sure Isaac was necessarily chomping at the bit to dish out sex advice, but I suggested it anyway. The point I wanted to get across to my boy was that he had a village to turn to, and that village was his family, not the internet.

If I could rewind to that day, I'd have handled it with less alarm, more humour. Still, as parents we must have grace for ourselves as well as our young ones. You're not always prepared to parent like a pro in the heat of the moment. Especially when you've just seen naked strangers grinding on your child's mobile device.

When our sons reached Year Four, we got letters home from school about their upcoming RSE – Relationships and Sex Education – lessons on the basics of sexual intercourse and puberty. Parents could opt out by signing a form. I always wondered about the parents who signed this form and left their kids clueless. Understandably, people have different personal and cultural attitudes around this. However, numerous studies show that children who are well informed about sex are more likely to delay sexual activity, to enjoy safe and consensual sex, to report sexual abuse and to protect themselves against unwanted pregnancies or sexually transmitted diseases.

Some might think Year Four is young (ages eight to nine). However, the average boy begins puberty at ages nine to fourteen, whilst for girls it's eight to thirteen, so it's important to prepare them for what's coming. I've heard of girls who didn't know what menstruation was, being terrified that they were bleeding to death when they got their first period.

Our kids' primary school was fairly progressive, and they called in specialists to host a workshop on talking to your child about sex. It was a diverse school, and this was reflected in the mix of parents who attended, from middle-class couples to single parents, grandparents,

RAISING BOYS WHO DO BETTER

women in hijabs, men in Sikh turbans. The session was open, informative and engaged, with lots of audience questions and an armful of pamphlets to take home. I felt empowered to take on this sensitive topic with my kids. Then my seven-year-old spotted a pamphlet on the kitchen table while I was grabbing breakfast and started to thumb through it.

'What's a wet dream?'

Despite my newfound bravura, I nearly choked on my toast. Keeping my expression as relaxed as I could manage, I gave him a basic explanation and he moved on to something else.

One thing about kids is that if you stick to the boring facts and keep your tone light, they'll acknowledge what you say (or not, depending on mood) and keep it moving. Some parents worry that talking about sex will be like opening up a Pandora's box. However, the average child is really not that interested beyond what they can readily absorb. Kids are curious, they're eager to get some kind of grasp on the topic, but they're mostly keen to see how you respond. The way you engage with your child on a subject this big can set the stage for important conversations you'll have with them throughout their lives.

With my boys, I try to make sure we're on the same page and that the page is a blank, open space. It's where we're free to ask big questions, sound a bit silly, mess up, provoke each other, disagree, revise ideas, teach each other and unlearn what we thought we knew. It's a space where we connect, and often that happens through humour. Even when I'm trying to get a serious point across, sometimes even with the most serious of points, I'll aim to find that sweet spot that brings up a smile or outright laughter, because for children, and indeed for grown-ups, being playful is one of the key ways we learn about life.

In their first sex-ed lesson, I'm not sure what the teacher said that set them off, but Ezra and his friend Mehmet got the giggles. We all know what it's like when you get the giggles in class; it's hard to stop. The teacher told them that sex was nothing to laugh about and sent them out of the class. What the actual . . . ?

I echoed Ezra's frustration afterwards. Of course kids should be allowed to have a giggle in sex education! There are many things about sex that are properly hilarious, especially to kids hearing about it for the first time. A child who's tittering in an RSE lesson is having a normal reaction, and when they're punished for it, that's like telling them: 'No, you're wrong, you can't feel or think this way.' It stops them from asking questions or feeling heard. As I always advise, try not to shut down future conversations with your child, even if you're uncomfortable. Leave the door open.

You shouldn't try to force conversations about sex on your child, however. This can get super-awkward and lead to them slamming that door in your face. One option is to provide some trusted resources for your child to explore on their own, and let them know that you're available for any questions.

Abiye came home one day with a book about bodies and growing up, and a book about sex for teens. He mentioned the books to the boys, then slid them into their baskets in the bathroom for future reference. After a quick flick through both books, I decided the book on sex was aimed at slightly older kids. So I told the boys I would put that book on a shelf in our living room. They would still have access to it if they wanted, but I thought it was more suited to when they were a bit bigger.

We left the other book in their toiletries basket, and over the years we've seen the book moved from bathroom to their bedrooms and back. It's been thoroughly fingerprinted and dog-eared.

Abiye got the idea for this approach from his own mum. He told me that one day when he was in his tweens, Helen had left a book on the table. It was a book that taught him all about sex and bodies, what to expect through adolescence, how to shave and more. As a single mum raising a boy, she knew he needed answers, but he was also at that age where he'd rather chew off his elbows than ask her directly.

Abiye said, 'When you think about it, it was a pretty badass move.'

The boys joke about us being 'boomers', but, despite our six-year age gap, Abiye and I are officially Gen X. And Gen X kids are the badasses of any modern era. Someone called us the original 'fuck around and find out generation' because we were raised like wildlings. Our parents drank and chain-smoked through our childhoods, sending us off to play in traffic, letting us get high on fizzy drinks and sweets, and pretty much leaving us to our own devices. That's at a time when devices didn't mean gadgets but could refer to anything from whizzing down a hill on a bike with no brakes to experimenting with sex, drugs and vinyl.

During school holidays, my parents would be doing their own thing while we got up to all sorts of mischief. Some of that mischief involved watching naughty videos. My older siblings and cousins would lock us little ones in the den with them so we wouldn't run off and tattle on them, then slide an unmarked video into the VCR. We were way too young to watch Emmanuelle's 'voyage of sexual discovery,' but curiosity kept us riveted.

As a young reader, I also had unfettered access to my parents' bookshelves. These included some Victorian smut, a memorable book called *The Games Grownups Play* (definitely not for little eyes), and that 1970s household manual, *The Joy of Sex*. I could get away with reading the former by slipping them in between larger books with more innocuous titles. However, *The Joy of Sex* was a thick tome that you had to sneak off into a quiet corner and look at when nobody was around. I was both fascinated and repulsed by the illustrations in the book. The guy with his unkempt beard and bits dangling between his legs. The woman's surprisingly hairy bush. I shuddered to imagine my parents in this array of positions and facial expressions.

Still, it was part of my education. For me, the facts of life were cobbled together from books, those glimpses of 1970s soft porn, 1980s sex comedies like *Animal House*, sneaking peeks at my brother's dirty magazines, playground chatter, whispers between friends after dark. Sex was not something my parents spoke about with me, certainly not in a specific conversation. Sometimes I wonder what those conversations might have been like. If they might have helped me understand my body more, enhanced my sexual self-worth, safeguarded me against the encounters that left me feeling broken inside.

I wonder what kinds of conversations are happening in homes around the country and at what stage. Are you one of those parents who started talking to your child early and often, because you knew that sex education starts as soon as your child gets curious about your body and their own? If so, take a gold star, because you're on the right track.

Experts agree that it's best to be proactive. Don't wait until you feel your child is mature enough, because by then you might be too late. You could start by having a conversation with yourself first. How do you feel about sex? What did you learn growing up? Have you read up on the latest literature? How has the landscape changed? What core values do you want to pass on to your child when it comes to sex, relationships and intimacy?

Exploring the subject with yourself, a partner or your closest peers, and arming yourself with more knowledge, can help create a steadier foundation for these important conversations.

When talking to a child, the things that work are similar to those that work when talking about race or other big topics. Stick to the basics. Keep it age-appropriate. Don't pretend you know it all. If you're feeling uncomfortable, acknowledge it so your child understands that the squirming is about you and not them. Younger kids in particular might pick up on your discomfort and attach that to what you're talking about, and internalize the idea that sex is bad, or else put it on themselves – 'I've done a bad thing'. You can break the ice by admitting, 'Talking about this is awkward for me but it matters, so I'm going to bring it up from time to time. I want you to be able to come to me about this stuff.'

Be the student, not the teacher. In other words, stay curious. In each conversation, you have an opportunity to discover more about your child, what they're learning, how they think and feel. I also advise asking simple, open-ended questions:

What do you know about . . . ? For example, what do you know about how babies are made?

What can you tell me about . . . ? What can you tell me about this body part?

Have you heard about . . . ? Have you heard about spermatozoa? (The long word is more fun.)

Do you have any questions about . . . ? Do you have any questions about how your baby brother got here?

With very young kids, you can begin by discussing bodies. Aim to be inclusive about different body types and skin tones as well as gender diversity. Authors and podcast hosts Jen Audrie and Lisa Lynn share how they talk to their young children about the gender spectrum in a relaxed and age-appropriate way. Jen says: 'We've talked about the LGBTQIA community and that some people are born a girl and feel like they're a boy. I didn't teach them the term transgender, we just talk about people feeling differently.'

Lisa says: 'We talk about what it means to be a boy and what it means to be a girl and how we don't assume, and we ask people how they like to be seen.'

Talk about bodily functions and body parts, such as, 'What's this body part for? How about this one? Do you know why these are called "private parts"? What are their actual names?' Healthcare experts note that it's important for children to learn the anatomical names for their genitals. This is to help normalize bodies and to raise awareness in case of any health or safeguarding issues.

Dr Cara Natterson, a paediatrician, author and co-host of the *Puberty Podcast*, laughs as she recalls some of the pseudonyms she's heard parents and kids use in her practice. She says: 'If we're not all using the same words, it's really hard to communicate with someone who doesn't understand your code language.'

A child who calls their vulva a 'fairy' or their penis a 'lightsaber' might struggle to explain to an adult if they have been hurt or inappropriately touched in those areas. Teach your child to label their genitals accurately, like any other body part. Although, once your child knows the correct terms, and spends the next week shouting 'PENIS!' and 'VULVA!' to everyone they meet, from our experience, it's fine if you still use slang too.

At this stage, you want your child to be comfortable with their body and also to start understanding boundaries – that is, that running around butt-naked might be fine at home, but it's not so fine in the post office.

You can talk about privacy, why genitals are called private parts, how we all deserve some privacy and why it's important to respect the privacy of others – for example, knocking if the bathroom door is shut.

Teach your child that their body belongs to them, so it's fine for them to explore it however they like. Masturbation and other forms of self-stimulation are perfectly natural for kids, but explain that touching private parts is not meant for public spaces. Your boy might spend all day with his hand stuffed down his trousers. Don't shame him if this happens out and about. Simply let him know this isn't the time and place and remind him to wash his hands.

Talk to your youngster about the select group of people (such as a parent or carer, a doctor or a nurse) who are allowed to see or touch their bodies, and when or why that might happen. It's also good to discuss what's OK to touch and what's not OK to touch. Some questions to consider together:

Who can see and touch me here?

How can they see and touch me there?

Why and where can they see and touch me?

Do I have to touch somebody if I don't want to?

Practise statements that can help to prevent boundary-crossing: 'No, I don't want it.' and 'Stop, I don't like that.'

The media tends to obsess about 'stranger danger', but I prefer to focus on strange behaviour, rather than the behaviour of strangers. Statistically, your child is most at risk of abuse from people they know than from people they've never met. Remind your child that if somebody asks or does something that seems strange or makes them feel strange, they should tell you right away. In our house, we always said 'secrets' were off-limits; instead, we talked about 'surprises', which allow for fun and mystery rather than shame and deception.

Of course, conversations about consent are not just about sex. You can model consent every day, from when your boy is in nappies, starting with those powerful two words: 'Can I?'

Can I have a hug?

Can I change your nappy now?

Can I come in?

Don't force your child to hug or kiss a relative if they're hesitant. You could say something like, 'It's OK if you don't want to kiss or hug, how about a high-five or a wave?' Respecting your child's boundaries will help them set and respect boundaries later in life.

As your child gets older, you should have more talks about what consent means and how it goes both ways. If your son is exploring dating, talk about how they can check in with themselves and with their dates to make sure everyone's on the same page.

Check yourself: Does this feel good? Does this feel right? Do I feel safe? Do I want to carry on doing this?

Check in with your partner: Is this OK? Can I touch you here? Does this feel good? Can we keep going?

Remind your son that, despite peer pressure and bro culture, it's perfectly normal for boys to say no too.

Dr Cara Natterson says:

The way we approach it in our house is in a non-gendered way. Consent is consent, and it must be given and received, full stop. It doesn't matter the gender of who you're with, there's no such thing as intoxicated consent, or forced or coerced consent. If the consent is not completely obvious and unquestionable, then it's not consent. When in doubt, walk away.

There's a rather sweet video titled 'Consent for Kids' on YouTube that you can watch with your little one. The video describes what consent is in a simple way, using friendly animations. It's made by Blue Seat Studios, the same company that created the popular video for older kids and adults on 'Tea and Consent', which uses the act of making tea as a metaphor for sexual consent. The videos are on YouTube and can be a primer for discussions at any age.

When your child blurts out a comment or a question about sex that catches you off guard, try not to panic. Remember, their curiosity is a part of growing up, so encourage discussion by asking questions for more context – for instance, asking, 'I'm curious, what made you think of that?'; offering up alternatives such as, 'That's an interesting idea. Actually, this is what I learned . . .'; gently correcting, saying, 'You said this and that's not quite right. Here's why.' Or admitting you don't know: 'Hmm . . . I'm not sure. Shall I find out and get back to you?'

One of the first questions a young kid might have is how babies are made. If they ask you, why not ask them what they think? It will give you a moment to recover, and also some of their ideas are so sweet. At age four, Ezra told me babies came from: 'Outside, from the town with lots of buildings.' Baby Town. I like the sound of that.

For little ones, Dr Cara Natterson recommends keeping it short and sweet: 'A sperm from a man and an egg from a woman join and then a baby grows in a womb and comes out.' At this point, she says, it's more inclusive not to talk specifically about who carries the baby for people in diverse set-ups, such as same-sex couples, those who've conceived through IVF, as well as foster or adoptive parents. By the age of around seven or eight, you can talk about the mechanics of intercourse and, again, try to keep it inclusive.

If your child is having their first sex-education lessons at school, you could try to get a lesson plan from their teacher. Also, ask questions when your son gets home. Laugh or cringe in sympathy. These classes are universally cringeworthy and sharing some of your own memories of sex ed can be a bonding moment.

By secondary school, most kids will have lessons on puberty, intercourse, safe sex, consent, sexual orientation and romantic feelings. At this age, it can feel harder to discuss with your child, since they rely more on peer relationships. However, you should still check in and offer trusted resources like educational websites, books or documentaries.

Multiple surveys of kids and teens reveal that they would prefer their parents to be a go-to source for learning about sex, alongside school and medical professionals.

Now that we're past the stage of bedtime reading, I like to watch TV shows with my sons. Depending on their age or viewing tastes, shows like *Grownish, Sex Education, Never Have I Ever, Atypical, Heartstopper* or *Big Mouth* can bring up talking points. The boys make fun of how I'll pause a show to discuss a 'teachable moment', but I don't care. I know some of what I say is sinking in. Mostly, I'm getting a glimpse of how they see dating and relationships, and how they see themselves.

Dr Natterson says what's often left out of school textbooks for tween or teenage kids is the small but mighty clitoris. This is largely down to a history of patriarchal repression of female sexuality and social stigmas around masturbation. I watched a video clip of men in the street asked to point at the clitoris on a 'vulva map' and the ignorance was shocking. It's a cliché that men don't read maps, but this is one map that they shouldn't ignore.

Can I urge you to make sure your son knows what the clitoris is, where to find it and what it does? Imagine it as a female superpower (it even has a cape) that's designed to spread pure joy.

Being open about the clitoris (and other erogenous zones) is one way to talk about pleasure and self-pleasure as a normal part of sex. Parents can get so awkward or anxious about the dangers of sex, like STDs or assault or unwanted pregnancies, that we forget to let our kids know about the fun and joy too.

If there's one key message to share with your son, it's this: sex is supposed to feel good. So, if you are in a sexual relationship, you should ask your partner what feels good and tell them if something does or doesn't feel right. Open communication can support your pleasure, safety and wellbeing. It can be the bedrock of relationships to come.

There's a lot to cover and we haven't even touched on sexual assault (more in another chapter). Whatever you do, try not to overwhelm your child with information. Drip-feed as needed. Sometimes, just listen and take notes.

Case in point: right after his GCSEs, Ezra is invited to go out with his friends. The hours go by, and he learns that some of his friends are together, but they've managed to get some girls along for the outing. So they've put a cap on the invitation as they don't want 'too many man' coming in case it upsets the balance or scares off their female companions.

'Imagine that!' He's indignant, talking across me to Jed at the other end of the sofa. 'These man have ditched me for *nyash*. And it's not even secure *nyash* but they've ditched me anyway. Nah, that's out of pocket.'

Slang translator: he's irritated that his friends have abandoned their boys' night out so they can be with some girls that they're not guaranteed to pull. That's out of order.

I'm listening but I don't comment. A while back, Ezra had told me that '*nyash*' was his generation's term for 'bum'. I couldn't help smiling as I explained that, although TikTok had made it global, '*nyash*' was a Nigerian pidgin term. It's the rapper Dave, of Nigerian heritage, who helped make it widespread when he warned: 'Don't die for nyash'. In other words, don't lose your head over booty.

In Nigeria, people say '*nyash*' to refer to a body part, but also as a coarser term for copulation. It's come to mean not just the sex act but the sex object.

As his mum, a part of me is disturbed to hear my sixteen-year-old using language that objectifies girls, especially in front of his younger brother. However, my strategy is not to jump down his throat. I make a mental note that this is a conversation to revisit when the timing's right, for whilst I am their mother I'm trying not to be a hypocrite. I've rapped those exact lyrics ('Don't die for *nyash*') alongside them with Dave blasting from our living-room speakers. So if I don't interrupt every wayward train of thought, I aim to follow up later. When they're in a mellow frame of mind, we'll discuss some of the language I've heard them use, and how it objectifies females; the importance of seeing a girl as a whole human being and not a piece or the sum of her parts. The boys will roll their eyes at me and say, 'We know, Mum, we get it.'

And I'll relax a little because I know this to be true. I know it in my bones. As a parent, there's a point at which you have to trust your children, and also trust yourself. Trust that the many talks you've had, the books you've read, the shows you've watched, the relationship you've built with your child will stand the test of time.

No matter what the world teaches them, or what mistakes they make along the way – and there will inevitably be many mistakes – nothing is more important than the true and loving connection you cultivate with your boy. It becomes their anchor, and it can inform how they connect with others throughout life.

I emphasize conversations because they're such a simple but powerful way to develop a relationship. Conversations don't always have to mean some long back-and-forth either. A conversation with your boy can be a few sentences, a question, a shoulder shrug, a nod. Kids are easily distracted, and teen boys might avoid eye contact. Neurologically, it's actually easier for them to process information this way. Try bite-sized chats on the school run, in the car, on a walk or, as Dr Natterson suggests, while doing a puzzle together. Remember to keep it playful and light if you can.

Dr Natterson says:

The greatest laughs we've had as a family is when our kids teach us the language, the realities, the trends of the moment and we can ask them questions; and, yes, we can teach and guide, but we're also learning the parlance of their world, which as a parent is amazing and so much fun.

Remember too that every child is different. Also, you don't have to be a sex guru to have these conversations, and there is no perfect sex chat. Whatever I'm talking about with my kids, I want them to feel safe to speak from the heart. In a banter-filled boy-zone, this can be tricky, but it's crucial. Too many of us, boys in particular, have barricaded our hearts behind padlocked chains.

Personally, I struggle with being vulnerable, and it's been a lifetime of unlearning. I want better for my boys. I talk to them about how you can only be intimate with someone when it's rooted in trust and vulnerability. Many people chasing sex are desperately seeking intimacy. The conundrum is that sex without intimacy can leave you feeling empty, cold and isolated.

I hope what our kids carry into future relationships is what they've learned at home. The intimacy of everyday connection; of shared moments and inside jokes; of nicknames and facial expressions and knowing whose toothbrush is whose and which end of the sofa everyone sits. Table talks and long, comfortable silences. Collapsing into a heap of arms, bellies, heads on shoulders, legs across thighs, forgetting where you end and your loved ones begin.

When the time is right, I want my sons to discover that good sex isn't about toned bodies climaxing in sync. It involves fun and fumbling around and laughter and trust and curiosity and safe touch and real emotions. Belonging to another but belonging to yourself first. Feeling free and comfortable in your skin so that you can let someone into the most intimate parts of who you are.

Conversation and Reflection Prompts

Did your parents have a sex chat with you? How did you learn about sex?

What stories did you inherit around sex and how has that affected the way you talk to your child about it?

Has your boy started sex education at school? How can you support this learning at home?

What conversations have you had around consent?

What conversations have you had around porn?

Do you use safety measures such as monitoring and blocking software on your family technology? What boundaries do you have in place?

Has your child asked you questions about sex? How have you responded? How might you respond next time?

FAMILY VIEWING

Watch one (or all) of the 'birds and bees' talk videos I referenced early in this chapter. Watch them with your child. Laugh. Cringe. Use them as a conversation starter.

THIS IS
HIS BRAIN

I magine you could peek inside the brain of a gamer and the brain of somebody taking Class-A drugs. What might you see? According to neuroimaging studies, the same areas light up when a gamer gets his 'fix'. Dopamine, the powerful neurotransmitter, creates a rush of pleasure that is similar to being high. The more he plays, the more dopamine is released.

MRI scans reveal that playing video games like *Fortnite* with addictive qualities can impact a child or a teenager's brain just like taking hard drugs or abusing alcohol. Apparently, the gamer brain's 'reward centre' mimics the same changes observed in alcoholics and drug addicts.

In 2016, researchers at California State University did a series of studies that revealed the brain's amygdala–striatal system, which controls impulses, was both smaller and more sensitive in children who played video games or used social media excessively. Professor Ofir Turel, who led the study, noted that kids and teenagers get especially triggered by video-game achievements or just the sight of a mobile-phone screen glowing with anticipation of being swiped.

Apparently, the structural changes in the brain allow for much faster processing of associations. 'But, like a car, you need to put more gas into it to generate more power,' Turel explained. The concern is that playing games non-stop could prime a youngster's brain for more noxious substances. Turel's initial research suggested a correlation between excessive gaming between ages thirteen and fifteen, and a heightened possibility of abusing at least one of fifteen addictive substances, including amphetamines and cocaine, later in life.

Hold up, wait a minute. Don't go running to unplug your kids' devices just yet. What I've outlined above is a worst-case scenario. *Fortnite* is not necessarily a gateway drug, and the average boy spending hours with his buddies on *Minecraft* is no more likely to start sniffing white powders than anyone else. Like pretty much everything in life, it's all about finding some balance.

I'm often fascinated by our children growing up in the digital age. How much quicker they make connections between ideas; how much more adept they are at adapting to rules that are constantly changing. Because it's not all bad news. Video-game players have also been shown to have increased abilities in problem-solving, hand–eye coordination, leadership, attention to detail, strategy and critical thinking, multi-tasking, creativity, focus and visual memory.

One study of laparoscopic (small-incision) surgeons found that, after playing video games for more than three hours per week, they actually made 32 per cent fewer errors during practise procedures compared to their non-gaming counterparts.

The best thing about gaming, in my opinion, is the social interaction. We used to have a strict rule about our boys only playing video games for a couple of hours on weekends. Then 2020 hit and everyone locked down. During the pandemic, I quickly relaxed those rules and let them play every day. So long as they'd done their home-schooling tasks and were keeping on top of homework, it seemed the easiest way to keep their minds off the world falling apart. More than that, it gave them constant access to the friends they weren't allowed to see face-to-face. The sound of Jed or Ezra spamming their Xbox controller buttons, laughing over their headsets as they battled, or teamed up with, up to fifteen other mates online is still one of the happiest soundtracks of our lockdown days. Sometimes I'd hear them playing with their cousins in Nigeria or the States. Occasionally, I caught Ezra speaking hesitant French with another gamer he'd met online. Playing immersive games in a foreign language can actually enhance conversational skills and vocabulary, but be prepared for your boy to pick up a few foreign cuss words.

Gaming can be good for older brains too. Another study showed an increase in cognitive functioning for gamers aged fifty and over after just ten hours of play. What's more, these improvements were said to last several years. Indeed, one of the tech-safety measures recommended by experts is to play with your child, or at the very least to make sure they play in communal areas. Our boys have whined about not being allowed to have devices in their bedrooms, but this is one rule we won't bend on. It means that I have a good sense of what they're playing, how they're interacting, if their moods are shifting and when it's time to switch off.

You need to stay plugged in to your child's habits because the dangers are still lurking. The World Health Organization has officially identified gaming addiction as a mental-health condition. If you notice your boy neglecting personal hygiene, schoolwork, regular eating, relationships or exercise so that he can log on, it might be time to intervene. Talk about his habits and how they might be affecting him and the rest of the family. Set some healthier limits around tech use. Find alternative activities that will get him out of the gaming chair and into real life.

According to some stats, fewer than 1 per cent of the general population fit the criteria for gaming addiction in the UK, US, Germany and Canada. However, one study found pathological levels of gaming in almost 12 percent of boys, but less than 3 percent of girls. If you have concerns about your boy's use of video games, there are some additional steps you can take before things get out of hand. I've mentioned in an earlier chapter that drawing up a family media contract can be a useful tool to start the conversation and to ensure everyone has the same ideas around what constitutes healthy and safe media use. You might consider attending an internet-safety workshop either online, at an after-school club or perhaps your child's school could set something up. Discuss with other parents and families in your network to find out what works for them. Every family is different, however, so don't be afraid to create your own rules.

Our sons are heavy gamers, and sometimes this has caused friction in our household. When this happens, we pause, discuss and establish some new guidelines. In my view, so long as they're still doing well in school, hanging out with their friends offline and engaging in genuine, human interaction, I'm generally cool with it.

What does give me moments of anxiety are shooter games. I've gone from romanticizing about children who will never own toy guns, to my boy shouting 'Peel, peel, peel!', to laser tag and paintball, to *Plants vs Zombies*, then *Fortnite*, then *Call of Duty*. The latter is something we've resisted at home, but Ezra's played it at his mates' houses. Right now, he's back on *Fortnite*. Sometimes I watch his entire frame tensed over his monitor as he rains virtual ammunition on some target. I can almost smell the adrenaline pumping through his body.

Most of the time, the boys assure me they're not playing realistic shooter games. 'There's no blood or anything, Mum.' However, Ezra's admitted to me that he feels desensitized to violence thanks to some of the stuff he's seen. Of course, this isn't just games, but other media like horror movies and, let's face it, world news.

When a White gunman attacked African Americans at a shopping centre in Buffalo, upstate New York earlier this year, murdering ten innocent people, he livestreamed the attack. Somebody sent Ezra a video clip of the killings. He opened it on WhatsApp.

'I thought it was a video game at first,' he told me.

I was horrified, not only that he'd seen live murders, but that people his age were sharing the videos. But that's the point of terrorism; its power to spread beyond the terror itself. Except that Gen-Z youths are so desensitized that what might have made a sixteen-year-old scream or cry in 1993 is now something to simply click 'Share' on and keep on scrolling.

Sometimes it feels like we're guinea pigs in an ongoing experiment. More and more studies are examining the impact of gaming, new media and the internet on the still-developing brains of children, but there's no way that the research can keep up. It's all happening too fast. As we meander into the metaverse age, one thing I can hold onto is how history moves in cycles, and that there will always be an analogue pushback. We see it in the ongoing love for physical books, the return of vinyl, even the sight of my sixteen-year-old stepping out in 1990s jeans that he deems 'drip' (cool fashion) makes my heart smile.

We watch old movies together, and some of my favourite reactions are when I've shared a film that I enjoyed when I was their age, like *Dirty Dancing*. Ezra's reaction: '*Dirty Dancing*. It's a bit of a mad one, my guy. She's like seventeen and he's about fifty.'

Then there was Jed's review of *Footloose*. 'So, basically, this entire movie is about a town that doesn't let people dance. Are you serious?'

'Yes. And Kevin Bacon frees them with his dancing feet. Awesome, right?'

'No, Mum. Just no.'

I might not be able to peek inside my boys' brains, but I love these little glimpses into how they think.

This is his brain. This is his brain on masculinity. Long before the advent of the computer, neuroscientists have been trying to figure out the male brain. Back in the day, common wisdom told us there was a male brain and a female brain. Men's brains were bigger and denser (make of this what you will). However, as I outlined in a previous chapter, the latest research shows minimal differences between genders in terms of brain structure.

Yet I have questions. How come so many more boys are diagnosed with conditions like ADHD, dyslexia and autism? Reportedly, girls often present differently with these conditions, as evidenced by the recent boom in women seeking diagnoses. I never considered that I might be on the ADHD spectrum until my husband sought a diagnosis for adult ADHD more than a decade ago. While reading a book on the subject to understand his mind better, I wound up understanding myself a lot more too. Experts say that girls tend to internalize, so a female with ADHD might not fit the more recognizable description of impulsive actions and hyperactive behaviour. They might look more absent-minded (tick), daydreamy (tick), anxious (tick), indecisive (tick), disorganized (tick).

Some studies suggest that females are under-diagnosed because female sufferers tend to internalize and are better at masking symptoms. Boys are more prone to expressing their ADHD symptoms outwardly. Research suggests that genetics, hormonal influence or social biases might be root causes. Most likely it's down to a complex mix of biology and environment. Either way, boys are more than three times as likely as girls to be diagnosed with ADHD and autism. Statistically, more young males engage in risky and compulsive behaviour like video-game addiction, gambling, sex addiction or drug and alcohol abuse.

Black males are being hospitalized with psychiatric disorders at an alarming rate. One statistic that is both disturbing and heart-breaking is that, up until age eleven, young Black boys don't show signs of having poorer mental health than other boys their age. However, as they get older, Black teens and men are diagnosed with more severe mental-health issues, and they are far more likely to be sectioned under the Mental Health Act. According to the charity Mind, this is down to a range of factors, including social pressures, stigma, cultural barriers and systemic racism. In *Bringing Up Race*, I explored how coping with an ongoing barrage of pressures from a racist and unequal society, known in psychological terms as 'weathering', can have a catastrophic effect on the mental and physical wellbeing of Black and Brown people.

Having to deal not only with the impact of racism, but the anticipation of racist behaviour, as well as the second-hand damage that comes from witnessing racism in our communities and in the media, can keep you in a state of hypervigilance. So, what happens when, as a Black man, you experience psychic trauma? When your worst nightmare comes true?

Elliott Rae, author and founder of *Music Football Fatherhood*, is one guy who nearly fell through the cracks. At one point, he had a successful job, a loving wife and a baby on the way. After a relatively smooth pregnancy, Elliott and his wife Soneni were in the labour room when things took a dramatic turn. His wife showed signs of a dangerous medical condition, the baby was in distress and the room filled with doctors. Elliott watched helplessly as their daughter was born, but she was grey and didn't make a sound. As doctors resuscitated his daughter at one end, while other medical staff attended to his wife, who was losing a worrying amount of blood, Elliott was in a state of shock.

With his baby girl wheeled to the neonatal intensive care unit (NICU), Elliott tried to call his mother but there was no reception. He said he felt like a lost little boy. Then a nurse told him to snap out of it, because he needed to be there for his family. Elliott says he was grateful for her words. But what I hear is somebody telling him to 'man up' and how difficult that must have been in that moment. From that point on, he went into survivor mode, taking care of business and not allowing himself to go to pieces because 'there wasn't the time'. He had to be strong.

Their daughter spent the first two weeks of her life in the hospital, and just when they thought she could come home, the doctors discovered an abnormal growth at the back of her head. Fortunately, medical tests ruled out anything sinister, and the young family were able to return to what Elliott thought was normal life, except he felt anything but normal.

Despite resuming at work, the new dad was struggling with depression, poor sleep and flashbacks of the traumatic birth. It was when he burst into tears on a packed tube that Elliott knew he needed help. Over the course of the next eighteen months, he was diagnosed with severe PTSD.

Elliott said: 'That was something I had associated with soldiers. I didn't realize you could get it outside wartime, like if you've had a traumatic life experience.'

Following his ordeal, Elliott began blogging, mainly as an outlet, and then, as more dads came on board, to start conversations around male mental health and other challenges of masculinity and fatherhood. The project grew into a website, a podcast, a documentary around Elliott's journey and a book featuring dads of all descriptions sharing their stories.

I asked Elliott how he found the courage to be so open about his mental-health struggles, especially given the man code that often shuts down emotion or expressions of vulnerability. He'd also have had to deal with the cultural stigma around mental illness or 'airing your dirty laundry' that can be such a hindrance in African and Caribbean communities. We are famous for suffering in silence.

'For a while, I didn't feel like I could speak to people,' Elliott admits.

That's why I started blogging. It took nearly a year before I actually went to the doctor. My wife has been very supportive throughout; I wouldn't have been able to do any of this without her. Also, when we did the book and I shared my story publicly, I was doing it with nineteen other people and all those people did it because they knew they weren't doing it by themselves. There was a safety in that. It illustrates the power of community.

Elliott is committed to bringing men together in different forums, including through his partnerships with Premier League football clubs, to talk about their lives and about manhood in a safe, non-judgmental space.

What we're doing is really counter to the narrative of manhood. Like, we held a session at the Emirates Stadium last Sunday and there were men talking about not getting to see their daughter, or that they're struggling because their son is autistic and about to get kicked out of school, or about when they told their partner they wanted to commit suicide. It was really honest, really powerful stuff.

One in five men will suffer from a mental-health problem during their partner's pregnancy and the first year after birth. Dads with mental-health problems during this perinatal period are forty-seven times more likely to be classed as a suicide risk than at any other time in their lives. This is shocking, particularly since suicide is the biggest killer of males under fifty in the UK.

Of all the many things we worry about as parents and caregivers of boys, the rates of suicide among young males tops the list. Every parent and professional I interviewed for this book was distressed about the statistic that young men are nearly three times more likely to die by suicide.

When I asked actor, comedian and author Rob Delaney about his biggest concern as a parent, he said: 'How can I help them weather the very real crisis in mental health for boys these days? How do I help them get to a mental or emotional space where suicide doesn't ever seem like an option? Can I?'

Rob is the father of four boys, including his late son Henry, who died of a brain tumour when he was just two. Rob has been open about his personal struggles with depression and alcoholism. His children are still quite young, though, so it's painful to hear that he's already thinking about male suicide as an impending threat.

However, I've interviewed parents who have lost children as young as eight to suicide. Those were some of the most heart-wrenching conversations I've ever had. Rob's questions touch on a very significant element of why boys and men might be more prone to suicide; the Man Box rules that prevent many males who are suffering from opening up or asking for help.

Elliott Rae says:

The suicide rate is very much linked to men being open to speak and seek support. A Movember survey showed that one in four men made contact with their mates less than once a month and one in ten couldn't recall the last time they saw their friends. Men are less likely to refer to Mind or Calm. We also know that men are more likely to throw themselves in front of a train or end things in a way that is more violent and more determined, whereas women might do it as a cry for help. All this does link into ideas of manhood, so there's loads of work to do.

Author and parenting coach Elaine Halligan says masculinity needs redefining urgently for the health of all concerned.

Society has some pretty clear ideas about what it is to be a man, i.e. to be strong, self-sufficient and not express emotions other than anger. If boys absorb these ideas about masculinity, it can lead to difficulty expressing or managing emotions and, sometimes, to aggression against others or against yourself.

So, to echo Rob's question, how do we get our boys and young men to an emotional and mental space where suicide isn't an option? Can we? This is such a sensitive area that requires a number of interventions, from social support to research, education and awareness. One of the concerns with raising awareness is that, according to the Samaritans, young people are at greater risk of suicide contagion. In other words, they are more likely to be influenced by hearing about suicide in the media than other age groups. Experts surmise that a young person has less impulse control, partly owing to a still-developing prefrontal cortex in the brain, and might not fully appreciate that suicide is a very permanent response to what are usually temporary problems.

Those of us left behind can never fully comprehend what has pushed our loved one past the point of no return. Recently, bestselling author Matt Haig, who wrote the book *Reasons to Stay Alive*, shared something on his Instagram that I thought was a helpful and poignant way to reframe things. He wrote:

> **Suicide is not a choice in the usual way of thinking about choice. It is a choice in the way jumping out of a burning building is a choice. If we could see inside minds the way we could see burning buildings, we would understand the real tragedy is the fire in the first place.**

We need to look for ways to stop the fires from happening, or to put them out before they rage out of control. What's hard is that sometimes that burning building looks like it's flickering with the warmest light. When dancer and entertainer Twitch died by suicide in December 2022, it sent shockwaves across social media. People couldn't stop sharing video clips of him, just the day before, performing and laughing and looking like he was at the top of his game. But depression doesn't always wear dark clothes and hide out in the shadows. Sometimes it's the brightest star coming apart right before your eyes, only you can't see past the brightness.

These days, with more conversation happening around what continues to be a taboo subject in many global cultures, there are more suicide-prevention programmes and mental-health support for families, children and young men. If you are a parent, not a professional, you might feel a bit lost as to what to do. There are no simple answers. The main thing is to be attentive, supportive, listen and, most importantly, give space for their feelings.

Author and educator Naz Ahsun says:

The real issue with 'boys don't cry' is the huge pressure that we put onto our young people. Not allowing them to feel. I think that's what has contributed to so much male depression and suicide. That's why I think men break. And when they do break, they suffer in silence.

Naz spoke with me about her son's mental-health challenges and how he came through it.

It started in his twenties, a consequence of unresolved trauma in his childhood and PTSD. I noticed he was down, and I noticed he was sleeping a lot. One day he came to see me and he simply told me. I think he was talking with friends online and probably did a lot of reading about it, and he said, 'I think I'm depressed.'

Naz's son was at university at the time but moved back home for a period and she found a psychotherapist to work with him. She feels his openness to the process helped him make progress and start to rebuild his life, although it hasn't been an easy road.

As a parent, you think, 'Oh God, I did something wrong,' but it's not anyone's fault. When they're a child, you can put a plaster on stuff and that's what I was looking to do, because it was an uncomfortable space for me too. What really supported me was listening to him and hearing what he needed, not what I thought he needed. That's where things really began to shift. With me recognizing he was growing up and needed to take care of this in his own way, with my support, but he needed to lead.

When your baby is little, they bump their heads and run to you, and you kiss everything better. When they grow, it's tempting to want to fix every issue that comes up. To cover them in bubble wrap or childproof the whole damn neighbourhood. More than that, you can start to analyse and pathologize every angle of your child's behaviour and worry it (and yourself) to shreds. But your child is not a problem to solve. I repeat, your child is not a problem to solve. He is a real, complicated human with his own identity that's partly formed by outside circumstances but mostly there from birth, or possibly earlier.

I carry a photo of Ezra on my keyring from when he was one day old and, honestly, I see the exact same temperament and character that he displays seventeen years later: wise, mischievous, thoughtful, stubborn to a fault. It's all right there in that little face. His brain might have adapted into the brain of a gamer (and a smart arse), but he's always known his own mind.

It's similar to what *Guardian* writer Tom Lamont said in our conversation, as he described coming to terms with the type of 'boyish boy' he never expected to be parenting.

At the end of the day, you know your kids; you know who they are. That's what I always think of parents with trans kids: they know. They just know their kids and that's the end of it. You've spent all that time with them, and you know them inside out. You know when they're faking and when they're really being themselves. They're not just figments in your mind, your kids are three-dimensional humans.

Dr Cara Natterson affirmed this from her background in paediatrics, and from parenting her own children.

What I saw in the medical world that has [been] borne out in my own life is that they are who they are when they come out. We meet them [in] minute one, and there are

RAISING BOYS WHO DO BETTER

**certain features and temperaments, certain personality
traits that are literally inborn and we can see them. Then
there are many other things that are socialized and
culturalized into them. But some things are there from day
one. Some kids come in packs. The much more common
path is that you do it once and you think you've got this
thing nailed and along comes a different person who
upends everything you know about parenting, and you
find yourself going, "Wait a second?!"**

I have it on good authority that *Wait a second*, or rather, '*What the fuck?*', is the accepted mantra for people raising children worldwide. This is your brain. This is your brain on parenting. WTF.

Conversation and Reflection Prompts

Does your boy play video games? What restrictions or safety
measures do you put around this?

Are you concerned about gaming addiction and have you
discussed this with your son?

Have you spoken about the dangers of other addictions,
e.g. substance abuse, gambling, social media?

Do you discuss mental health with your boy?

What practices can you encourage as a family to promote better
mental wellbeing?

Have you considered or used counselling, family therapy
or a family support group to help your boy open up?

If your boy is neurodiverse, do you feel supported by the system?
Where do you find community?

MOOD TRACKER

You can help a boy get more in touch with his emotions by listening to and identifying his own moods, thoughts and feelings regularly. One way to do this is by using a daily or weekly mood tracker (find one online or create your own) or a mood journal. If he's not keen on writing in a journal, he could use voice memos, e.g. on his phone.

Questions to consider:
How do I feel today? Where is this feeling located in my body?
Why do I feel this way? When did I last feel like this?
What can I do to feel better? Who can I turn to for help?
For younger ones, simply colouring in their feelings can offer an opportunity to discuss them and provide some support.
If you have specific concerns about a boy's mental health, do speak to a dedicated professional.

HOW TO KEEP A BOY SAFE

I am walking home along the route from the boys' primary school, carrying both of their backpacks. Ezra is on a scooter, his jacket flying behind him as he bumps over pebbles and pavement cracks.

'Careful,' I call to him.

Jed is walking just ahead of me when Frank* (*name changed), a boy in Ezra's class, jogs up to him from behind.

'Let's race.'

The two boys go running at top speed, down the slope, faster than I can possibly catch up.

'Watch the road!'

My voice is hoarse as I quicken my pace, eyes already scanning for incoming traffic. They race across the road without stopping.

'Boys!'

There are no vehicles in sight, but I'm annoyed now: how many times have I warned my sons to stop, look and listen? Jed and Frank have overtaken Ezra's scooter, they are neck-and-neck as they reach the park. Jed is inching ahead when Frank knocks into him and my little boy goes headlong into a park railing.

I don't know if I'm screaming at this point; all I know is that, when my four-year-old turns around, blood is gushing from the middle of his head. I fly to scoop him up before he collapses to the pavement. We sit on the ground, his head in my arms as I give a strangled plea for help to nobody in particular. Ezra kneels beside us and we're both crying. I can see strangers gathering, someone is calling an ambulance. A woman from the church across the road appears with a bandage and wraps it around Jed's head.

'Try and keep him awake.' Her voice is soothing. 'He'll be OK. You're OK. The ambulance is on its way.'

All I can see is Jed's blood seeping through the cloth and his eyes starting to close. I sing to try and keep him awake but my voice keeps catching.

From nowhere, Frank's dad appears and drags him away. Later, I will feel sorry for Frank and angry at his dad for leaving the scene. But right now, too many other thoughts are rushing through my head: *My boy is*

RAISING BOYS WHO DO BETTER

broken. Why didn't I run faster? So much blood. What am I going to tell his dad? Jed, please stay awake.

By the time the ambulance arrives, things are calmer. The siren has snapped Jed into focus, and he's excited to be inside this big vehicle and the centre of so much attention. The paramedics have refreshed his bandage and the bleeding has slowed.

'I know it looks scary,' one of the paramedics reassures me, 'Head wounds tend to bleed a lot. But he's alert and he's talking, so he should be fine.'

We get to the children's A&E, and they see us right away. The doctor is kind and chatty and the boys take to him instantly. When he removes the bandage, Ezra and I flinch because it looks like we can see through to Jed's skull. The doctor tells me that it's better than it looks and it's a clean wound, so Jed won't need stitches, he can use glue instead. None of us have heard of this technique and I'm amused to see Jed's eyes widen at the thought of his head being glued back together like an art project. The doctor points to a thin scar just above his own eye.

'You see that?'

Jed stares and nods.

'That happened to me when I was about your age.'

The doctor smiles at me.

'Boys,' he says. 'I'm surprised any of us make it to adulthood.'

You could argue that this was another example of implicit gender bias, although most statistics paint a different picture. Boys are more prone to injuries, bruises and head cracks, broken bones and 4 a.m. visits to the emergency room. My husband also has a thin line above his eyebrow from where he split his head open as a youngster.

We left the emergency room with a bloodied school jumper, an umbrella to stop rain from dissolving the surgical glue, and a wound that would develop into a faint pinkish-brown lightning bolt on Jed's forehead. We call it his Harry Potter scar.

I wish that was Jed's last trip to A&E as a little boy. The next time resulted in a typhoid shot, eight local-anaesthetic injections, twelve stitches and scars on his leg that look like he might have been attacked by a piranha. In Year Eight, Jed wrote his own account of the incident for a school essay. I loved his closing paragraph:

'My mum told me that I was a lion, strong and brave. I was treated by a very nice doctor. The one thing I learned was not to dance on a glass table or you won't be able to play football for a month.'

As a parent, you can guide and pray and plead and screech, but there's little you can do to stop a boy who wants to rush headlong into life. I've heard grisly tales of boys falling from trees, boys walking through glass doors, boys crashing off motorbikes, boys pinning each other to the point of near suffocation. This isn't to say that girls don't do wild and dangerous things too. All kids can get into scrapes, but, as noted, boys tend to sit at the sharper end of the spectrum.

The other day, I met a lovely guy called Justin, and when I mentioned this book, he said I could share this anecdote about his nephews.

My sister had three boys, one after the other. So, when they were around ages two, three and four, they were running about in the living room and making a racket, so she sent them to their bedroom to quieten down. A little while later, her front doorbell rang.

His sister went to answer the door and found a policeman outside.

He asked her if by any chance she had three boys. She answered yes, but told him that, whatever the issue was, her boys couldn't be involved because they were all upstairs in the bedroom. So, the policeman goes, 'Ma'am, can you come with me?'

The policeman led Justin's sister out to the side of the house and pointed up. She looked up to see her three boys sitting on the roof, shouting at the neighbours and waving a pirate flag. Apparently, they'd stood on top of each other and climbed out through the skylight!

You'll be pleased to hear that all three pirates successfully made it to manhood and are, according to their uncle, quite responsible individuals. For their mum's sake, I can't help wishing each one of them gets to experience the karmic force known as parenting a child who's even naughtier than you.

I asked Street Feast founder and entrepreneur Dominic Cools-Lartigue what the word 'boy' means to him, and he chuckled.

'The first thing that came to my mind is rascal, probably because my little boy is being a bit of a rascal right now,' he said.

> **You know what it's like, he's fourteen, and just this week got into the most trouble he's ever got into. I had to take a day off work to deal with it. We're trying to create the environment where he can be whoever he wants to be. But he needs not to be drinking vodka and coke after school on a Monday.**

Dominic acknowledged that it was tricky raising a child when you can see so much of yourself in them, including the rascally elements.

> **I love this stage, though, because we have some fantastic conversations, although I'm kicking myself now because we talk and it looks like he's looking me in the eye and he's listening, but it turns out nothing's getting through.**

I had two words for Dominic: frontal lobe. Those are the words I repeat to myself whenever my teenagers start acting in ways I can't fathom. I remember that the frontal lobe – in fact, the entire prefrontal cortex of their brains – is in a state of flux and doesn't fully mature until around your mid-twenties.

Dominic chuckled again.

> **Thank you for saying that. It's funny, I was talking to a few people recently about guys in their twenties, and I thought what assholes we were and what an asshole I was. I feel**

sorry for women in their twenties having to deal with boys in their twenties . . . and it is boys. Just the fully formed puppy, you know what I mean, with all the tools and no idea what to do. The arrogance, the entitlement. Thinking we can get away with everything. That's what we spoke to Remy about yesterday. I had a friend who wound up in prison because he thought he could get away with it.

Having grounded his boy for a month – 'He's got a spreadsheet of activities' – Dominic said he feels he let some balls drop over summer. 'I think we just lost him a little bit. The greatest influence in your teens should be his parents and not his peers, and that's where we slipped up this summer; the biggest influence was his peer group.'

The teenage years are actually when your peer group becomes more influential, and that's a normal developmental phase. Between the brain changes and the hormonal rollercoaster of adolescence, your child might start ignoring you and getting life hacks from YouTube, TikTok and some kid who's barely started shaving. They reach that stage Nigerians call ITK, which stands for 'I too know': in other words, they know absolutely everything. You can't tell them jack. And no matter how much wisdom you try to shovel their way, teenagers are gonna teenage.

I look back on some of my own teen behaviour and I pity my parents. I remember stumbling home drunk around 5 a.m. and grumbling to myself because my mum or dad were still sitting up on the sofa, wide awake. How irritating. Now I'd have to try and creep up to bed silently or pretend I hadn't been drinking. It never occurred to me that my parents weren't just staying up to catch me out. They were awake to make sure I came home alive.

These days, I sit up counting the minutes until I can send Ezra a text to make sure he's on his way back from a party. I wonder if he's listened to my advice or hopped on a street rental bike while drunk. When it snowed recently, he missed a day of school because, despite my warnings, he'd tried to ride one of these bikes along the icy road, skidded off and hurt his back. Fortunately, he was OK, but sometimes muttering 'frontal lobe' can't stop my heart hammering against my chest.

How do we keep our babies safe? To raise a child is to live with worry as your constant companion, almost as another family member. I wrote a list of one hundred things I worry about as a mother of boys, and I couldn't stop at a hundred. Some of this is amusingly neurotic. For instance, if you had told me before having kids how much I would fret over keeping their necks warm, I would have thought you or I were barmy. Once the temperatures drop, if I see a hint of skin between their chins and chests, my mother hen mind starts clucking. 'Where's your scarf? Put on a jumper. Zip up.' My siblings and I still laugh about what our mum used to stress about, like when my sister was on her way home from work in Lagos traffic and my mum called insisting that she bought a bathmat 'this very afternoon' because she'd had a dream about her slipping in the bath!

Journalist Tom Lamont said he doesn't think his nervous system has recovered from becoming a parent.

> **Naively, I never imagined it would be such a massive shock. But once you're blasted and knocked over and you've worked out how to cope with those new rhythms of your life, you realize nothing has really felt as savage as reshaping your life around a new child.**

In some ways, if you can survive the first year, you can survive anything, although that doesn't keep the worries at bay.

> **I think one of the things you do as a parent is you bury your head in the present. If you think too far forward, it's quite unnerving. Right now, with my son, it's the lack of self-restraint and no obvious understanding of limits and safety edges. I worry all the time about this little exuberant boy not realizing he's putting himself in danger.**

Tom is feeling some disquiet about the future too.

Social media, gaming, peer pressure, violence. Mostly, I'm nervous about teenage boys growing up in London. I feel like teenage boys are not top of anyone's list. At best, it's eye-rolling. At worst, it's labelling them as a troublemaker when they've barely had a chance to think for themselves what they are.

Let me calm your nerves a little if you are the parent of a child under ten, like Tom, and already peeking through your fingers at the teenager to come. It doesn't have to be all shouting voices and slammed doors. Generally, the teenage boys I know are funny – hilarious actually – sweet, thoughtful, focused. Kinder than you might expect. Anecdotally, they are better behaved than most of us were back in our rave and clubbing years. That doesn't guarantee that the teen years won't throw you and your boy off course sometimes, but there are steps you can take to get back on the right track.

My friend Verity has three boys, and one of them started hanging out with a rough crowd in his early teens. She said: 'He's always been drawn to that edgy side of things. Also, they were older, and he felt like they knew what life was about.'

He started sneaking off, not answering her phone calls, hanging out where she knew there was alcohol and drugs and no adults present. As a single mum, she struggled to get through to him. She sought help through his school, and right now he has a male support worker who makes sure he's attending classes and doing his scheduled after-school activities. He also joined a local sports club, which meant that she at least knew where he was and what he was doing during those periods.

That's one reason I'm grateful for my boys' interests in gaming and sports. For a good portion of their time, I know what they're doing because they're either at after-school practice or they're sitting in my living room, playing with their friends online. Parenting a boy can be scary, particularly a Black boy who is trying to walk the streets like he's already a man. The intersection of race and motherhood can feel like a tightrope. Every time another boy is stabbed, often in or around our neighbourhood, I wake up with my cheeks cut to ribbons. I've been grinding my teeth in my sleep.

The worst part is that the government still won't take proper action to stop knife crime, because the majority of the victims and perpetrators are Black or from disadvantaged backgrounds. It's the same story in countries like America, Brazil, France and Germany — Black and marginalized boys are disposable.

As an urban parent, you are caught between the fear of your son being stopped, searched, harassed or worse by the police, and the constant threat of a mugging or assault. These aren't just headlines and hashtags, these are everyday stories circling in our networks, like my friend Sam, whose son was robbed by a guy with a machete. Tales of mobile phones and winter coats and lunch money stolen outside the school gates by teens wearing face masks and brandishing kitchen knives. Both Ezra and Jed and their friends have been caught up in this a couple of times, and now they know to spot the 'roadmen' coming and to take off running, or duck into a shop for safety.

How can you unclench your teeth as a parent when all this is around the corner? Even if you are living with a certain amount of privilege, even if your boys are some of the lucky ones, there are no guarantees. Raising a child can feel like waking up and signing over a waiver form for your most precious thing, every single day. I'm reminded of something Tom Lamont told me, quoting *Karate Kid* and *Cobra Kai* actor Ralph Macchio, whom he had interviewed for an article. 'He said to me, "You know parenting isn't seasonal, man, it doesn't break for the summer."'

Ain't that the truth, Ralph!

Dr Cara Natterson, author and paediatrician, is the mother of a son and a daughter in their college years. She says:

As a parent, I'm terrified for both of my kids. I mean that not to be melodramatic, but I think, fraught is the best word. It is fraught for everyone. This concept of just

keeping them alive, when they're young, and now it's about keeping them alive with all the terrifying things in the world.

She spoke about how often boys around ages thirteen to fifteen 'turn down their volume' and retreat into themselves. 'It's about puberty and hormones and a little switch that goes off in their brain, where the peers take priority. They might be more talkative with their friends, but otherwise they might disappear into their bedroom or become more private.'

She said sometimes this gets confused with the 'strong and silent' stereotype of masculinity when it's really just a stage their body is going through. 'I think it's a disservice to imagine they don't want to communicate. Some of them just want to be left alone with their thoughts for a moment, or they don't have the right words yet, but they still want to talk.'

How can you reach out to a boy at this stage, especially when you might be concerned about him becoming withdrawn? Dr Natterson says the important thing is not to hound them but to stay connected.

Try asking questions in an open-ended way. Put down your phone. Engage them in conversations that show you care about the details, like remembering the names of their friends or stories that they told you. Not in an accusatory way but like, I heard you and I want to follow up with you.

Dr Natterson says her already quiet son, now seventeen, went through a super-quiet phase as he entered puberty. 'He went from monosyllabic to not syllabic. I got nothing. And, given what I do, that was very hard for me. My job is to keep him safe and healthy, so how do I do this when he's so quiet?'

Some strategies she came up with included listening and engaging with him on his terms. When he would shut his door around age thirteen, she would knock on the door – 'Always knock on a teen boy's door,' she warns – and wait for his response.

'Sometimes he would say "I'm in here," or whatever code it was for I'm not interested in you coming in. Then I would say "I'm gonna sit here" and I would literally sit on the ground outside the door, and we would talk that way for a few minutes, and it was easier for him because it avoided eye contact.'

She also recommended that, if your child has an older sibling, you could get them involved, not to rat each other out, but so there's a channel of communication. The other essential strategy we discussed was having a support network.

My podcast co-host Vanessa has four kids, and she talks a lot about the need for parents to have support networks. Because some of the things that parents need to say, they actively need to not say to their children, but they need to say them and that's so much of what your support network becomes. Kids need a support network too, and that can't just be a bunch of teenagers because they're going to get really bad advice!

What she encourages parents to do is to identify a surrogate that your child can turn to when they need advice or assistance, and they can't necessarily come to you first. This reminds me of a rite-of-passage tip: assemble their coming-of-age team.

When they're teenagers, I strongly recommend, every once in a while, you have a conversation where you say, if you can't come to me for this, who would you go to? Which adult? It's really important, because you are helping them identify an alternate person and giving them permission too. Also, when you learn who the right person is, you should give that person a heads-up.

She says that she identified as a surrogate parent/mentor for a colleague's daughter and, thankfully, she'd had fair warning before the girl called her in a sticky situation.

My phone rang at 2 a.m. and she was in the bathroom at her boyfriend's house. They'd been dating for months, and she called to say 'I thought I was ready to have sex, but I'm hiding in the bathroom.' Fortunately, her mom and I are very like-minded. So, I said to her: 'You love him, he loves you enough to know that if you're not ready, you're just not ready. So, you go out and tell him how you feel, and my guess is that it will be OK.' And she did, and it was.

I'm impressed by Dr Natterson's composure in the moment, as that's not an easy phone call to receive in the middle of the night. That scenario touches on another concern I have as a parent of growing men. What if my son was the boy in the bedroom waiting for their girlfriend to emerge from a locked bathroom? How would that conversation go?

The question for boys is not just 'Are you safe?' but also 'Are you safe to be around?' When I was a teenager, the talk about safe sex focused on condoms, the Pill and the spectre of HIV. As a mum in 2023, I worry about their physical wellbeing, but also about how well they understand boundaries and emotional cues. Dr Natterson said that raising a girl and a boy through their adolescence during the evolution of the #MeToo movement was interesting to say the least. We spoke about the need to have more open and nuanced conversations around stuff like porn, consent and hook-up culture.

At my company, Order of Magnitude, we have a band of about a dozen interns between the ages of eighteen to twenty-two at different colleges across the US. They are very articulate about what consent is supposed to look like, and then what it really looks like on a college campus. They tell me everyone's intoxicated all the time and that it's very hard to be in a dynamic in college where consent is

truly freely given because there's so much alcohol around.

Legally, you cannot give consent under the influence. I speak with my sons about enthusiastic consent and how anything that isn't a 'Hell, yes' is a 'Fuck, no' (I use cleaner language with them). But when everyone's hanging out and drinking or taking substances, things get slippery.

As a parent and a doctor, the right advice is consent must be given sober, period. However, as we raise our sons, if we don't acknowledge how this plays out in reality then we're doing them a great disservice. If we say, 'Yes, you can go to the party, college, whatever' and we haven't had the conversation about 'Here's really what's going to happen, let's figure this out together', then we've left them flat-footed.

These are essential conversations to keep having because while you might feel confident that your son is not the type of male who goes out and attacks women, what happens behind closed doors is just as crucial. We need to raise more boys and young men who are safe and trustworthy and who can hold themselves and each other accountable in everyday sexual encounters.

The week of Sarah Everard's murder, I sat in the kitchen reading the website Everyone's Invited. Tales of young girls lured into situations they couldn't handle. Coercion, guilt, shame, soft porn, dick pics, sexual assault. I felt appalled and triggered by how little has changed and, in some ways, how much more abusive these scenarios have become.

As I read, I heard the front door and Ezra's whistling as he came up the stairs.

'Hey Ezra,' I called out. 'How was school? Can we talk for a second?'

He eyed me warily. 'About?'

'Some stuff in the news. I'm sure you've heard about Sarah Everard.'

'The woman who got murdered? Yeah.'

'Well, I wanted to discuss it. Like, have they talked about it at school?

Do you know about this website Everyone's Invited?'

He shook his head.

'I wanted to talk about consent–'

Ezra held his hand up, cutting me off.

'Nah, mum, I'm not trying to have some big chat about that now. We did all that in RSE. I know all there is to know, trust me.'

And he left the room.

My instinct was to follow him crying: 'You know nothing (Jon Snow)!'

But when it comes to the big stuff, timing is everything. So is mood. My timing was totally off right then, but that didn't mean the conversation was over.

I looked for other opportunities, like when the boys and I were watching *Grown-ish,* a spin-off from the TV series *Black-ish,* which focuses on a group of college kids. They had a storyline about consent which was cleverly done in terms of addressing the nuances around boundaries and safety and intoxication. It's a comedy, so we were able to listen, learn and discuss the subject in a light-hearted space. What I appreciated about that episode is that it didn't lecture or moralize, it simply got us thinking. It allowed the boys to reflect and ask questions and that's a healthy goal for our sons in any given situation; that they can be more conscious, use their critical thinking, ask necessary questions and not assume their way is the right way or that their desires are the only desires. For children aged sixteen and older, Michaela Coel's award-winning BBC drama *I May Destroy You* can provoke powerful discussions around consent and sexual assault.

Raising critical thinkers is key, but so much of this comes back to raising boys who are in touch with their feelings. For, as parenting coach Elaine Halligan says:

We need to allow boys to be hurt, upset, and to cry if they want to. Moving on and getting over it can be good advice from time to time. But over the longer term, it tells our boys not to listen to how they feel. If they can't listen to how they feel, how can they listen to how someone else feels?

Educator Zahara Chowdhury suggests that active listening is often the missing piece.

Listening is a core skill that none of us are taught really, we're just conditioned to listen without knowing whether we're doing it well or not! The whole premise behind #MeToo can be termed a failure to listen and be heard too, so I think this is very important as a starting point to raising and educating boys.

You might be surprised at how much a boy does listen to what you say, even when you're talking to his back, or he hasn't looked you in the eye since he turned thirteen. Elliott Rae, founder of *Music Football Fatherhood*, shared something he remembered from his youth. A PE teacher at school told him that if he was walking down the street late at night, and he saw a woman coming, he would cross the road to help her feel safer.

'I was very young, maybe Year Eight [around age twelve]. Out of all my schooling, that's what I remember best. Just understanding how a woman late at night might be feeling.'

I was curious about what conversations Elliott has with his community around sexism and gender-based violence. What was his intersectional experience as a Black man and as the father of a young girl?

I never used to worry. My mum was a big worrier, and I didn't understand why. But now I'm worried about everything. Unfortunately, we have to prepare our children physically and mentally for the world they're growing up into. The other side is about conversation. The more we can talk about this as men, test our beliefs, learn through people's stories, see a different way of thinking and doing, I believe that will have a positive impact.

He shared another anecdote that had us both laughing and musing on the intersectionality of race, gender, parenthood and puppy ownership!

'It's funny, we got a cute little dog called Jessie,' he said.

When he was a puppy, I was walking him down a quiet backstreet around 8 p.m. It was dark. And I've never experienced this before but this White woman on the other side of the road crossed over to walk in front of me. She walked right in front of me! I was like, this has never happened in my life! But because I have this cute little dog, suddenly I'm approachable.

As I often say, context is key, and perspective is everything. The way we see the world, how others see us, how we see ourselves; the stories we tell to construct our own realities. We don't have much control over how our kids' lives will turn out. But as a parent, you have the power of a storyteller. The stories we tell can chart new paths for our children to walk. We cannot follow all the way, but we can meet them where they are and walk with them as far as we can go.

For there is no safety in the road ahead, there is only the road and your courage to keep on walking. I learned this from Rob Delaney and his beautiful, heart-wrenching memoir, *A Heart That Works*. In our interview, Rob described the simple joys of living in a house full of boys. 'I'm surprised by how much I love it. I'd wanted girls, or at least a girl but now I'm at peace with my insane, loud family. I love the chaos. It's physically intense and pulls you through the day. I'm rarely bored around them, and never with them.'

He describes his sons as fairly typical, in boy terms. 'So far, they're all within the bounds of what's reasonably common. Nothing that would have really raised eyebrows in the 1950s or whatever.'

However, there's nothing typical about their story. When Rob's third son, Henry, began vomiting as a baby, they thought it was a stomach problem. After months of seeking specialist advice, they learned that it was a brain tumour. In his memoir, Rob writes about the shock of the diagnosis, the brain surgeries, the trauma of Henry's tracheostomy, his facial paralysis and hearing loss, his relapses and, finally, the day they removed his body in a bag. I'm writing this like it's just another list, but my heart is in my throat because I've never read anything so moving, so brutal, so crystal clear in its depiction of loss and raw grief. I had to read the book in stages because it was so overwhelming, and yet throughout I felt as though Rob was giving me a gift. The gift of getting to know his little boy. The gift of understanding that even through the shittiest of life's shitstorms, you can find humour and wonder and connection, even moments of joy.

'I don't think I could bear to read that,' my sister said when I told her what I was reading, and yet I urge everyone to read it. It is beautiful and funny and true. It is absolutely bursting with love.

Rob told me his experience of losing Henry had changed the way he parented.

It showed me that kids can and do die before their parents. Now I know my other kids can and absolutely will die one day, it's not an abstraction like it is for most parents. Thus, I am very consciously aware of their impermanence and how lucky I am to have them for this day.

Parenthood is an exceptional act of courage. I don't mean the accidental or intentional collision of sperm and egg, but the conscious choice to raise a child into adulthood and beyond. To see them through the loops and curveballs that life throws at you. To give them your entire heart, while knowing that you are just one chapter in the story they are still writing. To reckon with the hard fact that the story might end before either of you are ready. To give them your heart anyway.

This book was never about one-size-fits-all strategies or simple workarounds. Even the medical professionals I've spoken with throughout agree there's no prescription for raising humans. One thing I do believe in is that love is powerful medicine and love out loud is everlasting magic. So, speak words of love to your boys and over your boys, as often as you can. Speak love. If their lack of frontal-lobe development is making you come unstuck right now, or you're finding it hard to know what to say, you can take some inspiration from the next chapter.

Conversation and Reflection Prompts

How can we hold ourselves, our schools, our communities and our leaders more accountable for the wellbeing of boys (and girls) across society?

When have you been the most scared for your boy? Have you spoken with him about it?

How can you talk to your boy about keeping himself physically safe?

How can you talk to your boy about being safe around girls or in sexual encounters?

Have you or your child experienced any of the following: bullying, cyberbullying, physical violence, peer pressure, crime, unsafe sex, sexual assault? How have you handled this as a family?

Who can you identify as a surrogate for your boy to turn to in times of trouble (if and when he can't come to you)?

Who is part of your own support network?

CHOOSE A SAFE WORD

Sometimes in risky situations, or when boundaries might become blurry, a safe word is necessary. You could talk with an older boy about agreeing on a safe word with his partner in a romantic relationship or sexual encounter. A word that clearly means stop. As a family, you might also agree on a safe word for your boy to help get him out of difficult circumstances. A safe word for someone picking your child up at school, for instance. Or a safe word for a child who has experienced unsafe or unwanted behaviour. Some families have a word or an emoji that their son can text home if he wants to leave a sleepover early. Talk about safe words and choose one that works for you.

TO OUR SONS, WITH LOVE

Around a year before the pandemic shook the world, I figured out three of the great mysteries: the meaning of life, our purpose in life and the ultimate life lesson. I felt pretty smug about it, and also a bit dumb because it had been staring me in the face for forty-plus years. Apparently, I had to go through several country moves, including a trip to hell and back, personal losses, marriage, childbirths, burying both my parents, reading and writing hundreds of thousands of words before I realized what it was all about. Are you ready?

The meaning of life is a story. The purpose of life is to love and grow. The ultimate life lesson? Let go.

That's it. This applies to every aspect of existence, no matter your background or your career aspirations. You are here because you are part of the story, both character and co-writer. Your purpose, no matter what you attach it to, is simply to love and grow. It's what we're meant to do as individuals, as parents, in our relationships, in our communities, in our vocations, for the planet as a whole. When the ancient scripts stated: 'Go forth and multiply', or 'Live long and prosper' if *Star Trek* is more your thing, what that really meant was 'Love and grow'.

The ultimate lesson? It's the central tenet of every world faith. Let go of hate, greed, small-mindedness, attachment to earthly things, the illusion of separation. Let go of what you think you can control. Let go of the child you have raised, so they can walk on their own. Let go of this mortal flesh and become one with everything beyond.

Love, grow, let go. And as we have been told, the greatest of these is love.

As soon as I committed to writing this book, I knew I wanted to end it with love notes. We spend so much time managing, feeding, wrangling, educating, feeding, worrying, feeding, cajoling, advising, feeding and feeding our boys that we forget the most basic thing: love. Most of us love our children dearly, but how often do we let them know it? How often do we allow ourselves to feel it?

If we want to raise boys with big hearts, we need to model it for them. So much of raising kids is about examining our own upbringing and how that impacts our behaviour. Most of us are still walking wounded from our childhoods. Dr Deryl Goldenberg said:

As a civilization we're still learning how to manage our cruel impulses and traumas without revisiting them on our children and the people we govern. You can see it acting out on the world stage. Look at what Putin is doing. We see it all over the place; people that have power and act out on others what we can only assume was visited upon them at one point in their development. I think psychology and therapy is one way through this; most people could benefit from some kind of therapy.

I've found talk therapy helpful, not just for specific issues like anxiety, but for getting in touch with real feelings. Since childhood, I've often kept them locked in. Now, as a mother, I'm aware of when I've been parcelling out my affection, holding back sometimes for fear of letting all the love I have for my boys consume us. However, holding back on love serves nobody. It leaves us bereft of the very thing that makes any of this worth it.

I asked my interviewees to write or share love notes, or words of hope, and I've included some of my favourite responses here.

LOVE NOTES

Haha, I write my boys love notes all the time. I tell them things like
I'm happy to be around them and I love them as they are. No
conditions. Just by showing up here in this life they deserve love.

Rob Delaney

I write my son a diary – or try to, it's not very consistent. I end
each entry along the same lines: I pray, hope and desperately
wish that you are always kind, happy, confident, strong and so
loved for ever. Always do good and do your best. Smile and learn
to laugh, but it's also OK to cry and be sad, even if you don't have
a reason. And please be a good dancer . . . don't let the side
down! To me you are so perfect, and I thank Allah every day for
blessing me with such a genuinely wonderful little boy. I love you
so very much and I hope you'll always love me too.

Zahara Chowdhury

You were two years old when you started to understand that the
world was made up of difference, and that people came in a
variety of shades and colours. You knew far earlier than I
thought you would that I am Black and your father is white. I
wondered if you were confused about that – whether it meant
anything to you. I wondered whether any children had pulled
your hair or excluded you or made you feel like you did not
belong. I wanted to wrap you up in love and shut out a world that
ever made you question your worth.
When we asked you what colour you were, you looked puzzled
and answered: grey. Grey; like an overcast day. And we knew
right then that we would have to work hard to protect you from a
world that might make you feel disappointed in yourself, one that
might make you long for summer when your smile was already a
sunbeam. You will always be our summer. So your dad told you
that you were not grey, but golden brown. And your eyes lit up.

You saw in golden brown your own radiance and worth. In golden brown we saw the image of God in you. And God said that grey, black, white or golden brown – it was always there.

Chine, *God Is Not a White Man: And Other Revelations*

It's 6.45
Most of the curtains on our road are still closed.
Lauren is asleep upstairs
And we're saying goodbye
As we hug and you walk out the door,
I try to get a sense of you,
A glimpse of your vibe.
Are you in a good place?
Are you ready for what this day has in store for you?
'Make good decisions,' I say
As you leave the house so early,
off to school on your own.
I stand at the door,
watch you walk and disappear down the road
On the mornings that you turn back and smile
It lights me up.
I'm set.
I'm good.
You're good
My boy
Dom

Dominic Cools Lartigue

To My Boy Sam, I have so much to thank you for, as your arrival into our world twenty-six years ago has been the most exhausting and exhilarating rollercoaster ride I've even been on and continues to elate and thrill me.
You bring us and everyone you encounter profound joy and entertainment, with your infectiously positive outlook on life. You

have an innate ability to make people feel good about themselves, a creative mind, an ability to problem-solve, and a great sense of humour, not to mention an incredible spirit for adventure that is anxiety-inducing for this mum!
I adore the fact that the brilliant diamond I always sensed was there is now gleaming for all to see, and as a natural entrepreneur, you really do add value to people's lives, in terms of contributing to their happiness and enjoyment of life. People now know what you have been through or what your eyes have seen, and I can assure you, all you have conquered shines through your personality and mind. I love that you know your passion, your zone of genius and what your legacy will be. Keep enjoying the intoxication of life, being happy and contented and a positive influence on so many.
Love you now and always x'

Elaine Halligan

Zach and Ben, your empathy and awareness surprise me every day. Thank you for allowing me to take your initials off my neck and to add an E instead. For pushing me to be me, knowing I will be a better parent to you.

Eve Rodsky

Sorry that I was so immature and hurt you
in the ways that I did.

Dr Deryl Goldenberg

Son, remember how loved you have been
and how loved you are.

Vanessa Walters

MESSAGES OF HOPE

It's hard not to fear for our sons, especially if they're young men of colour. There's a lot of danger out there for our boys in so many ways. It's important that we don't let our fear get in the way of just loving and appreciating and hanging out with them. So that whatever happens they know we're there. We want to be able to walk with them through these hard times.

Paul Kivel

What gives me hope is seeing progress. On Sunday at the Emirates Stadium, I was sitting there and I was nearly in tears to be honest. We were facilitating a conversation with men in our community. Guys come up and start sharing and I'm sitting there thinking *Wow, this is happening*. It's progress because the work is happening. I'm having more conversations like this and when I'm emailing people about positive masculinity, people are getting it now. They fully understand why it's needed. It's very easy to feel like nothing has changed, but things do change. It's about celebrating the incremental steps along the way. None of us in our lifetimes are going to solve any one problem. Our contributions to anything are just contributions, like those who came before us and those after and it's the culmination of all our work that will get us to that point. But seeing progress is where I get hope.

Elliott Rae

The last line of our book is that the reason why we do this work is that we're planting trees we'll never enjoy the shade of but we know that it's worth it. That's what I'm trying to do with my sons, trying to imbue them with a sense of responsibility but a sense of sweetness and kindness and a vulnerability that allows them to move through the world in a loving way. And that's hard to do, so hard to do, but I'm hopeful.

Lisa Lynn

I love what I see happening with the Gen Z kids, they are not afraid to speak up, there is a sense of entitlement but whatever. I love they're not afraid to call it out and that's what we'll need. And also the way we're allowing our kids to know right from wrong, everyone's accepted, everyone has as much of a right to be in the room as everyone else. And knowing that there are so many other people doing the same thing makes me really excited to see what happens when these dinosaurs fade away.

Jen Audrie

TO OUR SONS

Dearest Isaac,

I don't write or blog about you often because I feel it's not my place. You have your own mother with her own tales to tell. However, you are such a huge part of our family's unfolding story. There are no rulebooks for being a stepmother, but I'm glad we've built such a close relationship in our own time, in our own way. I see so much of you in your little brothers, and of course they've always looked up to you even when you couldn't really see yourself clearly or the path ahead. You might be interested to hear what Jed said when I asked him about his brothers. He said: 'We're all quite similar. I'd say Isaac and Ezra are more similar. We're all quite jokey and always joking around with each other. They talk about more serious stuff, and also more silly stuff than me.' I'd say he's right. You are one of the funniest people I know and as snappy as your humour can be, you've always had a serious core and the sweetest nature. Don't let life knock any of that out of you. Remember, you control the decks, and your music fills the room. Years ago, you must have been about eleven and you said to me: 'You know those films and books where there's a stepmother and she's really evil and cruel to her step-kids? Well, you are the exact opposite of that.' I hold those words, and you, Isaac, close to my heart always.

Darling Ezra,

The last public love note I wrote to you was on my blog when you turned eight. I marvelled at how you were halfway to sixteen. Now you are halfway to thirty-two, and writing that not only makes me catch my breath, it makes me feel like Old Mother Time. I try to picture the man you will be then. Whether you will still make weird noises and balance in ridiculously awkward positions in your chair and crack every joint in your body to make me shudder. Whether you will still come into the kitchen doing funny dances. I suspect you will. After all, you get it from your mama and I'm a perennial kitchen raver. I wonder if you will have met the love of your life yet. How many times you will have broken hearts and had your heart broken. If you've had the courage to give your heart freely. I hope so.

You don't know what you want to be yet when you grow up. On your seventeenth birthday interview, you wished for money, money and more money. I know that whatever you do will involve more substance than that, and I hope it will make use of your quick wit, analytical mind and natural gift of the gab. I pray that you have learned to manage your hanger by then, the hunger and anger that transforms you from cheeky Zen master to Mr Hyde. I feel like we've been working on that all your life, so you know what to do. Take a breath, have a snack and recover yourself. Sometimes when we're chatting, I feel like Bo in *Black-ish,* when her kids come to her for advice and she's not listening because she's congratulating herself in her head on what a great mum she is. It always cracks us up. But I'm a little bit Bo (although a lot more like Grandma Ruby). I feel like I'm winning at this mothering thing. The truth is, for the most part, you make it look easy.

My boy Jed,

Do you remember when I asked you to stop filling the dishwater half-heartedly and you looked at me shocked. 'I don't have half a heart. Do I have half a heart?' And you burst into tears. Ezra and I hugged you and I assured you that there was nobody I had met with more heart than you. These days, you act like that never happened. You say you were only joking but those tears were real and I want you to know, it's OK. You don't have to put on a front with the world outside and certainly not with me. You've always been a boy with big feelings. We used to call you our emo gangsta. Funny, because I'm the one who'll be crying thug tears in a matter of years, when you close this door and walk into the next phase of your life. When you were about to turn thirteen, you told me: 'Mum, in about five days, I'll no longer be a child.' I reminded you that technically you were a child and that you would for ever be my baby. My squish. I can't call you Squish in front of your mates, but I love that you still give me extra squeezes when we hug. Promise to keep doing this even when I'm ninety and my bones are brittle. I'm so proud of who you're becoming, although you are who you've always been: a quirky Aquarian, an Ox at heart, a Jedi by name, an accidental poet, a three-quarters maniac and a beautiful human being. I'm so lucky to know you.

To my sons and to all our sons with love,
Uju

For You

There are no conversation or reflection prompts for this final chapter, just a single task. If you could write a love note to your son or to a boy in your life, what would you say? Write it down and let him know. Don't hold back.

RESOURCES AND RECOMMENDATIONS

INTRODUCTION
BOOKS
Bobbi Wegner, Raising Feminist Boys: How to Talk to Your Child About Gender, Consent, and Empathy, New Harbinger, 2021

Sonora Jha, How to Raise a Feminist Son: Motherhood, Masculinity, and the Making of My Family, Sasquatch Press, 2021

1. HOUSE OF BOYS
PODCASTS
Dear Patriarchy https://podcasts.apple.com/gb/podcast/dear-patriarchy/id1535820167

FILMS
The Mask You Live In documentary, Jennifer Siebel Newsom (director) https://therepproject.org/films/the-mask-you-live-in/ (5 January 2015)

WEBSITES
Festival of the Girl https://www.festivalofthegirl.com/

A Call to Men https://www.acalltomen.org/

Paul Kivel (Act Like A Man Box) https://paulkivel.com/

2. MOTHERS AND SONS
BOOKS
Laura Bates, Men Who Hate Women: From Incels To Pick-up Artists, The Truth About Extreme Misogyny And How It Affects Us All, Simon & Schuster UK, 2020

PODCASTS
On Boys https://podcasts.apple.com/gb/podcast/on-boys-podcast/id1358171705

MAGAZINES
Sonshine magazine https://sonshinemagazine.com/

3. HOW NOT TO RAISE A CHAUVINIST
BOOKS
Michael Ian Black, A Better Man: A (Mostly Serious) Letter to My Son, Algonquin Books, 2020

Eve Rodsky, Fair Play: Share The Mental Load, Rebalance Your Relationship And Transform Your Life, Quercus, 2021

PODCASTS
The Guilty Feminist https://guiltyfeminist.com/

FILMS
Fair Play documentary, Jennifer Siebel Newsom (director) https://www.fairplaylife.com/documentary (July 8, 2022)

RESOURCES
Fair Play Card Deck https://www.fairplaylife.com/the-cards

4. LESSONS FROM OUR FATHERS

BOOKS

Franz Kafka, Letter to the Father, translated by Ernst Kaiser and Eithne Wilkins, Schocken Books, 2015

Elliot Rae (editor), DAD: Untold Stories of Fatherhood, Love, Mental Health and Masculinity, MusicFootballFatherhood, 2021

FILMS

Beyond Men and Masculinity documentary, Alex Gabbay (director), 29 October 2022, https://thefutureishumane.com/

5. HOW TO TRAIN YOUR DRAGONS

BOOKS

Cressida Cowell, How to Train Your Dragon: Book 1 (of 12), Hodder Children's Books, 2003

6. WHAT BOYS LEARN AND HOW IT'S TAUGHT

BOOKS

Elaine Halligan, My Child's Different: The lessons learned from one family's struggle to unlock their son's potential: How positive parenting can unlock potential in children with ADHD and dyslexia, Crown House Publishing, 2018

PODCASTS

School Should Be https://www.schoolshouldbe.com/

WEBSITES

The Parent Practice https://www.theparentpractice.com/

7. HOW TO RAISE A GOOD SPORT

BOOKS

Emma Brown, To Raise a Boy: Classrooms, Locker Rooms, Bedrooms, and the Hidden Struggles of American Boyhood, Atria/One Signal Publishers, 2021

ORGANIZATIONS

Music Football Fatherhood https://musicfootballfatherhood.com/

8. BOYS AND BODIES

FILMS

Free The Nipple documentary, Lina Esco (director), https://www.ifcfilms.com/films/free-the-nipple, 12 December 2014

WEBSITES

Body Happy Kids by Molly Forbes https://www.bodyhappyorg.com/

9. HOW TO TALK ABOUT PRIVILEGE

BOOKS

Jennifer Audrie and Lisa Lynn, Dear Patriarchy: The Gaslit Woman's

Guide to Surviving the
(Corporate) World, Warren
Publishing, 2022

10. RAISING BLACK BOYS
BOOKS
Uju Asika, Bringing Up Race: How to
Raise a Kind Child in a Prejudiced
World, Yellow Kite (September 24,
2020)

Chine McDonald, God Is Not A White
Man: And Other Revelations,
Hodder & Stoughton, 2021

Kyle 'Guante' Tran Myhre (Guante),
Not A Lot of Reasons to Sing, But
Enough, Button Poetry (2022)
https://guante.info/enough/

FILMS
National Theatre Live: Barbershop
Chronicles, Inua Ellams (writer)
and Bijam Sheibani (director), 9
January 2018, https://www.imdb.
com/title/tt12300964/

11. RITES OF PASSAGE
BOOKS
Arnold van Gennep and David I.
Kertzer, The Rites of Passage (2nd
edition), translated by Monika B.
Vizedom and Gabrielle L. Caffee,
University of Chicago Press,
2019

WEBSITES
Stop Hazing https://stophazing.org/

12. HOW TO TALK ABOUT SEX
BOOKS
Lynda Madaras, Area Madaras and
Simon Sullivan (Author), The
'What's Happening to My Body?'
Book for Boys(3rd edition),
William Morrow, 2007) https://
www.amazon.co.uk/Whats-
Happening-Body-Book-Boys/
dp/1557047650

Nikol Hasler, Sex: An Uncensored
Introduction, Zest Books, 2015
(Best For Older Teens)

PODCASTS
Puberty Podcast https://shows.acast.
com/the-puberty-podcast

WEBSITES
Sex Education Forum https://www.
sexeducationforum.org.uk
The Rap Project (Raising Awareness
and Prevention) https://
therapproject.co.uk/

13. THIS IS HIS BRAIN
WEBSITES
Young Minds https://www.
youngminds.org.uk/
InternetMatters.org https://www.
internetmatters.org/
Man Up (mental-health charity)
https://www.manup.how/

14. HOW TO KEEP A BOY SAFE

BOOKS

Rob Delaney, *A Heart That Works*, Coronet, 2022

Dr Cara Natterson, *Decoding Boys: New Science Behind The Subtle Art Of Raising Sons*, Yellow Kite, 2021

WEBSITES

Order of Magnitude https://www.orderofmagnitude.co/

Everyone's Invited https://www.everyonesinvited.uk/

The Ben Kinsella Trust https://benkinsella.org.uk/

Jags Connect https://jagsconnect.org/about-us/

ADDITIONAL RESOURCES

Beyond Equality https://www.beyondequality.org/

Everyday Sexism https://everydaysexism.com/

Fawcett Society https://www.fawcettsociety.org.uk/

He for She https://www.heforshe.org/en

Men's Story Project https://www.mensstoryproject.org/

Next Gen Men https://www.nextgenmen.ca/

The Good Men Project https://goodmenproject.com/

INTERVIEWEE WEBSITES

Abi Wright https://www.festivalofthegirl.com/

Tom Lamont http://tomlamontjournalist.com/

Rob Delaney https://www.robdelaney.com/

Chine McDonald https://www.chinemcdonald.com/

Eve Rodsky https://www.everodsky.com/

Jennifer (Jen) Audrie and Lisa Lynn https://dearpatriarchypodcast.com/home or https://podcasts.apple.com/gb/podcast/dear-patriarchy/id1535820167)

Paul Kivel https://paulkivel.com/

Kirstie Beaven https://sonshinemagazine.com/

Zahara Chowdhury https://www.schoolshouldbe.com/

Vanessa Walters https://www.vanessawalters.net/

Dr Cara Natterson https://www.linkedin.com/in/cara-natterson-md-13aa9552/

Dr Deryl Goldenberg https://drderylgoldenberg.com/

Elliott Rae https://elliottrae.com/

Dominic Cools-Lartigue https://dml-uk.com/our-clients/dominic-cools-lartigue/

Naz Ahsun https://www.naseemahsun.com/

Elaine Halligan https://www. elainehalligan.com/

For more resources (e.g. Conversation and Reflection worksheets or a sample Family Media agreement), sign up to Uju's mailing list: https:// bit.ly/boysbetter

NOTES AND
SOURCES

INTRODUCTION

1. Tom Lamont, 'How to raise a boy: my mission to bring up a boy fit for the 21st century', *Observer*, 1 August 2021, https://www.theguardian.com/lifeandstyle/2021/aug/01/how-to-raise-a-boy-my-mission-to-bring-up-a-son-fit-for-the-21st-century

2. Samuel Osborne, 'Brazil must stop being "a country of sissies" over coronavirus, says President Jair Bolsonaro', *Independent*, 11 November 2020, https://www.independent.co.uk/news/world/americas/brazil-coronavirus-cases-jair-bolsonaro-president-b1721337.html

1. HOUSE OF BOYS

1. All quotes from Abi Wright from an interview on 13 September 2022

2. Kim Elsesser, 'Gender Stereotypes in Hulu's Baby and Toddler Programming May Have Lasting Effects For Kids', Forbes, 23 May 2022, https://www.forbes.com/sites/kimelsesser/2022/05/23/gender-stereotypes-in-hulus-baby-and-toddler-programming-may-have-lasting-effects-for-kids/

3. Melissa Hogenboom, 'The Gender Biases that Shape Our Brains', BBC Future, 25 May 2021, https://www.bbc.com/future/article/20210524-the-gender-biases-that-shape-our-brains

4. 'No More Boys and Girls: Can Our Kids Go Gender Free?', BBC, 25 August 2017, https://www.bbc.co.uk/programmes/b09202jz

5. All quotes from Tom Lamont from an interview on 6 October 2022

6. Pennie Brownlee, 'Bang bang! You're dead', 2008 (originally published in *The First Years: Nga Tau Tuatahi. New Zealand Journal of Infant and Toddler Education* 10(2), pp.38+), https://penniebrownlee.weebly.com/uploads/1/0/4/3/10437917/bang_bang_youre_dead.pdf

7. All quotes from Rob Delaney from an interview on 8 October 2022

8. All quotes from Chine McDonald from an interview on 2 November 2022

9. All quotes from Eve Rodsky from interviews on 19 and 28 October 2022

10. All quotes from Jen Audrie and Lisa Lynn from an interview on 13 September 2022

11. Michael Feola, 'How 'Great Replacement' Theory Led To The Buffalo Mass Shooting', Washington Post, 25 May 2022, https://www.washingtonpost.com/politics/2022/05/25/buffalo-race-war-invasion-violence/

12. Madison Park and Jacqueline Howard, 'Why Female Shooters Are Rare', CNN, 8 May 2019, https://edition.cnn.com/2019/05/08/health/female-shooters-rare/index.html

13. Julia Jacobo and Nadine El-Bawab, 'Timeline: How The Shooting At A Texas Elementary School Unfolded', ABC

News, December 12, 2022, https://abcnews.go.com/US/timeline-shooting-texas-elementary-school-unfolded/story?id=84966910

14. Olivia Riggio and Julie Hollar, 'Mass Shooters' Most Common Trait—Their Gender—Gets Little Press Attention', FAIR, 30 June 2022, https://fair.org/home/mass-shooters-most-common-trait-their-gender-gets-little-press-attention/

15. 'APA Guidelines For Psychological Practice With Boys And Men', American Psychological Association, Boys and Men Guidelines Group, 2018, http://www.apa.org/about/policy/psychological-practice-boys-men-guidelines.pdf

16. *The Mask You Live In,* directed by Jennifer Siebel Newsom, The Representation Project, 2015, https://therepproject.org/films/the-mask-you-live-in/

17. 'A Call to Men', Tony Porter, TEDWomen, 2010 https://www.ted.com/talks/tony_porter_a_call_to_men

18. All quotes from Paul Kivel from an interview on 1 September 2022

19. 'Act Like a Man Box', Paul Kivel, https://paulkivel.com/wp-content/uploads/2011/09/actlikeamanbox.pdf (also see https://prezi.com/ikyv9sbxws45/act-like-a-man-box/)

20. Brian Heilman (Promundo-US), Gary Barker (Promundo-US), and Alexander Harrison (Unilever), 'The Man Box: A Study on Being a Young Man in the US, UK, and Mexico', Equimundo and Axe, March 30, 2017 https://www.equimundo.org/resources/man-box-study-young-man-us-uk-mexico/

21. 'Māori Culture – Five Surprising Facts About The Haka', Te Pa Tu, https://te-pa-tu.com/our-stories/maori-culture-five-surprising-facts-about-the-haka/

22. Young people are taught this haka as it contains an appropriate message for many adolescent males, particularly at that point in their lives where they are making the difficult transition into adulthood.

23. Te Taitimu Trust, *Tika Tonu* Haka and Full Meaning, https://www.facebook.com/tetaitimu/posts/tika-tonu-haka-and-full-meaning-ki-rarotaringa-whakarongo-kia-mau-hi-ringaringa-/1098489470265298/

2. MOTHERS AND SONS

1. All quotes from Kirstie Beaven from an interview on 14 October 2022

2. Elle Krupnik, 'Science Shows Why It Seems Impossible for Men and Women to "Just Be Friends"', MIC, 30 January 2015, https://www.mic.com/articles/109480/science-shows-why-it-seems-impossible-for-men-and-women-to-just-be-friends

3. Milan Dinic, 'YouGov Friendship Study Part Four: Friendship And Gender - Can

Men And Women Be Friends?', YouGov, 16 December 2021, https://yougov.co.uk/topics/society/articles-reports/2021/12/16/yougov-friendship-study-part-four-friendship-and-g

4. All quotes from Zahara Chowdhury from an interview on 20 October 2022

5. 'Mothers "harder on daughters than sons", poll suggests', BBC, 6 October 2010, https://www.bbc.co.uk/news/education-11476561

6. Susan Scutti, 'Climate Change Will Affect Gender Ratio Among Newborns, Scientists Say', CNN, 20 January 2019, https://edition.cnn.com/2019/01/23/health/climate-change-infant-sex-ratio-intl/index.html

7. Darcia F. Narvaez, PhD, 'Be Worried About Boys, Especially Baby Boys', *Psychology Today*, 8 January 2017, https://www.psychologytoday.com/us/blog/moral-landscapes/201701/be-worried-about-boys-especially-baby-boys

8. Ida Eriksen, 'Mothers to All Boys Have Shorter Life Expectancy and More Illness', *Science Nordic*, 11 April 2017, https://sciencenordic.com/denmark-videnskabdk-womens-health/mothers-to-all-boys-have-shorter-life-expectancy-and-more-illness/1444340

9. All quotes from Vanessa Walters from interviews on 14 October and 2 November 2022

10. All quotes from Dr Cara Natterson from an interview on 7 October 2022

11. Kate Stone Lombardi, 'Research Indicates Boys Who Are Close to Their Moms Are Less Anxious and Do Better in School', *Good Housekeeping*, 30 April 2019, https://www.goodhousekeeping.com/life/parenting/a25802255/mamas-boy-myth/

12. R. Winston, R. Chicot, The importance of early bonding on the long-term mental health and resilience of children. London J Prim Care (Abingdon). 2016 Feb 24;8(1):12-14. doi: 10.1080/17571472.2015.1133012. PMID: 28250823; PMCID: PMC5330336. https://www.ncbi.nlm.nih.gov/pmc/articles/PMC5330336/

13. Joanna Neary, @JoannaNeary https://twitter.com/MsJoNeary/status/1448217101425168386

3. HOW NOT TO RAISE A CHAUVINIST

1. 'WNBA Dunks: 29 Slams & 8 Players in League History', Queen Baller's Club, 2 October 2020, https://queenballers.club/basketball/wnba-dunks

2. Brian Palmer, 'Below The Rim: Why Are There So Few Dunks In Women's Basketball?', Slate, 23 March 2012, https://slate.com/culture/2012/03/brittney-griner-dunk-why-are-there-so-few-jams-in-womens-basketball.html

3. 'Toni Young Suffers Season-Ending Injury', Oklahoma State University Athletics News, 18 March 2011, https://okstate.com/news/2011/3/18/Toni_Young_Suffers_Season_Ending_Injury

4. Adam Rosenberg, 'A Bunch of Men Foolishly Think They Could Score Against Serena Williams In Tennis', Mashable, 13 July 2019, https://mashable.com/article/serena-williams-poll-yougov-score-a-point

5. Anil Ananthaswamy and Kate Douglas, 'The Origins of Sexism: How Men Came to Rule 12,000 Years Ago', New Scientist, 18 April 2018, https://www.newscientist.com/article/mg23831740-400-the-origins-of-sexism-how-men-came-to-rule-12000-years-ago/

6. 'Nicolas Chauvin', Encyclopaedia Britannica, https://www.britannica.com/biography/Nicolas-Chauvin

7. Black Codes and Pig Laws, PBS https://www.pbs.org/tpt/slavery-by-another-name/themes/black-codes-and-pig-laws/

8. Richard Sydenham, 'They Call Me a Chauvinist Pig. I Am, and I Don't Give a Damn': The Sensational New Steve McQueen Biography', Daily Mail, 16 November 2013, https://www.dailymail.co.uk/home/event/article-2507268/Steve-McQueen-They-chauvinist-pig-I-I-dont-damn.html

9. Scott Dutfield and Alina Bradford, 'Pigs, Hogs & Boars: Facts About Swine', Live Science, 5 October 2018, https://www.livescience.com/50623-pigs-facts.html

10. Sabrina Imbler, '"Botanical Sexism" Could Be Behind Your Seasonal Allergies', Atlas Obscura, 17 May 2019, https://www.atlasobscura.com/articles/seasonal-allergies-blame-male-trees

11. Nicole Fallert, 'It Was Supposed To Be A Benign TikTok On "Botanical Sexism," But Then It Spiraled Into A Huge Social Media Debate', BuzzFeed News, 27 August 2021, https://www.buzzfeednews.com/article/nicolefallert/botanical-sexism-male-trees-theory-controversy

12. Michael Ian Black Discusses "A Better Man", On Boys podcast, 9 June 2022, https://podcasts.apple.com/au/podcast/michael-ian-black-discusses-a-better-man/id1358171705?i=1000565742729

13. Jonathan Chadwick, 'Five-Year-Old Children Are Sexist And Become Less So As They Grow Up - But Boys Still Display 'Benevolent' Sexism At The Age Of 11, Study Shows', Daily Mail, 23 April 2020, https://www.dailymail.co.uk/sciencetech/article-8246085/Five-year-old-children-inherently-sexist-study-claims.html

14. Ben Paynter, 'Around The World, A New Survey Finds That Sexism Starts Early', Fast Company, 11 October 2017, https://www.fastcompany.com/40479388/

around-the-world-a-new-survey-finds-
that-sexism-starts-early

15. Saadia Zahidi, 'Here Are Two
Approaches To Accelerate Gender
Parity For A Gender-Equal Future', World
Economic Forum, 18 June 2019, https://
www.weforum.org/agenda/2019/06/
approach-to-accelerating-gender-
parity-gap-equality/

16. Fanpage.it, 'The Effects Of Sexism On
Children. Reactions To Female
Discrimination', 11 January 2019, https://
youtu.be/ibi4noJRtps

17. Fair Play Card Deck, https://www.
fairplaylife.com/

18. Shanti Das, 'Inside the Violent,
Misogynistic World of Tiktok's New Star,
Andrew Tate', *Guardian*, 6 August 2022,
https://www.theguardian.com/
technology/2022/aug/06/andrew-tate-
violent-misogynistic-world-of-tiktok-
new-star

4. LESSONS FROM OUR FATHERS

1. Alfred Ajayi, 'Disinheritance: Widows in
Igboland battle against culture that men
love to preserve (Part 2)', ICIR, 27
October 2022, https://www.icirnigeria.
org/disinheritance-widows-in-igboland-
battle-against-culture-that-men-love-to-
preserve-part-2/

2. 'Fresh Prince of Bel-Air – Will's Father
Leaves', YouTube, https://www.youtube.

com/watch?v=PI4Mv8R0mE0

3. Deryl Goldenberg, PhD, 'The Psychology
Behind Strained Father Son
Relationships', Psych Alive, https://www.
psychalive.org/psychology-behind-
strained-father-son-relationships/

4. All quotes from Dr Deryl Goldenberg
from an interview on 13 October 2022

5. Franz Kafka, *Letter to the Father*,
translated by Ernst Kaiser and Eithne
Wilkins, Schocken Books 2015, https://
www.waterstones.com/book/
letter-to-the-father-brief-an-den-vater/
franz-kafka/ernst-
kaiser/9780805212662

6. E. T. Gershoff, Should Parents' Physical
Punishment of Children Be Considered a
Source of Toxic Stress That Affects Brain
Development? Fam Relat. 2016
Feb;65(1):151-162. Doi: 10.1111/fare.12177.
Epub 2016 Mar 22. PMID: 34334857;
PMCID: PMC8323998.

7. *Beyond Men and Masculinity*
documentary, Alex Gabbay (director), 29
October 2022,https://thefutureishumane.
com/

8. Anne-Marie Gambelin, 'Relax, Mama:
Dad's Roughhousing With Your Kids Is
Good For Them—Really', Motherly, 7
January 2022, https://www.mother.ly/
health-wellness/the-science-benefits-
of-roughhousing-with-your-kids-that-
will-make-you-less-anxious/

9. Micah Toub, 'The Science of How

Fatherhood Transforms You', *Today's Parent,* 18 June 2021, https://www.todaysparent.com/family/parenting/the-science-of-how-fatherhood-transforms-you/

10. Nikhil Swaminathan, 'Strange but True: Males Can Lactate', *Scientific American,* 6 September 2007, https://www.scientificamerican.com/article/strange-but-true-males-can-lactate/

11. Rosenberg, Jeffrey. The importance of fathers in the healthy development of children. US Department Health and Human Services, Administration for Children and Families, Administration on Children, Youth and Families, Children's Bureau, Office of Child Abuse and Neglect, 2006.

12. All quotes from Elliott Rae from an interview on 5 December 2022

13. All quotes from Dominic Cools-Lartigue from an interview on 6 November 2022

5. HOW TO TRAIN YOUR DRAGONS

1. Roger Moore, 'Jay Baruchel Lets His Inner Canadian Out with How to Train Your Dragon 2', Buffalo News, 10 June 2014, https://buffalonews.com/entertainment/movies/jay-baruchel-lets-his-inner-canadian-out-with-how-to-train-your-dragon-2/article_14f79c7a-0307-5fb9-8e3c-a1482758a9f6.html

2. All quotes from Naz Ahsun from an interview on 30 August 2022

3. 'Niger, Wodaabe Tribe', Atlas of Humanity, https://www.atlasofhumanity.com/wodaabe

4. Cressida Cowell, Scholastic Kids Book Clubs, https://clubs-kids.scholastic.co.uk/authors/61054

6. WHAT BOYS LEARN AND HOW IT'S TAUGHT

1. M. Inglis, S. O'Hagan, 'Stereotype threat, gender and mathematics attainment: A conceptual replication of Stricker & Ward'. PLoS One. 2022 May 27;17(5):e0267699. doi: 10.1371/journal.pone.0267699. PMID: 35622813; PMCID: PMC9140291.

2. Lisa Aro, 'When Math Just Doesn't Add Up: Understanding Dyscalculia', *ADDitude* Magazine, 7 June 2021, https://www.additudemag.com/dyscalculia/

3. 'Diversity And Inclusion in Schools Report', Pearson, https://www.pearson.com/uk/educators/schools/issues/diversity-and-inclusion/diversity-and-inclusion-in-schools-report.html

4. James Tunnell, 'Do Boys Learn Differently To Girls?', Rising Stars and RS Assessment, https://www.risingstars-uk.com/blog/may-2018/do-boys-learn-differently-to-girls

5. Richard Adams, 'Girls overtake boys in A-level and GCSE Maths, so are rhey "smarter"?', *Guardian,* 13 August 2021,

https://www.theguardian.com/
education/2021/aug/13/girls-overtake-
boys-in-a-level-and-gcse-maths-so-are-
they-smarter

6. 'Gender Inequalities In Education And
Outcomes', Gender Equality Index:
Sweden, Organisation for Economic
Cooperation and Development (OECD)
Library, https://eige.europa.eu/
gender-equality-index/2021/country/SE

7. Sweden, https://www.oecd-ilibrary.org/
sites/0c2e0513-en/index.html?itemId=/
content/component/0c2e0513-
en#section-d12020e20314

8. Lise Eliot, 'Brain Differences in Boys and
Girls: How Much Is Inborn?', Scientific
American, 1 March 2016, https://www.
scientificamerican.com/article/
brain-differences-in-boys-and-girls-how-
much-is-inborn

9. Joan Raymond, 'The "Baby Talk" Gap?
Moms May Favor Girls When Talking To
Infants', Today, 14 May 2014, https://www.
today.com/parents/baby-talk-gap-
moms-may-favor-girls-when-talking-
infants-1d80257873

10. Nasser, Amany, 'The Difference Between
Girls and Boys in Learning', 2016,
https://www.researchgate.net/
publication/311855897_The_Difference_
Between_Girls_and_Boys_in_Learning

11. Clare Roth, 'Has Anyone Found a
Gendered Brain Yet?', DW (Deutsche
Welle), 28 September 2022, https://www.

dw.com/en/gender-and-the-brain-why-
neuroscience-is-still-searching-for-
evidence

12. Kendra Cherry, 'What Is Neuroplasticity?',
Verywell Mind, 8 November 2022, https://
www.verywellmind.com/what-is-brain-
plasticity-2794886

13. All quotes from Elaine Halligan from an
interview on 8 December 2022

14. Grace Chen, 'How Well Do Single-Sex
Schools Really Work?', Public School
Review, 20 May 2022, https://www.
publicschoolreview.com/blog/
how-well-do-single-sex-schools-really-
work

15. T. Benton, 'Attitudes to learning
– questioning the PISA data', Cambridge
Assessment Research Report,
Cambridge, UK: Cambridge
Assessment, 2015

16. Banerjee, Robin, and Vicki Lintern, 'Boys
will be boys: The effect of social
evaluation concerns on gender typing',
Social Development 9, no. 3 (2000):
397-408

17. 'Cork Students Win Young Scientist
Award For Project On Gender
Stereotypes', RTE, 10 January 2020,
https://www.rte.ie/news/
ireland/2020/0110/1105661-young-
scientist/

18. Belinda Luscombe, 'Kids Believe Gender
Stereotypes by Age 10, Global Study
Finds', Time, 20 September 2017, https://

time.com/4948607/gender-stereotypes-roles/

19. 'The Forgotten: How White Working-Class Pupils Have Been Let Down, and How to Change It', UK Parliament, 22 June 2021, https://publications.parliament.uk/pa/cm5802/cmselect/cmeduc/85/8503.htm

20. Gemma Moss and Liz Washbrook, 'Understanding the gender gap in literacy and language development' (2016): 1–61. https://www.bristol.ac.uk/media-library/sites/education/documents/bristol-working-papers-in-education/Understanding%20the%20Gender%20Gap%20working%20paper.pdf

21. Kim Elsesser, 'Is Reading Just For Girls? 3 Reasons We're Failing Boys', *Forbes*, 29 October 2018, https://www.forbes.com/sites/kimelsesser/2018/10/29/is-reading-just-for-girls-3-reasons-were-failing-boys/?sh=1f1444674f47

22. David Reilly, David Neumann, PhD and Glenda Andrews, PhD, Griffith University, 'Gender Differences in Reading and Writing Achievement: Evidence from the National Assessment of Educational Progress (NAEP),' *American Psychologist*, 20 September 2018 https://www.breakingthecode.com/boys-are-falling-behind-in-reading-worldwide/

23. 'Gender gap in children's reading grew in UK lockdown – survey', *Guardian*, 13 July 2020, https://www.theguardian.com/education/2020/jul/13/gender-gap-in-childrens-reading-grew-in-uk-lockdown-survey

24. Rebecca Joy Stanborough, 'Benefits of Reading Books: How It Can Positively Affect Your Life', Healthline, 15 October 2019, https://www.healthline.com/health/benefits-of-reading-books

25. 'The Books by Women Every Man Should Read', Women's Prize for Fiction, https://womensprizeforfiction.co.uk/features/features/news/men-reading-women

26. Campbell Leaper and Christia Spears Brown, 'Sexism in schools', *Advances in child development and behavior* 47 (2014): 189–223. https://courses.lumenlearning.com/suny-educationalpsychology/chapter/gender-differences-in-the-classroom/

27. Fullard, Joshua, 'Teacher Diversity in England 2010–2021', ISER Working Paper, 2022. https://www.iser.essex.ac.uk/research/publications/publication-547538

28. Yolanda Young, 'Teachers' implicit bias against Black students starts in preschool, study finds', *Guardian*, 4 October 2016, https://www.theguardian.com/world/2016/oct/04/black-students-teachers-implicit-racial-bias-preschool-study

29. 'Break The Cycle: Ending School-To-

Prison Pipelines In The UK', We Are
Breakthrough,
https://www.wearebreakthrough.org/
blog/break-the-cycle-ending-school-to-
prison-pipelines-in-the-uk

30. 'Why Are So Many Roma Young People
Excluded from School?', 22 August 2019,
https://coram-i.org.uk/why-are-so-many-
roma-young-people-excluded-from-
school/

31. Michelmore, O., and Mesie, J., 'Unfair
results: Pupil and parent views on school
exclusion' (2019), https://www.coram.org.
uk/resource/unfair-results

32. UK government response to the petition,
'Add education on diversity and racism to
all school curriculums', 30 July 2020,
https://petition.parliament.uk/
petitions/323808

7. HOW TO RAISE A GOOD SPORT

1. 'World Cup: Women Prepare For
Increased Domestic Abuse', Unison, 21
November 2022, https://www.unison.org.
uk/news/article/2022/11/world-cup-
women-prepare-for-increased-
domestic-abuse/

2. Colleen Walsh, 'Taking Your Kid's Sport
Too Seriously', Harvard Gazette, 18
November 2019, https://news.harvard.
edu/gazette/story/2019/11/psychologist-
explains-the-problem-of-angry-parents-
and-coaches/

3. Emma Brown, To Raise a Boy:
Classrooms, Locker Rooms, Bedrooms,
and the Hidden Struggles of American
Boyhood, Atria/One Signal Publishers,
2021, https://www.amazon.co.uk/
Raise-Boy-Classrooms-Bedrooms-
Struggles/dp/1982128089

4. Adele Diamond and Kathleen Lee,
'Interventions shown to aid executive
function development in children 4 to 12
years old." Science 333, no. 6045 (2011):
959–964. https://www.science.org/doi/
abs/10.1126/science.1204529

5. 'Arts and sport to be prescribed to
adolescents with mental ill health',
University College London, 27 October
2022, https://www.ucl.ac.uk/news/2022/
oct/arts-and-sport-be-prescribed-
adolescents-mental-ill-health

8. BOYS AND BODIES

1. 'Forcing 8-Year-Old Girl To Wear Shirt At
Pool 'Completely Sexist': Parent', CTV
News, 22 June 2015, https://kitchener.
ctvnews.ca/forcing-8-year-old-girl-to-
wear-shirt-at-pool-completely-sexist-
parent-1.2435042

2. Free the Nipple documentary, Lina Esco
(director), https://www.ifcfilms.com/films/
free-the-nipple (12 December 2014)

3. Alaina Demopoulos, 'Free the nipple:
Facebook and Instagram told to overhaul
ban on bare breasts', Guardian, 18
January 2023, https://www.theguardian.

com/technology/2023/jan/17/
free-the-nipple-meta-facebook-
instagram

4. Adele Jackson-Gibson, 'The Racist and
Problematic History of the Body Mass
Index', *Good Housekeeping*, 23 February
2021, https://www.goodhousekeeping.
com/health/diet-nutrition/a35047103/
bmi-racist-history/

5. Bruce Ettinger, Stephen Sidney, Steven
R. Cummings, Cesar Libanati, Daniel D.
Bikle, Irene S. Tekawa, Kimberly Tolan,
Peter Steiger, 'Racial Differences in Bone
Density between Young Adult Black and
White Subjects Persist after Adjustment
for Anthropometric, Lifestyle, and
Biochemical Differences', *Journal of
Clinical Endocrinology & Metabolism*,
Volume 82, Issue 2, 1 February 1997, pp.
429–34, https://doi.org/10.1210/
jcem.82.2.3732

6. Rob Henderson, '5 Reasons Why
Women and Men Care About Height',
Psychology Today, September 24, 2019,
https://www.psychologytoday.com/gb/
blog/after-service/201909/5-reasons-
why-women-and-men-care-about-
height

7. Guido Heineck, 'A note on the height–
wage differential in the UK–Cross-
sectional evidence from the BHPS',
Economics Letters 98, no. 3 (2008):
288–93. https://www.sciencedirect.com/
science/article/abs/pii/

S0165176507001681

8. Height of all US presidents from 1789 to
2021, Statista, https://www.statista.com/
statistics/1115255/us-presidents-
heights/

9. 'In Politics, Height Matters', Economist, 19
February 2020, https://www.economist.
com/graphic-detail/2020/02/19/
in-politics-height-matters

10. Jadie Troy-Pryde, 'Can You Spot What's
Wrong with All of Charles and Diana's
Photos?', *Marie Claire*, 2 November 2021,
https://www.marieclaire.co.uk/news/
celebrity-news/prince-charles-princess-
diana-photos-height-486035

11. Elamin Abdelmahmoud, 'He Was 5'7".
After Surgery, He'll Be 5'10".', *BuzzFeed
News*, 29 April 2022, https://www.
buzzfeednews.com/article/
elaminabdelmahmoud/limb-
lengthening-surgery-height-stigma-
short-kings

12. 'Limb-Lengthening Surgery Creates
Controversy', NBC San Diego, 30 July
2014, https://www.nbcsandiego.com/
news/local/limb-lengthening-surgery-
creates-controversy/56079/

13. J. Robert Staffieri, 'A study of social
stereotype of body image in children',
*Journal of personality and social
psychology* 7, no. 1p1 (1967): 101. https://
psycnet.apa.org/record/2005
-11105-001

14. 'Children As Young As 3 Unhappy With

Their Bodies', PACEY, 31 August 2016, https://www.pacey.org.uk/news-and-views/news/archive/2016-news/august-2016/children-as-young-as-3-unhappy-with-their-bodies/

15. National Geographic: Health At Every Size https://education.nationalgeographic.org/resource/health-every-size/

16. Judith Burns, 'Body Image 'A Problem For Boys', Says Advertising Think Tank', BBC, 8 August 2016, https://www.bbc.co.uk/news/education-37010205

17. 'Manorexia: Causes & Signs of Anorexia in Men', The Bulimia Project, https://bulimia.com/anorexia/manorexia/

18. Cerea, S., Bottesi, G., Pacelli, Q.F. et al., 'Muscle Dysmorphia and its Associated Psychological Features in Three Groups of Recreational Athletes', Sci Rep 8, 8877 (2018). https://doi.org/10.1038/s41598-018-27176-9

19. 'Anabolic Steroid Misuse', NHS, https://www.nhs.uk/conditions/anabolic-steroid-misuse/

20. 'Beat Eating Disorders', https://www.beateatingdisorders.org.uk/media-centre/eating-disorder-statistics/

21. 'Politics: Prescott Praised After He Admits to Eating Disorder.' The Free Library, 2008 Birmingham Post & Mail Ltd, 20 March 2023 https://www.thefreelibrary.com/POLITICS%3a+Prescott+praised+after+he+admits+to+eating+disorder.-a0178071377

22. 'Sam Claflin's Body Issues', Elle UK, 12 November 2013, https://www.elle.com/uk/fashion/celebrity-style/articles/a1927/hunger-games-star-sam-claflin-on-having-to-get-finnick-odair-s-body/

9. HOW TO TALK ABOUT PRIVILEGE

1. "Forgotten' White Working-Class Pupils Let Down by Decades of Neglect, MPs Say', UK Parliament Committees, 22 June 2021, https://committees.parliament.uk/committee/203/education-committee/news/156024/forgotten-white-workingclass-pupils-let-down-by-decades-of-neglect-mps-say/

2. Funmi Olutoye, 'The Outrage Over Sainsbury's Christmas Ad With A Black Family Proves It: Racism In The UK Never Stopped', Independent, 18 November 2020, https://www.independent.co.uk/voices/sainsburys-christmas-advert-black-family-racism-b1724922.html

3. Emily Ratajkowski, 'Emily Ratajkowski on Pregnancy and Why She Doesn't Want to Reveal the Gender of Her Baby', Vogue, 26 October 2020, https://www.vogue.com/article/emily-ratajkowski-pregnant-announcement-digital-cover

4. Sarah Silverman @SarahKateSilverman,

'EXPERIMENT.', Instagram, 8 September 2022, https://www.instagram.com/p/CiQrv2njqvQ/?hl=en

5. Emma W., 'Terminology: It's Not Black And White', National Cyber Security Centre, 30 April 2020, https://www.ncsc.gov.uk/blog-post/terminology-its-not-black-and-white

6. 'What Is Privilege?' by *BuzzFeed* (As/Is), 4 July 2015, https://youtu.be/hD5f8GuNuGQ

7. David P. Fessell and Karen Reivich, 'Why You Need to Protect Your Sense of Wonder — Especially Now', Harvard Business Review, 25 August 2021, https://hbr.org/2021/08/why-you-need-to-protect-your-sense-of-wonder-especially-now

10. RAISING BLACK BOYS

1. 'How Systemic Racism Affects Young People In The UK', Barnardo's, 21 July 2020, https://www.barnardos.org.uk/blog/how-systemic-racism-affects-young-people-uk

2. Jon Ungoed-Thomas, 'Elite football in England has 40 referees – all white. Why don't Black officials get top jobs?', *Observer*, 20 November 2021, https://www.theguardian.com/world/2021/nov/20/elite-football-in-england-has-40-referees-all-white-why-dont-black-officials-get-top-jobs

3. Black Lives Matter, https://blacklivesmatter.com/about/

4. Annual statistics: a youth justice system failing Black children https://www.gov.uk/government/news/annual-statistics-a-system-failing-black-children

5. 'The Myth of the Black Rapist', Sexual Assault Prevention & Awareness Center, University of Michigan, https://studentlife.umich.edu/files/sapac/assault-black.pdf

6. Jayland Walker, PBS News Hour, https://www.pbs.org/newshour/tag/jayland-walker

7. Sana Noor Haq and Zayn Nabbi, 'No Firearm Found At Scene Of Rare Fatal Police Shooting In England, Watchdog Says', CNN, 8 September 2022 https://edition.cnn.com/2022/09/08/uk/chris-kaba-police-shooting-intl-gbr/index.html

8. Sophie Sherry, 'Park Ridge Family Says Off-Duty Chicago Cop Pinned 14-Year-Old on Sidewalk, Pressed Knee Into His Back', NBC Chicago, 5 July 2022 https://www.nbcchicago.com/news/local/park-ridge-family-says-off-duty-chicago-cop-pinned-14-year-old-on-sidewalk-pressed-knee-into-his-back/2874082/

9. 'How to Explain White Supremacy to a White Supremacist,' by Kyle 'Guante' Tran Myhre, *A Love Song, A Death Rattle, A Battle Cry,* Button Poetry, 2016, https://guante.info/

10. Inua Ellams in conversation at Leeds

Playhouse (via Charles Hutchinson

11. https://charleshutchpress.co.uk/
why-barber-shop-chronicles-was-the-
hardest-play-inua-ellams-had-to-write/)

12. National Theatre Live: *Barbershop
Chronicles,* Inua Ellams (writer) and Bijam
Sheibani (director), 9 January 2018,
https://www.imdb.com/title/tt12300964/

13. Susannah Butter, 'Unicorn Pool Floats,
Community Spirit and Sheer Decency:
Why We Love The England Team',
Evening Standard, 12 July 2021, https://
www.standard.co.uk/insider/england-
team-euros-pool-floats-unicorn-
tiktok-b944792.html

11. RITES OF PASSAGE

1. Emily Bazelon, 'Bar Mitzvah Madness',
Slate, 19 May 2005, https://slate.com/
news-and-politics/2005/05/saving-the-
bar-mitzvah.html

2. Quinceañera, *Encyclopaedia Britannica,*
https://www.britannica.com/topic/
quinceanera

3. Dennis O'Neil, 'Rites of Passage', 8
January 2007, https://www.palomar.edu/
anthro/social/soc_4.htm

4. Rachel Nuwer, 'When Becoming a Man
Means Sticking Your Hand into a Glove of
Ants', *Smithsonian* Magazine, 27 October
2014, https://www.smithsonianmag.com/
smart-news/brazilian-tribe-becoming-
man-requires-sticking-your-hand-glove-
full-angry-ants-180953156/

5. National Geographic, Land Divers, 18
October 2007, YouTube https://youtu.
be/I0Mq6rCfYtU

6. Holiday, Online Etymology Dictionary,
https://www.etymonline.com/word/
holiday

7. Colin Blakemore and Shelia Jennett,
'Rites of Passage', *The Oxford
Companion to the Body,* Encyclopedia.
com, 22 February 2023, https://www.
encyclopedia.com/medicine/anatomy-
and-physiology/anatomy-and-
physiology/rites-passage

8. David Adam Lertzman, 'Rediscovering
rites of passage: Education,
transformation, and the transition to
sustainability', *Conservation Ecology* 5.2
(2002). https://ecologyandsociety.org/
vol5/iss2/art30/

9. Andrew Lawrence, '"Nobody called 911":
what can be done to change the culture
of hazing at US colleges?', *Guardian,* 23
June 2022, https://www.theguardian.
com/us-news/2022/jun/23/us-
colleges-university-hazing-fraternities-
sororities

10. 'Two Former Fraternity Members
Sentenced In Hazing Death At Bowling
Green State University', Associated
Press, via NBC News, 18 August 2022,
https://www.nbcnews.com/news/
us-news/two-former-fraternity-
members-sentenced-hazing-death-
bowling-green-sta-rcna43662

11. 'Family Settles Lawsuit Over Stone Foltz's Hazing Death In "Largest Payout" by a public university in Ohio history', CBS News, 23 January 2023, https://www.cbsnews.com/news/stone-foltz-hazing-death-lawsuit-three-million-bowling-green-university-ohio/

12. StopHazing.org https://stophazing.org/issue

13. Bill Plotkin, *Nature and the human soul: Cultivating wholeness and community in a fragmented world*, New World Library, 2010

14. Ron Fritz, 'An Exploration of Coming of Age Rituals & Rites of Passage in a Modern Era', YouTube, 6 July 2017, https://www.youtube.com/watch?v=Obta5WPfse4

15. Claire Potter, 'Fred's modern rite of passage', *Guardian*, 28 July 2012, https://www.theguardian.com/lifeandstyle/2012/jul/28/modern-teenage-rite-of-passage

12. HOW TO TALK ABOUT SEX

1. 'Todd Chrisley's Awkward Sex Talk with His Kids', Yahoo! Entertainment, 30 June 2015, https://www.yahoo.com/entertainment/video/todd-chrisley-awkward-sex-talk-201830701.html

2. LetsBePandas, 'The Simpsons - Homer Gives Bart Advice On Women', YouTube, 26 February 2016, https://youtu.be/ToTRAhmnxls

3. Comedy Central, 'What "The Sex Talk" Looks Like Now – Alternatino', YouTube, 10 June 2019, https://youtu.be/1j4rrgr0KeU

4. Cut, 'The Birds and the Bees, Parents Explain', YouTube, 10 January 2015, https://youtu.be/iKlgqcjKpl8

5. 'Children See Pornography As Young As Seven, New Report Finds', BBFC, 26 September 2019, https://www.bbfc.co.uk/about-us/news/children-see-pornography-as-young-as-seven-new-report-finds

6. Porn Industry Archives, Enough is Enough, https://enough.org/stats_porn_industry_archives

7. Tanith Carey, '"Don't wait": how to talk to teenagers about porn', *Guardian*, 31 August 2019, https://www.theguardian.com/lifeandstyle/2019/aug/31/how-to-talk-to-teenagers-about-porn

8. 'Relationships and Sex Education – The Evidence', Sex Education Forum, https://www.sexeducationforum.org.uk/resources/evidence/relationships-and-sex-education-evidence

9. 'Talking with Teens about Relationships', Office of Population Affairs, https://opa.hhs.gov/adolescent-health/healthy-relationships-adolescence/talking-teens-about-relationships

10. Early or Delayed Puberty, NHS, https://

www.nhs.uk/conditions/early-or-delayed-puberty/

11. Nikol Hasler, *Sex: An Uncensored Introduction,* Zest Books, 2015 https://www.amazon.co.uk/Sex-Uncensored-Introduction-Nikol-Hasler/dp/1936976846

12. Blue Seat Studios, 'Consent for Kids', YouTube, 4 October 2016, https://youtu.be/h3nhM9UlJjc

13. THIS IS HIS BRAIN

1. 'Videogames Affecting Children's Brains Like Drugs And Alcohol', Matrix Diagnostics, 17 February 2020, https://www.matrixdiagnostics.co.uk/videogames-affecting-childrens-brains-like-drugs-and-alcohol/ (see also https://onlinelibrary.wiley.com/doi/abs/10.1111/adb.12894)

2. J. C. Rosser Jr, P. J. Lynch, L. Cuddihy, D. A. Gentile, J. Klonsky, R. Merrell, 'The impact of video games on training surgeons in the 21st century'. *Arch Surg.* 2007 Feb;142(2):181–6; discussion 186. Doi: 10.1001/archsurg.142.2.181. PMID: 17309970. https://pubmed.ncbi.nlm.nih.gov/17309970/

3. Isabela Granic, Adam Lobel and Rutger C. M. E. Engels, 'The benefits of playing video games', *American Psychologist* 69.1 (2014): 66.

4. 'What Is "Gaming Addiction" and How Can You Prevent Children from Developing It?', Internet Matters, https://www.internetmatters.org/hub/question/gaming-addiction-can-prevent-children-developing

5. Drew Harwell and Will Oremus, 'Only 22 Saw The Buffalo Shooting Live. Millions Have Seen It Since', *Washington Post,* 16 May 2022, https://www.washingtonpost.com/technology/2022/05/16/buffalo-shooting-live-stream/

6. Lise Eliot, 'Neurosexism: The Myth That Men And Women Have Different Brains', Nature, 27 February 2019, https://www.nature.com/articles/d41586-019-00677-x

7. Dr Neetu Johnson, 'How Does The Clinical Picture Of ADHD Differ In Males And Females?', Psychiatry-UK, 26 May 2020, https://psychiatry-uk.com/adhd-in-girls-and-women/

8. Joanna Martin, 'Why Is ADHD More Common In Boys Than Girls?', *The Conversation,* 13 March 2018, https://theconversation.com/why-is-adhd-more-common-in-boys-than-girls-92151

9. Reema Rattan, 'Mothers' Genes May Be Why Autism Is More Common In Boys', *The Conversation,* 27 February 2014, https://theconversation.com/mothers-genes-may-be-why-autism-is-more-common-in-boys 23727#:~:text=Boys%20are%20more%20likely%20to,Journal%20of%20Human%20Genetics%20today.

10. V. Tamás, F. Kocsor, P. Gyuris, N. Kovács,

E. Czeiter, A. Büki, 'The Young Male Syndrome-An Analysis of Sex, Age, Risk Taking and Mortality in Patients With Severe Traumatic Brain Injuries', *Front Neurol.* 2019 Apr 12;10:366. doi: 10.3389/fneur.2019.00366. PMID: 31031696; PMCID: PMC6473461.

11. 'Working with Young Black Men', MIND https://www.mind.org.uk/about-us/our-policy-work/equality-and-human-rights/young-black-men/

12. '"Weathering": What Are the Health Effects of Stress and Discrimination?', *Medical News Today,* https://www.medicalnewstoday.com/articles/weathering-what-are-the-health-effects-of-stress-and-discrimination

13. 'Ask DadPad: Why Suicide Prevention Matters for Dads', The DadPad, 10 September 2021, https://thedadpad.co.uk/ask-dadpad/suicide/

14. 'This Year the Focus of Mental Health Awareness Week is on Relationships.', Movember, 17 May 2016, https://uk.movember.com/story/view/id/11258/movember-foundation-research-identifies-need-for-action-on-male-friendships-and-social-connections

15. Suicide Facts and Figures, Samaritans, https://www.samaritans.org/about-samaritans/research-policy/suicide-facts-and-figures/

16. Matt Haig, @MattZHaig, Instagram, 18 December 2022, https://www.instagram.com/p/CmTcnA_sc58/?utm_source=ig_web_copy_link

14. HOW TO KEEP A BOY SAFE

1. Joany M. Zachariasse et al., 'Sex-specific differences in children attending the emergency department: prospective observational study.' *BMJ open* 10.9 (2020): e035918. https://bmjopen.bmj.com/content/10/9/e035918.abstract

2. Sanjeet Bagcchi, 'Adolescent Boys More Prone To Injury, Death Than Girls', SciDev.Net, 7 November 2020, https://www.scidev.net/asia-pacific/news/adolescent-boys-more-prone-to-injury-death-than-girls/

3. Julia Scott, KQED, 'Why Is the Teenage Brain So Unpredictable? A Neurobiologist Explains', PBS, 24 May 2017, https://www.pbs.org/newshour/health/teenage-brain-unpredictable-neurobiologist-explains

4. Michael Goodier, 'Black people four times as likely as white people to be murdered, ONS data shows', *Guardian,* 9 February 2023, https://www.theguardian.com/world/2023/feb/09/black-people-in-england-and-wales-four-times-more-likely-to-be-murdered

5. 'Calls for a commission on knife crime in the Black community', London Assembly, https://www.london.gov.uk/press-releases/assembly/commission-on-knife-crime-in-black-community

ACKNOWLEDGEMENTS

First, I would like to thank my beloved husband Abiye (no, you are the GOAT), my sons Ezra and Jed, my stepson Isaac, my late father Ukpabi, my brother Obi, my nephew Seyi, my father-in-law Patrick Dele Cole and all the males in my life who inspired me to want to write this book. Each one of you has shown me so many colours and layers of masculinity and I am grateful for your presence in my life.

To my wonderful interview subjects Abi Wright, Tom Lamont, Rob Delaney, Chine McDonald, Eve Rodsky, Jen Audrie, Lisa Lynn, Paul Kivel, Kirstie Beaven, Zahara Chowdhury, Vanessa Walters, Dr Cara Natterson, Dr Deryl Goldenberg, Elliott Rae, Dominic Cools-Lartigue, Naz Ahsun and Elaine Halligan: thank you for your time, insights and conversations. Thanks also to Atti, Tom, Cruz, Wyndham, Thomas, Teddy, and Tom. This book wouldn't be the same without your contributions.

Immense thanks also to my incredible agent Rachel Mills and the Rachel Mills Literary team (Nelle, Charlotte, Alex), my editor Becky Alexander and copy editor Sarah Hulbert and everyone at DK Life who helped get this book out into the world. An extra special thanks to Marleigh Price, who championed my voice and vision from the start and guided me through rough draft to first-round edits. It was such a pleasure working with you, Marleigh.

To the many mothers and particularly mothers of boys (#BoyMom) whose friendship and kinship, wisdom, stories, insider jokes, tea breaks and wine o'clocks have helped me ride the ups and downs of parenting these past seventeen years. Big love to Vicki, Laura, Tunde, Gonca, Mercy, Dee, Sam, Gill, Harriet, Luisa, Meena, Louise, Jo, Lou and Sarah, Lisa, Annie, Storm, Nina, Emily, Amaka, Nneka, Mona and Brooke.

Eternal gratitude also to the boys' aunties, godmamas, nanas and guardian angels, especially Nana Helen, Mira, Bat Auntie Nnenna, Chenna, Rachel, Reem, Jolade, Seun, Queen, my auntie Obii, my late

mother-in-law Mina, my sister Nkiru and my late mother Chinyere.
Thanks again to the people who have supported my work over the years and particularly Orla Keating, Jules West-Erhabor, Gary Belsky, my partner in memes Natasha Atherton, Obianuju Ellen Asika, Mary Stretch and my girl Nomita for your constant encouragement.

This book centres on boys, but I wrote much of it with my little sister Nwando and my nieces Mayowa and Nuli in mind. Because I want a better world for girls too.

Finally, thanks to everyone who has read my work and is helping to change the story for future generations. If you enjoyed this book, please do consider leaving a review to help spread the message far and wide.

ACKNOWLEDGEMENTS

INDEX

A

B

C

D

E

F

G

H

DK LONDON
Acquisitions Editor Marleigh Price
Senior Acquisitions Editor Becky Alexander
Editorial Assistant Charlotte Beauchamp
Art Director Maxine Pedliham
Publishing Director Katie Cowan
Production Editor David Almond
Senior Production Controller Samantha Cross

Editors Monica Chakraverty and Sarah Hulbert
Indexer Ruth Ellis
Jacket Designer Luke Bird

DK INDIA
Pre Production Manager Balwant Singh
DTP Coordinator Pushpak Tyagi
DTP Designer Umesh Singh Rawat

First published in Great Britain in 2023 by
Dorling Kindersley Limited
DK, One Embassy Gardens, 8 Viaduct Gardens,
London, SW11 7BW

The authorised representative in the EEA is
Dorling Kindersley Verlag GmbH. Arnulfstr. 124,
80636 Munich, Germany

Copyright © 2023 Dorling Kindersley Limited
A Penguin Random House Company
10 9 8 7 6 5 4 3 2 1
001–334536–June/2023

Text copyright © Uju Asika

A CIP catalogue record for this book
is available from the British Library.
ISBN: 9780241608418
Printed and bound in the United Kingdom

This book was made with Forest
Stewardship Council™ certified
paper – one small step in DK's
commitment to a sustainable future.
**For more information go to
www.dk.com/our-green-pledge**

For the curious
www.dk.com